ST   ST⁓IAS

Sojourner Truth

A Life, A Symbol

Also by Nell Irvin Painter

STANDING AT ARMAGEDDON
The United States, 1877–1919

THE NARRATIVE OF HOSEA HUDSON
His Life as a Black Communist in the Deep South

EXODUSTERS
Black Migration to Kansas After Reconstruction

Sojourner Truth

A Life, A Symbol

Nell Irvin Painter

W · W · Norton & Company

New York   London

For information about permission to reproduce selections from this book, write to
Permissions, W. W. Norton & Company, Inc., 500 Fifth Avenue,
New York, NY 10110.

The text of this book is composed in 12/14 Berthold Bodoni Light
with the display set in Cochin Bold Roman and Italic
Composition and manufacturing by the Haddon Craftsmen, Inc.
Book design by Margaret M. Wagner

Library of Congress Cataloging-in-Publication Data

Painter, Nell Irvin
Sojourner Truth, a life, a symbol / by Nell Irvin Painter.
p.   cm.
Includes bibliographical references (p.) and index.
ISBN 0-393-02739-2
1. Truth, Sojourner, d. 1883.   2. Afro-American abolitionists–Biography.
3. Abolitionists–United States–Biography.   4. Women abolitionists–United States–
Biography.   5. Social reformers–United States–Biography.   6. Women social
reformers–United States–Biography.   I. Title.
E185.97.T8P35   1996
305.5'67'092–dc20
[B]   95-47595
                                                                                                      CIP

W. W. Norton & Company, Inc., 500 Fifth Avenue, New York, N.Y. 10110
http://web.wwnorton.com
W. W. Norton & Company Ltd., 10 Coptic Street, London WC1A 1PU

1   2   3   4   5   6   7   8   9   0

For Glenn
love of my life

Contents

List of Illustrations

I

Isabella

I

Isabella

1

Isabella, Sojourner Truth, and American Slavery

SOJOURNER TRUTH, born Isabella, is one of the two most famous African-American women of the nineteenth century. The other, Harriet Tubman, the "Moses" of her people, also came out of slavery. Many people confuse the two because both lived in an era shadowed by human bondage, but Truth and Tubman were contrasting figures. New York was Truth's Egypt; Tubman's was in Maryland, these respective places marking each woman with a regional identity that Truth, at least, later came very much to prize. Born in about 1797, Truth was a generation older than Tubman, born in about 1821. Tubman will walk these pages from time to time, but only as a guest.

A woman of remarkable intelligence despite her illiteracy, Truth had great presence. She was tall, some 5 feet 11 inches, of spare but solid frame.[1] Her voice was low, so low that listeners sometimes termed it masculine, and her singing voice was beautifully powerful. Whenever she spoke in public, she also sang. No one ever forgot the power and pathos of Sojourner Truth's singing, just as her wit and originality of phrasing were also of lasting remembrance.

As an abolitionist and feminist, she put her body and her mind to a unique task, that of physically representing women who had been enslaved. At a time when most Americans thought of slaves as male and women as white, Truth embodied a fact that still bears repeating: Among the blacks are women; among the women, there are blacks.[2]

We think of Truth as a natural, uncomplicated presence in our national life. Rather than a person in history, she works as a symbol. To appreciate the meaning of the symbol—Strong Black Woman—we need know almost nothing of the person.[3] Because we are apt to assume that the mere experience of enslavement endowed Truth with the power to voice its evils, we may forget a shocking fact: No other woman who had been through the ordeal of slavery managed to survive with sufficient strength, poise, and self-confidence to become a public presence over the long term. Harriet Tubman spoke up occasionally at antislavery meetings, and the drama of her actions lent weight to her words. But she could not sustain appearance after appearance.

Only Truth had the ability to go on speaking, year after year for thirty years, to make herself into a force in several American reform movements. Even though the aims of her missions became increasingly secular after midcentury, Truth was first and last an itinerant preacher, stressing both itinerancy and preaching. From the late 1840s through the late 1870s, she traveled the American land, denouncing slavery and slavers, advocating freedom, women's rights, woman suffrage, and temperance.

Pentecostal[4] that she was, Truth would have explained that the force that brought her from the soul murder of slavery into the authority of public advocacy was the power of the Holy Spirit. Her ability to call upon a supernatural power gave her a resource claimed by millions of black women and by disempowered people the world over. Without doubt, it was Truth's religious faith that transformed her from Isabella, a domestic servant, into Sojourner Truth, a hero for three centuries—at least.

SOJOURNER TRUTH was one born again, not only in the evangelical sense of the phrase and not merely because Isabella Van Wagenen rechristened herself Sojourner Truth. She was, all through, a self-made woman, and that was so much the case that

beginning to write her biography becomes a challenge to definition as well as genealogy.[5]

Biographies normally set the stage for the appearance of the protagonist by examining ancestors for portents of greatness. I will do
what I can along those lines, though the track leading backward
from Isabella quickly grows faint. Tracing the genealogy of any
slave is a difficult thing to do. I know Isabella's parents' names but
can go back no further into her family history with any certainty.
The genealogical task is also complicated by the relationship between Isabella Van Wagenen and Sojourner Truth, each of whom
has her own separate birth date. Isabella's is in the late 1790s on
a day that cannot be designated exactly; Sojourner Truth's is 1 June
1843.

We know that Isabella created Sojourner Truth by reinventing
herself and leaving her old vocation and habitat, but Isabella is not
all there is to Truth's ancestry. The symbols of American history
come into play here, for Sojourner Truth presented herself as a
former slave, and we still identify her with the movement to abol-
ish slavery in the United States. The allegorical territory of American slavery is always situated somewhere—everywhere—in the
South. Thus, to a great extent, Sojourner Truth appears to emerge
out of a generalized southern setting. Here lies a conundrum—
separating person from symbol and Isabella from Sojourner—for
Isabella was a slave in New York State, one of tens of thousands
of enslaved New Yorkers. The history and human geography of Isabella's New York were worlds away from the mythic South we associate with American slavery and with Sojourner Truth.[6]

ISABELLA was born in the village of Hurley, in Ulster County, New
York, about seven miles west of the Hudson River. Hurley (its first
Dutch name was Niew Dorp) lies about ninety miles north of New
York City and sixty miles south of Albany.[7] The county's original
inhabitants were Waroneck (Mohawk) Indians, who called a creek
that empties into the Hudson River "Esopus," meaning small river.
After much struggle in the mid-1610s that came to be known as
the Esopus Wars, Dutch settlers overwhelmed the Indians without entirely displacing them. For more than a hundred years af-

terward, large numbers of Indians remained in a region that, with the arrival of Africans, would become tri-racial.[8]

A hilly region of frigid, fast-running streams and rivers, Isabella's birthplace belongs to the New England upland of forested mountains, and lies west and slightly to the north of Hartford, Connecticut; Providence, Rhode Island; and Cape Cod, Massachusetts. A cold, rocky place of long winters and short summers, Ulster County is covered with northern flora: spruce, balsam fir, hemlock, red cedar, yellow birch, as well as the oak, hickory, and pine that are found throughout the eastern United States. If she stood in a field with time to enjoy the scenery to the west, Isabella would have been able to see the Catskill Mountains, whose highest peak, Slide Mountain, rises to 4,180 feet.

Ulster County was one of New York's original counties, organized in 1683 and named after the Irish title of the Duke of York. At the turn of the nineteenth century it was overwhelmingly rural, producing wheat that was fair-to-middling in quality and lots of decent wool.[9] When Isabella was born, before the advent of railroads and before New York City became a lucrative market, Ulster County was a backwater. Beautiful in a cold and craggy fashion akin to New England, it was not easy to traverse by road. Travelers used the river or bogged down trying to cross difficult terrain.

In rural counties like Ulster—in the Hudson Valley, on Long Island, and in New Jersey—the culture of local blacks was likely as not to be Afro-Dutch, although some blacks were Afro-Indian. They worked for Dutch farmers in areas where as many as 30 to 60 percent of white households owned slaves.[10] At the turn of the nineteenth century Ulster County's total population was 29,554, of whom more than 10 percent, 3,220, were black people scattered widely across the countryside.[11]

Most slaveholding New York State households owned only one or two slaves; a large slaveowner, like Isabella's first master, might have six or seven at a time, but New Yorkers who owned more than twenty slaves could be counted on the fingers of one hand. In the late eighteenth century, of course, no stigma attached to the trafficker in people, and masters did not hesitate to break up slave fam-

ilies through sale. But all was on a much smaller scale than the
southern system of slavery.

Several factors, including the wide distribution of slaves among
white families, combined to give rural black New Yorkers a singular culture. The contrast was especially sharp in comparison with
southern blacks, often living in much larger homogeneous communities, who developed a vibrant Anglo-African culture revolving
around plantation slave quarters. Half of all black southerners
lived in communities of twenty or more African Americans, large
concentrations that allowed them to learn their culture from other
blacks and to create a distinctive way of life.

In New York State, by contrast, there were large numbers of
blacks only in New York City. On the farms of rural New York,
where slaves like Isabella lived and worked, one or two Africans
commonly lived with a Dutch family and remained too isolated and
scattered to forge any but the most tentative separate culture. Surrounded by Dutch speakers, rural black New Yorkers grew up
speaking the language of their community. A good 16 or so percent, perhaps more, of eighteenth-century black New Yorkers,
like Isabella and her family, spoke Dutch as their first language.[12]

Such sound from black folk astonished those who were not
from New York. A southern slave, accompanying his owner on a
trip to New York, grew frustrated trying to extract directions from
an Afro-Dutch woman. To his query about the way to New York,
she answered: "Yaw, mynheer," pointing toward the town, "dat is
Yarikee."[13] Isabella as a young woman would have spoken in just
this way. Over her lifetime she learned to speak English fluently,
but she lost neither the accent nor the earthy imagery of the Dutch
language that made her English so remarkable.

It is not possible to know exactly how Sojourner Truth spoke,
for no one from her generation and cultural background was
recorded. Isabella was the slave of the Dumont family from about
twelve until about thirty, and many years later the daughter,
Gertrude Dumont, protested that Truth's speech was nothing like
the mock-southern dialect that careless reporters used. Rather, it
was "very similar to that of the unlettered white people of [New
York in] her time."[14] As an older woman, Truth took pride in

speaking correct English and objected to accounts of her speeches in heavy southern dialect. This seemed to her to take "unfair advantage" of her race.[15]

Living so closely with Boers, Afro-Dutch New Yorkers imbibed other aspects of Dutch culture. If Afro-Dutch New Yorkers went to church—and in the countryside most, like their poor white neighbors, did not—they might join churches that were Dutch Reformed (as did Isabella's oldest daughter, Diana) or Methodist (as did Isabella). In Ulster County in the very early nineteenth century, young Isabella learned the Lord's Prayer in Dutch from her mother, and she may have attended Reformed churches as a child and young woman. This Afro-Dutch world was distinct, first culturally, then economically, from the slaveholding South.

ISABELLA'S birth coincided with a climactic invention—the cotton gin—which made slave-grown, short-staple cotton the economic underpinning of the American South. During the antebellum era of cotton as king, the economic and political interests of elite southerners increasingly diverged from those of elite northerners. This polarization was as yet embryonic in the late 1790s, because the political tensions that finally led to civil war had not yet acquired the agonizing sharpness that would dominate the middle of the century and bring Sojourner Truth into the public eye. When Isabella was born, the American North as well as the American South was a land of bondage.

The effacement of the memory of northern slavery has skewed American regional identities by exonerating white northerners and blaming white southerners. This erasure complicates the task of situating Isabella's life history, for by the mid-nineteenth century, when Sojourner Truth was a familiar presence in antislavery circles, New York belonged to the metaphorical land of liberty. With *southern* slavery as the symbol of *American* slavery, Truth's early life automatically migrated into a vague, composite antebellum South, a Southern Nowhere that for all its lack of specificity is definitely south of the Mason-Dixon line.

This metaphorical slave South appears in classic form in Harriet Beecher Stowe's phenomenally popular 1851–52 novel, *Uncle Tom's Cabin*. Its types and themes had arisen in the antislavery press and slave narratives in the generation before Stowe published, supplying her with a stock of characters familiar in outline: the long-suffering, Christian slave, the cruel master with his whip and his mulatto concubine, the outraged slave mother, the slave trader, even the kind master and the jealous mistress.[16] By the time Sojourner Truth became an antislavery speaker, this South had become a taken-for-granted setting antithetical to the free North.

Though foreign to northerners, the metaphorical slave South was at the same time familiar by dint of having so often been described. In this South, slavery was everlasting; slaves could not marry, own property, or learn to read or write. Their masters' powers were absolute, with the corruption that accompanies absolute power. Sex and violence suffused the entire institution. This slave South was a purgatory from which only the strongest, bravest, and most intelligent of slaves could flee, men and women like Frederick Douglass and Harriet Tubman. Even these exceptional figures came from Maryland, right next door to the North. The Deep South was a hell that allowed no escape. In the far-away states of Alabama, Mississippi, and Louisiana, unspeakable atrocities seemed to occur on a routine basis. Nothing was too awful to happen there.

Such a facile symbolic opposition: slave South and free North. But realities in Isabella's time were not so neat.

Slavery was an important part of northern life before 1800, however latter-day historical symbolism may have erased its stigma from the North. When Isabella was born, only Charleston among American cities had a larger black population than New York, and New York City's 5,865 blacks (including five slaves owned by Founding Father John Jay) accounted for about 10 percent of the total population. Almost 1,000 of the 6,281 black people in Connecticut and 12,422 of the 16,824 black people in New Jersey were still enslaved; black people were scattered throughout the North, and former slaves were to be found even in Massachusetts.[17]

In the nineteenth century—as in our own times, *mutatis mutandis*—northerners preened themselves in their moral superiority to the slave drivers of the South, as though their own section had remained innocent of involuntary servitude. Such self-righteous censure of the South exempts northerners from their own slaveholding legacy, for when Isabella was born a slave, a commonplace national institution bound her.

2

Isabella, A Slave

ISABELLA was born in the late 1790s on Roundout Creek, near where it joins the Wallkill River in rural Hurley, in the town of Rosendale, Ulster County, New York. No one wrote down and kept information of where or when she was born, because no one who could write anticipated that an enslaved baby would become an American legend. Now that the legend requires a place of origin, local people have identified two old stone cottages on the eastern side of Roundout Creek as likely birthplaces of Sojourner Truth.[1]

Isabella's parents were James and Elizabeth, the slaves of Colonel Johannis Hardenbergh, a Revolutionary War colonel who died not long after Isabella's birth. As a young man, James was tall and straight, as Isabella would become, and he was known as "Bome-free," meaning tree. Elizabeth was known as Betsey or as Mau Mau ("Mama" in Dutch) Bett.[2] Neither Betsey nor James was young when Isabella was born: James was probably born in about 1760, his wife perhaps in the 1770s. He had lost two wives to sale before Betsey.

Isabella was the youngest of James and Betsey's ten or twelve children, but as a child she knew only one sibling. Her parents cherished her and her older brother Peter, as they cherished all their children—with an affection colored by the certainty of loss. One of Isabella's indelible childhood memories—mentioned five times early in her *Narrative*—is her parents' grieving over their children who had been sold. Seared by frequent, detailed tellings of these losses, Isabella's earliest years lay in the shadow of her parents' chronic depression and her own guilt as a survivor. A fear of inevitable disaster, a "cruel foreboding," lay over this home: Isabella dreaded separation, which she would experience when she herself was sold.

Isabella's parents were hardworking people whose emotional lives were blighted by loss but whose material circumstances were relatively advantageous, if not entirely unusual for faithful New York slaves at the turn of the eighteenth–nineteenth century. Their owners, descended from one of Hurley's earliest settlers, were among Ulster County's wealthiest land- and slaveowning families. Colonel Johannis Hardenbergh had owned six slaves in the middle of the eighteenth century, only one less than Hurley's largest slaveholder.[3] When Isabella was born, James and Betsey were cottagers farming a hilly lot lent them by their master. They grew tobacco, corn, and flax, which they sold for cash to buy food and clothing for their children.

As cottagers, James and Betsey would have owed Hardenbergh a set number of days' labor in exchange for their small house (the cottage) and farmland. James and Betsey would not have held legal title to the land, making it impossible for them to pass it on to Isabella or their other heirs. Had Johannis Hardenbergh not died, they might have found themselves in perpetual debt to him, as would southern sharecroppers in the late nineteenth and early twentieth centuries.[4] As it happened, Johannis Hardenbergh's death had a worse result—it deprived James and Betsey of both their cottage and their land.

Hardenbergh's son and heir, Charles, removed James and Betsey from their cottage to his great stone house. Here Isabella and the other slaves slept in a cold, dark, and damp cellar that bred illnesses of the joints and lungs. It was in the dark of this miserable pit that her parents told little Isabella the horror of the kidnapping of two of her siblings, Nancy (three) and Michael (five), some years before. A story much retold, its anguishing details were still vivid in Sojourner Truth's memory nearly half a century later.

Michael had arisen early on a winter's morning and made his

mother's fire. The morning was snowy, and at first the child was delighted by the appearance of Colonel Hardenbergh's big sleigh. He grew frightened, though, when strange men placed him in the sleigh and when his little sister Nancy was brought out and locked into the sleigh box. Michael panicked. Betsey and James saw the boy jump off the sleigh and seek refuge in the house by hiding under a bed. Hardenbergh's agents quickly recaptured Michael and drove off with both children. Their parents were left bereft, suffering both the pain of loss and the agony of impotence.[5] Such bereavement would recur five years later.

After the death of Charles Hardenbergh and the auction of his property in 1807 or 1808, nine-year-old Isabella went to an English-speaking family named Neely, who lived in Twaalfskill, near Kingston.[6] For $100 she was torn from her parents and her brother. According to her *Narrative*, Isabella dated her "trials in life" from this sale, when she entered into the painful business of working as a slave: *"Now the war begun."*[7] Her parents, too old and infirm to fetch any price, were sent to live in a hut belonging to a family named Simmons who did not own slaves. Until she became free almost twenty years later, Isabella's only knowledge of even nominal freedom for black people was as a condition of age, infirmity, and destitution.

Years later, Isabella recalled that her parents had ended their days "ignorant, helpless, crushed in spirit, and weighed down with hardship and cruel bereavement." In wretched health and without income or farmland, they experienced all the tribulations of rural poverty. Betsey died first, quite suddenly, perhaps in 1809. James lingered on in poor health for several years. As a young mother, Isabella wished that she could nurture and protect her old father, take care of him as though she were his parent, but she could not. Lame and blind, James died "chilled and starved," after years of hobbling back and forth between various Hardenbergh relatives. Before she was half-grown, Isabella had lost both parents and some ten siblings.

ISABELLA'S life in the workforce began in earnest at the Neelys', where she was the only slave and did household labor under execrable conditions. Inadequately clothed, she suffered terribly from the cold Ulster County winters. A language barrier aggravated her problems. Neither of her owners spoke Dutch, and Isabella spoke no English. When Isabella could not understand commands, her mistress flew into rages and her master whipped her savagely. Especially remembered was a whipping whose motive she never discovered, when John Neely beat the nine-year-old girl so cruelly that blood streamed down her back. These scars she bore for the rest of her life. At this time she prayed for her father to come to her, and he somehow managed not only to make his way, but also to help rescue his young daughter through sale to yet another set of masters.

Within about a year of her sale to Neely, Isabella became the property of the innkeeping and fishing Schriver family of Kingston. In her year and a half with the Schrivers, Isabella performed a variety of chores. She carried fish, farmed, gathered herbs, made beer, shopped—whatever needed to be done. Although the Schrivers were pillars of the Klyn Esopus Dutch Reformed Church, the atmosphere of their tavern did not encourage Christian deportment; Isabella soon learned to curse as well as perform her many tasks. And then she was sold again in 1810, at the age of twelve or thirteen, to Martin Schriver's fellow parishioner, John Dumont, who bought her for £70, the equivalent of $175.

Here her travels stopped for a long while, for Isabella would live with the Dumont family for some sixteen years, during which she passed through puberty, married, and had five children. She became in fact very attached to the Dumonts, with whom she lived longer than with her own parents.

It was an attachment profoundly ambivalent, however, the product of a painful relationship.[8] Isabella had already experienced terrible beatings at the Neelys', but with the Dumonts she was subject to two kinds of abuse: physical and sexual. Such mistreatment, endemic to slavery North and South, left scars as much psychological as physical.

DOING farm labor for John Dumont and household labor for his wife, Sally, Isabella worked long and hard. The Dumonts disagreed on the degree of her efficiency. John Dumont boasted that Isabella "could do as much work as half a dozen common [white] people, and do it well, too." Sally Dumont complained that Isabella could do so much work because it was only "half performed."

In 1812, an incident occurred in the Dumonts' complex household that implicated not only both adult Dumonts, but also one of the two white hired girls and the Dumont's ten-year-old daughter, Gertrude. As often happens in abusive situations, brutality has its friends, in this case Kate, one of the hired girls, who identified with the aggressors and inflicted her own kind of attack on Isabella. Several mornings when Isabella was out milking the cows, Kate threw ashes into the potatoes that Isabella was boiling for breakfast. Although Sally Dumont saw the dingy potatoes as just another instance of Isabella's carelessness, Gertrude Dumont took Isabella's side. One morning Gertrude got up early, hid herself in the kitchen, and witnessed Kate's dirtying the potatoes. Gertrude told on Kate, which, Isabella felt, vindicated not only herself but her master as well. Her attachment to John Dumont grew in tandem with her estrangement from her mistress. Indeed, Isabella's affection for him would prove lasting, despite his cruelty.[9]

Isabella was an abused child, and her strategies for survival resembled those of other abused children. As is often the case, she found ways to explain and excuse the abuse. Dumont only beat her when she deserved it, she said later, but her narrative attests to her hypervigilance, the wariness of a person who lives with the specter of violence. Isabella would sometimes stay up all night, afraid to sleep, trying to do her work well enough to gain approval. Like many other people who had been beaten as children, she would later reenact her torment with her own children and beat them into silence when they cried out from hunger.[10] Her anxiety to please Dumont earned her the scorn of his other slaves, who may have isolated her even before the sexual abuse began. Evidently older than she, they probably were not subject to the further, insidious abuse of which young Isabella was the resentful but not entirely candid victim.

Although John Dumont beat Isabella, this was not so far from ordinary. Isabella accepted the patriarchal order in which she lived and blamed herself. Even as an adult, she reckoned that he was in a position of authority over her, and when she did wrong, it was fitting that she pay the price. In her *Narrative*, Sojourner Truth was open about this. But the *Narrative* also indicates that something less well recognized than *master*-slave sex was going on.

Truth makes no mention of sexual abuse from John Dumont, although master-slave sex was a standard part of the abolitionist bill of indictment against the slave South. Had Truth wanted to say that her master had raped her (as have some of her biographers), she probably would have mentioned it as part of the evil of slavery.[11] Then, as now, the sexual abuse of young women by men is deplored but recognized as common. Less easily acknowledged, then and now, is the fact that there are women who violate children.

The sexual abuse came from her mistress Sally Dumont, and Truth could tell about it only obliquely, in scattered pages in her *Narrative*. Truth spoke straightforwardly about most of her suffering in slavery, "this putrescent plague-spot," but only vaguely about this. Despite all the abolitionists' investigations, she said, "there remained so much unseen."[12] We have no statistics for the early nineteenth century, but in the late twentieth century, the assailants of about 5 percent of sexually abused girls are women.[13] In Isabella's hierarchal, slaveholding family, she responded to John Dumont's beatings by identifying with him. But she despised Sally Dumont.

Here we lack details, for Truth had two motives for keeping secrets by the time she told her story. Having come through a libel trial in the mid-1830s, she was concerned about her credibility. She also feared that because what had happened to her was "so unaccountable, so unreasonable, and what is usually called so unnatural," readers who were "uninitiated" would not believe her.[14] Besides, she added, her assailant had died, and she did not want to distress the innocent who were still living. When Truth dictated her story to her amanuensis Olive Gilbert in the late 1840s, Sally Dumont had been dead for three years, but John Dumont was still alive and in touch with Truth.[15]

Looking back from the vantage point of more than twenty years, Sojourner Truth saw her extreme anxiety to please Dumont as absurd. But at the time, she said, she "looked upon her master as a *God*," assuming even that he could read her thoughts, a power she did not then concede to God.[16] She had believed that submission to Dumont was the same as being true to God, a reasoning that also prevailed among slaveowning southerners with regard to their wives and children as well as their slaves.

Sojourner Truth, recalling herself as a slave, realized that she had been incapable of separating John Dumont's interests from her own, even when serving him meant depriving her own children and setting herself against her fellow slaves. Without knowledge of our phrase "slave mentality," Truth depicted young Isabella as a prime case, which is also how several other people at the Dumonts' saw her.

Slave mentality does not appear in a vacuum. Its characteristics—a lack of self-confidence, personal autonomy, and independent thought, a sense of one's own insignificance in comparison to the importance of others, a desire to please the powerful at any cost, and, finally, a ferocious anger that is often turned inward but can surge into frightening outbursts—are precisely the traits of vulnerable people who have been battered. Isabella arrived at the Dumonts' large household as an isolated child, and the elder Dumonts' age and authority over her made them into substitute parents. They subjected her to sustained and multifaceted abuse of the sort that destroys self-esteem and distorts reality. Yet she, like any young person living closely with her elders, became attached to them as family.

The relationship was ambivalent for all parties. To the Dumonts, she was daughter, servant, farm worker, and black person; later they depended upon her as a nurse. On her side, the connection was distorted by the need to manage sexual abuse and beatings. She denounced Sally Dumont, adored John Dumont, and took satisfaction when, after his wife's death, it seemed that he had converted to a recognition that slavery was wrong. Isabella returned to the Dumonts' after her emancipation, after her move to New York City, even—as Sojourner Truth—after her relocation to Northampton, Massachusetts. She attended Sally Dumont on her deathbed in 1846 and said good-bye to John Dumont when he left

Ulster County with his sons in 1849. This attachment reached into Sally Dumont's extended family of Warings and Gedneys, who employed Isabella's children fifteen years after she had left Ulster County.

WHILE Isabella's relationship with the Dumonts preoccupied her as a slave, she did forge additional ties. She married Thomas, another of Dumont's slaves, in about 1815, and had five children.[17] Isabella's friends included her longtime confidante, an older slave-woman named Soan who cared for Isabella's widowed father James and died before him. The only character in the *Narrative* who speaks straightforwardly of retribution and wreaks vengeance against her owner while she is still enslaved, Soan tortured her master and lied to her mistress with a fearlessness that amazed Isabella.[18] Deencia, mentioned only briefly, was Isabella's peer, someone who had, according to the *Narrative*, "so often befriended her."[19]

Considering that Isabella was a poor woman and that romantic love has been a luxury for the leisured classes, the rarity of romance in her life is not surprising. Her marriage seems to have conformed to the working-class model of people attached to one another without the gloss of what middle-class people prize as love. But the *Narrative* also contains a somewhat vague anecdote meant to portray a love affair that occurred before her marriage, the sole romance of Truth's entire life. Olive Gilbert writes that an "attachment sprung up" between Isabella, as a budding young woman of sixteen or seventeen (this would have been in 1813–14), and Robert, a slave on a neighboring farm.

Robert may have been the father of Isabella's first child, Diana, who was born some seven years before the next, Peter, but this is only conjecture based on the wide spacing of the first two children compared with the rest. Whatever its nature, the relationship between Isabella and Robert ended tragically.

According to the *Narrative of Sojourner Truth*, Robert's owner, a man named Catlin, did not want his slave having children off his premises. He forbade Robert to see Isabella, and when Robert disobeyed this command, Catlin beat him within an inch of his life.

The beating broke Robert's will, convinced him to marry a woman whom Catlin owned, and condemned him to a premature death. The nuances of this story, especially as they relate to the attraction between Isabella and Robert, will never be recovered, but one of its main points is perfectly clear: This tragedy, like so many in slavery days, turned on a savage beating whose psychological and physical consequences were devastating.

At this time, marriages between slaves were legally sanctioned in New York. Olive Gilbert's explanation in the *Narrative* that slave marriages like that of Isabella and Thomas were not recognized in law drew on southern rather than northern practice. In 1809, New York had enacted laws recognizing slave marriages, declaring the children legitimate, prohibiting the separation of married partners, and conceding the rights of slaves to own and transfer property.[20]

The possibility of having a marriage recognized in law seems not to have allowed Isabella or Thomas any increased autonomy of choice, for John Dumont seems to have picked their spouses. Thomas was older than Isabella, having been married twice previously and having lost at least one wife to the trade in slaves. After the sale of one of his wives, Thomas had run away to New York City but had been dragged back to Ulster County. He may have subsequently inspired Isabella's interest in the city, although the *Narrative* gives few clues as to the nature of Isabella and Thomas's relationship. Between about 1815 and about 1826, Isabella at any rate bore five children; the names and birthdays of only four of them, who are named after her mother and siblings, are known: Diana, born about 1815; Peter, 1821; Elizabeth, 1825; and Sophia, about 1826. The fifth, perhaps named Thomas, may have died in infancy or childhood and may have been born between Diana and Peter.[21]

Of Isabella's children, Diana most resembled her in physique and experience. In her old age, Diana was "a perfect picture of her mother. She is tall, strong, and boasts of a color which never fades. Her voice is less masculine than that of Sojourner Truth, and her talents are less visible, although she possesses an unusual intelligence for her race."[22] Like Isabella, Diana had spent sufficient years in slavery to speak its meaning later on: She had worked like

Isabella at the same "man's" tasks on Dumont's farm, hoeing and planting corn, pulling flax, and picking stones out of Ulster County's rocky fields.

Diana remembered being sent at an unspecified age to school, a baffling experience. She had "no idea what the school was for or why she was sent there." During her week as a scholar, the teacher never spoke to her. Beside this perplexing memory, Diana carried another of herself, her siblings, and her mother: "her mother used to sit with her children on the floor in their cabin on the Dumont farm, before a fire place, with a pine knot for a light, and mend her clothing, and talk with them. This was Sojourner's dream. She told the children that some day they would have a home of their own, and that the family would all be together."[23] Diana related no memories of Thomas.

Though almost silent on the character of their marriage, the *Narrative of Sojourner Truth* indicates that Isabella and Thomas cared enough for one another to have once planned to live together in a cottage that their master Dumont had promised them after their emancipation under state law in 1827. The cottage never materialized, and the plans proved chimerical. One shred of evidence—an undated document saying that Isabella was not happy with Thomas—exists to impugn the marriage.[24] In any event, as soon as Isabella could act autonomously, she left her husband and her children (except the baby Sophia) with the Dumonts. Over the course of about a year, from 1826 to 1827, she turned herself into a free woman.

3

Journey Toward Freedom

FREEDOM represented a complete novelty to Isabella. She had been born a slave of slave parents, and her children were still slaves. The only free black people she knew were old and wretched. No matter how ardently she wanted to be free, the actual prospect would have been daunting. Her husband reduced the uncertainty by staying in a familiar routine, the least disruptive reaction to upheaval.[1] Acting alone, Isabella took her first step into emancipation by setting her own timetable.

To calculate the moment at which she should be free, Isabella weighed the action of the state of New York against a bargain she had struck with John Dumont. She fixed the right time at a little over one-half year before the last of the slaves in New York were to be emancipated—on the Fourth of July 1827. Isabella and Dumont were not in disagreement on the timing of state action, but they fell out of accord over the fate of his earlier promise to free her a year in advance.

After Dumont had made this commitment, Isabella injured her right hand and lost the ability to work with maximum efficiency. (Her misshapen fingers are apparent in photographs taken thirty-five years later.) Calculating the seriousness of the injury and his attendant loss of labor, Dumont reneged on his promise. Isabella reached another conclusion: She reckoned that even though she was injured, she had accomplished as much as an ordinary worker, and, therefore, that she had done enough work for the bargain to hold. She was an extraordinarily efficient worker in the house and in the field. It was said that she could do a day's work in the house, then go into the field and work faster than any man. When it came to binding grain, she would "bind a sheaf, throw it up in the air, and have another one bound before the other fell."[2] Dumont may have made and broken his commitment lightly, but for her part, hardworking Isabella still had not forgotten the agreement twenty years later.

ISABELLA freed herself in several steps and in three dimensions: She left slavery with the Dumonts when *she* thought the time was right; she freed herself from fear through a discovery of Jesus' love; and, empowered by her new religious faith, she broke out of the passivity of slavery by using the law toward her own ends. In so complicated a process, no one date captures her passage out of bondage. Citing the moment in July 1827 when she became legally free may conveniently date her liberation, but focusing mainly on the aspects of slavery that affected owners—the legal and the economic—obscures much of emancipation's larger significance.

There is no denying that legal and economic status counted enormously in circumscribing slaves' chances in life; but the injuries of slavery went much deeper, into the bodies and into the psyches of the people who were its victims. In their experience, slavery meant a good deal more than lack of standing before the law and endless, unpaid labor, just as there would be a good deal more to freedom than being able to make a contract or earn a shilling.

In the North, the process of emancipation was made personal by the very gradualness of the laws of most states. Slaves surely preferred to be free sooner rather than later, but their desires were hardly uppermost in the minds of state legislators. Rather, northern abolition moved incrementally, seeing to it that owners were not deprived abruptly of their accustomed labor.

In New York, discussion of abolition began in earnest in the 1780s, and in 1799 the state began the process of gradual emancipation. Slavery would end on the Fourth of July 1827. For those born before 1799, emancipation would be unconditional; but those born after 1799 might have to serve a further period of indentured servitude: until they were twenty-eight, if male, or twenty-five, if female.[3]

This legislation would have kept Isabella and Thomas slaves until 1827. Their children owed indentured servitude for much longer: Diana until about 1840, Peter until about 1849, Elizabeth until about 1850, and Sophia until about 1851. Requirements of law and work kept the family scattered. Indentured, the children could not follow Isabella into freedom, and as a live-in domestic servant, she lacked the home she had dreamed of as she mended by firelight with her children.[4] When Sojourner Truth became an abolitionist, some of her children were still not free.

ISABELLA wanted to be fair. Determined to become free on her own terms, she was not willing to leave John Dumont in the lurch. Never mind that he had reneged on their agreement. Into her reckoning went an attempt to balance his needs against her freedom.[5] So, instead of leaving on the Fourth of July 1826, as their agreement had stipulated, she worked for Dumont throughout the summer of 1826 and, in addition, accomplished a crucial part of the work of the fall—the spinning of Dumont's wool, about one hundred pounds, representing full discharge of her responsibilities. A time-consuming job, spinning by hand nowadays is done mostly as a labor of love, like hand-knitting. The amount of time required to spin wool into yarn depends upon many variables: whether the wool is clean or dirty, how fine or coarsely it is to be spun, and how many hours a day the spinner puts into the work. Isabella had other farm and household chores, so her hours at the wheel were limited.

Ulster County was known as a wool-producing region, but this reputation rested more on the mediocrity of its wheat than the splendor of its wool. As neither Isabella nor Dumont took pride in the production of fine woolen yarn, the raw material was certainly not impeccable and the yarn probably qualified as homespun. The task of spinning Dumont's one hundred pounds of wool into yarn would have taken Isabella four to six months, which would mean that her work as a slave came to an end in November or December 1826.[6]

When Isabella left Dumont of her own volition, she forfeited the possibility of a house and plot for herself and her husband as cottagers, as Isabella's parents had been before Johannis Hardenbergh's death. In the event, neither Isabella nor Thomas would ever have a house in Ulster County, either together or alone. With no home to anchor her in the Hudson Valley, she made her way to the booming city that unbeknownst to her was also becoming the media capital of the United States, a move that made it possible for later generations to know her. Had she stayed around Kingston—even if she had become the most prominent figure in antebellum Ulster County—she most likely would not have found her way into print, the necessary first step into historical memory.

HOW TO start a new life? What to take? What destination to seek? Looking back, Sojourner Truth said in the late 1840s that the answers came from someone she identified as God, a God of her own making, very different from that of the Methodists she met in Ulster County. Early on, Isabella had conceived of a mode and a setting for godly communication, which, in retrospect, seemed to her naive and magical.

On an island in a stream, she built herself a brush arbor, much like the outdoor shrines of black southerners, and worshipped God as though she were in a West African river cult.[7] Like English, French, and American peasants whose concept of religion also encompassed magical practices, Isabella bargained with her God. By midcentury, the memory of such "blasphemous conversations" shocked Sojourner Truth.[8] But Isabella's original concept of God was both distant and familiar; he was a "great man," literate unlike Isabella, one who kept track of what should not be forgotten in a "great book."[9] God and John Dumont had ways of knowing and habits of recall in common.

By the end of the year 1826, Isabella was moving toward

Methodism, but her religious sensibility was syncretic—which is the very essence of African-American culture—and also very much in flux. Her religious foundation was that of country people in New York and New England, a blend of beliefs and habits from animist West Africa and pagan Europe, the Calvinist Dutch Reformed Church and the Arminian Methodists. To this was added the enthusiasms of the Second Great Awakening, when Methodist-style camp meetings affected even Presbyterians and Congregationalists. Isabella's notion of the deity was changing from the distant, judgmental, Calvinist God to whom her mother had taught her to pray, to a closer, more caring God she was encountering with Methodists she had met recently.

In 1826, Isabella heard the voice of her God instructing her when to set out on her own as a free woman. Just before dawn in the late fall, she left the Dumonts' carrying only her baby, Sophia, and a supply of food and clothing so meager that it fit in a cotton handkerchief. She intended only a short journey, so as to save John Dumont trouble when he came looking for her, which she knew he was bound to do, for she was depriving him of two servants—herself and her baby—whom, according to law, he still owned. About five miles away, she called upon an old friend, Levi Rowe, who welcomed her from his deathbed and directed her to Isaac and Maria Van Wagenen of Wagondale, whom she had also known for years.[10] Like the Dumonts, the Van Wagenens were prominent members of the Klyn Esopus Dutch Reformed Church. Unlike the Dumonts, the Van Wagenens opposed slavery. When John Dumont came to fetch Isabella, the Van Wagenens paid him $25:$20 for Isabella for a year, $5 for baby Sophia. Taking the Van Wagenens' last name (often rendered "Van Wagner" outside Ulster County), she lived a "quiet, peaceful life" with "excellent people" there for about a year.[11]

4

Sanctification

BY ISABELLA'S time, Methodists were no longer always proud to be seen as a peculiar and plain people. When they could afford it, many Methodists were as likely as Episcopalians to build expensive churches with rented pews and hire educated ministers who delivered closely reasoned sermons instead of stem-winding, soul-warming preaching. But in the eighteenth century, Methodism had originated as a return to the purity of the primitive church. Holiness had permeated early Methodism and meant living one's life in a holy way by avoiding alcohol, ostentatious dress or furnishings, dancing, and profanity. Eighteenth-century Methodists shouted, cried, fainted, went into trances, and, above all, sang ingenuously in meeting, on ferryboats, on street corners, and wherever else the spirit moved them.[1] But by the nineteenth century, Methodism had been routinized and was moving away from strict holiness, closer to the materialist values of the larger society.

The Second Great Awakening of the early nineteenth century sought to turn this materialist tide in all the American denominations, including Methodism. It brought in thousands of Americans who, like Isabella—and southern slaves and poor whites in the North and South generally—had hitherto been unchurched. But change bred controversy. Even as holiness attracted members and

preachers from all the Protestant denominations, it divided church
people among themselves over preaching styles, manners in worship, and whether believers could know for sure if they were saved
from the fires of hell. The tension between respectability and fervor split Methodists in New York City and New England, and leaders of both camps had allies in the Hudson Valley—in Ulster
County, in fact.

Isabella, being poor and fervent, belonged to the holiness tendency within New York Methodism, which meant that she now
believed in dressing and living simply, subduing anger, and avoiding dissipation. Holiness represented her conversion, for as a young
woman, she had been something of a hell raiser, as her young
mistress, Gertrude Dumont, recalled sixty years later. Gertrude
Dumont remembered that Isabella was long "fond of liquor and
tobacco, and used both when she could get them . . . but she became greatly changed in these respects afterwards."[2] This trajec-
tory from corruption to holiness set Isabella firmly within the
evangelical tradition of sinners who find Jesus, leave off their bad
habits, and save their souls. Isabella quit drinking when she embraced Methodist holiness in the 1820s, but it was another forty
years before she gave up smoking.

In early 1827, Isabella helped to found the Kingston Methodist
Church. Her very inclusion situates it in the democratic, enthusiastic strand of Methodism called "perfectionism" in the late 1820s
and early 1830s. In our time, the term that best describes the religion Isabella believed in and felt in her heart is "pentecostal."
Isabella and her fellow worshippers laid great emphasis on the
Holy Spirit, or, as they said often, simply, "the Spirit." The moment they concentrated on most was Pentecost, the time after
Jesus' resurrection when the Apostles, filled by the Holy Spirit,
spoke in tongues, a practice that has long characterized pentecostalism.[3]

For Isabella, the significance of these "pentecostal outpourings
of the Holy Spirit" was amplified by the approach of Pinkster in
1827. Not only was Pinkster the Dutch celebration of Pentecost and
hence of the Holy Spirit, it had also become the moment in which
black New Yorkers came together and celebrated as a people.

"Pinkster"—Dutch for "Pentecost" (the English Whitsuntide)—

occurs seven weeks after Easter.[4] Initially the Dutch in New Netherland celebrated Pinkster as a religious holiday, but after the American Revolution, the class, racial, and religious character of the holiday shifted. No longer primarily a Dutch Reformed commemoration of the Apostles' baptism by the Holy Spirit, Pinkster by the early nineteenth century had become a carnival week in which Afro-New Yorkers celebrated on a grand scale. The biggest and most elaborate Pinkster celebration took place in Albany, on "Pinkster Hill," now the site of the state capitol, where black people crowned a king, drummed, paraded, danced, sang, drank, and staged elaborate ceremonies in which those who had been born in Africa instructed the American-born. Blacks in New York City and other towns also celebrated Pinkster, though less elaborately. For so scattered a people as Afro-Dutch New Yorkers, Pinkster served as a unique racial jubilee, what an observer termed "the perfect Saturnalia."[5]

Before Isabella became a Methodist trying to live out holiness convictions, she would have eagerly anticipated Pinkster as a great good time; but for a Methodist committed to living a holy life and resisting worldly temptations, Isabella's anticipation of Pinkster represented a spiritual rebuke. The revels of Pinkster became her consummate symbol for backsliding, saturated with racial and religious meaning.

In 1827, Pinkster fell on the 4th of June, exactly one month before the general emancipation, a coincidence that would have endowed the holiday with added significance. At this point Isabella had been living with the Van Wagenens for several months, but their virtue proved no match for the prospect of Pinkster in the year of freedom. Isabella "looked back into Egypt" and imagined the good times to come with Pinkster among her black friends back at the Dumonts'. Pinkster in 1827 bore a bundle of meanings for Isabella: slavery and blackness, freedom and apprehension, hope and vice and pleasure, and commitment to a life of religious purity—the old world and the new order all at once. Isabella's near relapse into celebrating freedom with the pleasures of the flesh provoked a crisis that led to her sanctification.

Isabella nursed her anticipation in secret, until one morning she told Maria Van Wagenen she had an intimation that John Dumont would come to fetch her. Isabella said she would go back with him. In the course of that very day, Dumont appeared, as her father had appeared years earlier to deliver her from the Neelys.

As a middle-aged Sojourner Truth retold it twenty years later, her interchange with John Dumont was playful. She does not explain why he said he came by or stopped at the Van Wagenens' house, but she says that she told him she was going home with him. She thought "his manner contradicted his words" because he was smiling at her when he said he would not take her back. After all, she had run away from him. And yet he waited—or so Isabella thought—while she readied herself and her baby to leave.[6] As Olive Gilbert retells what Sojourner Truth said happened next in her *Narrative*, Dumont sat himself in his open carriage, and Isabella was about to join him. Then came the moment. Before she climbed into the back of the vehicle,

> God revealed himself to her, with all the suddenness of a flash of lightning, showing her, "in the twinkling of an eye, that he was *all over*"— that he pervaded the universe—"and that there was no place where God was not." She became instantly conscious of her great sin in forgetting her almighty Friend and "ever-present help in time of trouble." All her unfilled promises arose before her, like a vexed sea whose waves run mountains high; and her soul, which seemed but one mass of lies, shrunk back aghast from the "awful look" of Him whom she had formerly talked to, as if he had been a being like herself; and she would now fain have hid herself in the bowels of the earth, to have escaped his dread presence.[7]

She feared certain, awful annihilation should she receive "another such 'a look,' " but the second look did not come.

When Isabella regained consciousness of the world around her, Dumont was gone. She walked back into the Van Wagenens' house to resume her work, but work lost out to the travail of sanctification, as she wrestled with ambivalence and the experience of God's awesome, immediate presence. She wanted to talk to God, to mollify Him, but "her vileness utterly forbade it." She felt worthless before God's immensity, and, cowering in her degradation, she wished for an intercessor to plead against her extinction. After such tremendous spiritual turmoil came blessed relief. She felt that a

friend had come to shield her from the "burning sun" of God's
wrath.

In the peaceful aftermath of torment, she found an ally. "Who
are you?" she asked of the vision that beamed "with the beauty of
holiness, and radiant with love." Evoking images of light and asking a version of Paul's emblematic question, "who art thou?" Isabella was, like countless evangelicals before her, reenacting Paul's
conversion on the road to Damascus.[8] Her vision was of Jesus, who
loved her, had always loved her, who would stand between Isabella
and God's fury. "When he came," she recalled, "she should go and
dwell with him, as with a dear friend." She was radiantly happy,
with a heart as "full of joy and gladness" as it had been of terror
and despair. The liberating presence of Jesus eased Isabella's
pain.[9]

ISABELLA would speak later of being baptized in the Holy Spirit.
Experiencing a second birth of entire sanctification, she had been
born again with an assurance of salvation that gave her the self-
confidence to oppose the rich and powerful of this world.

As a vulnerable young woman—deprived of her parents, over-
worked, neglected, beaten, and sexually abused—she had approached this world with a vivid sense of her worthlessness,
convinced that insuperable barriers separated her from the prominent people she worked for. Now she had a friend in Jesus, whom
she sometimes likened to "a soul-protecting fortress," sometimes
to a power that raised her "above the battlements of fear." The assurance of her sanctification and God's constant support released
Isabella from the crippling conviction that she was nothing. She
discovered a new means of power, what pentecostals call the power
of the Spirit, that redressed the balance between someone poor and
black and female and her rich white masters.[10]

Isabella discovered the secret power that black women have
tapped into over the generations to counter the negation they experience in the world. In sanctification, they have located a power
that has made possible survival and autonomous action when all
other means fail. More than anything else she did or said in her
life, this ability to act with the support of a powerful supernatural

force and to mine its extraordinary resources made Sojourner Truth a representative African-American woman.[11]

A century later, Isabella would have fallen within the ranks of those identified as "sanctified" or "holiness" or "pentecostal," perhaps in the Church of God in Christ, which has proved so hospitable to black women's spiritual gifts.[12] Those churches had not yet been formed, but even without an institutional identity, her faith placed God on her side in a way that still serves people without worldly resources.[13] Such faith would buttress her will in the struggle now almost upon her.

5

Plaintiff and Witch

As ISABELLA went about her housework, she preached and sang, learning a new vocation through practice. The Van Wagenen family quite approved of her Methodism and were impressed by her preaching. Surely she ought to live somewhere that could provide the big audiences her preaching was coming to deserve.[1] A place to find work and save souls in abundance lay a hundred miles to the south, beckoning to Isabella, as it did to country people all around its upstate and New Jersey hinterlands. She would have been free to leave the Van Wagenens and go to New York City in early 1828, had her plans not been disrupted by some very bad news.

At the end of 1826, John Dumont had sold her son Peter to one of his in-laws, a Dr. Gedney, who was probably Sally Dumont's cousin. Gedney had taken Peter to New York City, evidently bound for England. But Peter, only five or six years old at the time, proved too young to carry out the tasks that Gedney had in mind. Even so, the child's youth did not protect him from the trauma of multiple sales and removals. Gedney sold Peter to his brother, Solomon Gedney, who then resold the boy to his brother-in-law, an Alabama planter named Fowler, who had married Solomon Gedney's sister

Eliza, Sally Dumont's second cousin. Six-year-old Peter found himself enslaved in Alabama, a thousand miles from mother and home.

Solomon Gedney's impulse was fairly common in New York State in the mid-1820s. As slavery was coming to an end, New York owners sought to cash in on the still vigorous southern market by selling their slaves south. Although state law prohibited the sale of New York slaves into places where slavery would continue to be legal after 1827, the law was subject to routine and massive contravention. Peter was only one of thousands of black New Yorkers illegally sold into perpetual bondage in the South.[2] Had Isabella not acted, she would have joined her parents and countless other black families who experienced the searing, permanent loss of children. Slavery was ending in New York, but not this all-too-familiar bereavement.

But now Isabella was a new woman who believed that her God would help her recover her son. She called first at the Dumonts', where Sally Dumont scoffed: *"Ugh! a fine fuss to make about a little nigger!"* Sally Dumont expressed surprise at "such a halloo-balloo about the neighborhood; and all for a paltry nigger!!!" To which Isabella replied, with immense determination, *"I'll have my child again."* Isabella had no money, the key to justice, but, she said, God had the means to regain her son. She felt, she recalled much later, "so *tall within*—I felt as if the *power of a nation* was within me!"[3]

Isabella then went to Mrs. Gedney—the mother of Solomon Gedney, mother-in-law of Fowler, and the aunt of Sally Dumont. Gedney's response was self-pitying. She missed her daughter Eliza so far away in Alabama and scoffed at Isabella's reminder that Gedney's daughter was grown up, but Peter was too young to be so distant from his mother. Finding the Dumont-Gedney-Waring family utterly unsympathetic, Isabella did not despair. "Oh, God, you know I have no money, but you can make the people do for me, and you must make the people do for me," she said to her ally. "Oh, God, make the people hear me—don't let them turn me off, without hearing and helping me."[4]

The only way to retrieve Peter was by going to court, something normally far outside the experience of poor women like Isabella. With the aid of the Holy Spirit, she acted. She sought and received advice and money for legal fees, above board from Ulster County Quakers and in secret from John H. Rutzer and A. Bruyn Hasbrouck, prominent Dutch lawyers with whom she would live and work in 1828. Although intimidated and naive, she entered a complaint with the Ulster County grand jury.[5]

The process of getting Peter back took about a year, but by the spring of 1828, while Isabella was working at the Rutzers', Peter returned to Kingston. It was a homecoming that nearly broke his mother's heart. When his master brought Peter to Isabella, the child shrieked piteously and refused to go to her. Regarding his mother as though she were a monster, he clung to his "dear master," with whom he begged to stay. Isabella was utterly disconcerted. She knew she had gotten out of her place and run afoul of a prominent family by going to court, and here, at the culmination of her efforts, her boy was hysterically denying her. She could lose her child and her year's efforts through his refusal to acknowledge her as his mother. Isabella had no way of knowing that Peter's response after so tragic a separation was characteristic of children who feel themselves abandoned by the adult to whom they are most attached, no matter what the objective circumstances of the loss.

Peter had over the course of this most traumatic year become detached from Isabella, the second stage of his reaction to the loss of his mother. At first, when he had been sold away, he would have been deeply distressed, disconsolate, and despairing. Isabella was seeing the middle stage, when, reunited with his mother, he acted as though she were a terrible stranger. In the third stage, after reconciling with her, he would have become intensely clinging and perhaps aggressive and defiant. This kind of behavior might help explain why Isabella took Peter with her to New York City instead of leaving him in Ulster County with his father and his sisters.[6]

On the day of their reconciliation, several adults—Isabella, the lawyer, and the clerks of the county court—soothed Peter and convinced him that Isabella was, indeed, his own mother. Once he was mollified, Isabella got a good look at him, and again, her spirits

fell: "Oh, Lord Jesus, Look! see my poor child!" Peter was covered with scars from head to toe, and his lacerated back was as
rough as a washboard. Isabella discovered that Fowler had
whipped, kicked, and beaten Peter, though the boy was not yet
seven years old. Peter told his mother that Fowler had also attacked
a young slave mother, whipping her "till the milk as well as blood
ran down *her* body." Fowler's assaults had distressed Cousin Eliza
as well as Peter.

Seeing her child's tortured body overwhelmed Isabella with sor-
row—"Oh my God! Pete, how *did* you bear it?"—and with anger. In
this moment of anguish, Isabella forgot her Methodism, forgot the
faith that does not seek retaliation. She returned to the magic of
the rural culture in which she had grown up, and sought vengeance
in an act of everyday witchcraft. Cursing Fowler and his family, she
called upon her God to "render unto them double" for what they
had done to Peter.[7] Among country people of Isabella's time,
witchcraft usually dealt in *maleficium*—curses aimed at neighbors
who withheld needed favors or who spat out insults. As the curse
of one who was poor and afflicted, her malediction was likely to
work.[8]

Isabella remained in touch with the Dumont-Gedney-Waring
family after Peter's return, living with and working for various
branches in a seeming act of forgiveness that astonished even
John Dumont. As she explained it to her old master, she hoped
her efforts would lessen Solomon Gedney's anger toward her,
which had nearly caused her to lose a job with his cousins. Then
one day when she was working for the first time in the home of
Frederick Waring (Solomon Gedney's and Sally Dumont's uncle),
one of Waring's daughters rushed up with shocking news. The
same Fowler who had abused Peter so brutally had beaten Eliza
Gedney Fowler to death.

Isabella's feelings were contradictory. She mourned Eliza and
grieved for Eliza's family, even for her mother, who had laughed
at Isabella's appeal for assistance in rescuing Peter. Nonetheless
she recognized—as the Gedneys had not—that a man who would
abuse a black child so cruelly could murder someone white, even
one of his own, especially a woman.

The coincidences were remarkable. Isabella was only once in her life in the house of Frederick Waring, on the very day when news of Eliza's murder arrived. Twenty years later, Sojourner Truth was convinced that "a special providence of God" was at work, that the Gedneys' anguish was an act of "retributive justice," God's answer to her curse. In 1828 and perhaps also in 1848, she inwardly remarked, "Oh, my God! that's too much—I did not mean quite so much, God!"[9] The news and circumstances of Eliza's death unhinged the Waring household. Eliza's mother lost her mind and spent her days pacing about, crying Eliza's name; one of Eliza Fowler's children grew chronically depressed.

The Methodist perfectionist that Isabella became in the late 1820s would not ordinarily have used witchcraft, but in a moment of extreme provocation, a mother who had only recently been born again into the assurance of Jesus' love could be understood for uttering a curse that would bear more bitter fruit than she might ever have imagined. After the recovery of her son and the death of Eliza Gedney Fowler, Isabella may never again have turned to witchcraft; waging and winning a struggle with her superiors in a court of law may have given her sufficient courage not to need it any more. But she never lost that force of character.

DURING the time that Isabella was working for various wealthy families around Kingston, her daughters remained bound to their master. Her later efforts to have her children with her point to the conflict she felt between motherhood and ambition, between staying in Ulster County with her children and seeking well-paid work in the metropolis. In the late 1820s, she resolved that tension in the favor of bettering her fortunes.

Peter's situation was less agonizing, for the one redeeming feature of his ordeal in Alabama was his release by law from additional years of indenture, a burden carried by others born into slavery in New York in the early nineteenth century. Peter was free to accompany his mother, but his sisters had to stay with the Dumonts. While Isabella prepared to leave the country, she put Peter to work tending locks on the Delaware-Hudson Canal in Wagondale.[10]

In September 1828, a way opened toward the city. Isabella and Peter moved to New York with a Mr. and Miss Grear, who were, like Isabella, Methodist perfectionists. It was the Grears who put her in touch with the people who would influence her life profoundly during the next fifteen years.

6

New York Perfectionism

HOW FINE it would be to sit in an archive, open a document to
the page dated 1828, and read from Isabella's own hand how it
came to be that she left Ulster County for New York City: to learn
from her directly what she thought of the prospect of city life. What
went through her mind during the day-long boat trip, and why she
went with the traveling companions she chose, whom we know
only as Mr. and Miss Grear. Miss Grear was a teacher who knew
her way around the city, and she and her father found Isabella
work in the homes of their friends.

Among those friends were the Latourettes, a zealous Methodist
family who lived on Bowery Hill. Their patronage would prove crucial in Isabella's life, for the Latourettes influenced the course of
Isabella's experiences in New York, immediately and for many
years to come.[1] Access to direct testimony would be gratifying; but
lacking the document, lacking the archive, and, indeed, lacking any
word whatever from Sojourner Truth or the Grears or the Latourettes, the biographer continues the process through piecing.
Luckily, James Latourette and the people known as perfectionists who shared his convictions—some of whom called themselves
prophets—attracted commentary. I am thankful for it, even though
it comes mainly from their critics.

Isabella brought from Ulster County a prized possession, one of
the few material items that she carried out of slavery and kept always: the ticket that certified her conversion to Methodism and admitted her to the John Street Methodist Church in New York City.
Like thousands of other poor, mobile English, Irish, and American people, Isabella preserved this ticket as an assurance of community in a vast city of strangers, for Methodist societies were
divided into classes that met weekly, small groups of fellowship that
today would seem akin to group therapy.[2] Isabella's group at the
John Street Church in 1829–30 was the segregated black class
meeting.

Uncomfortable at John Street Church, she soon moved on to the
Zion African Church, which later became the mother church of
the African Methodist Episcopal Zionists. Zion Church had been
formed in 1796 by seceders led by Peter Williams and others,
when racism became too onerous at the John Street Church. In
this black congregation in the early 1830s, Isabella found family
as well as fellowship; but as had so often been her case, the re-
discovery of family meant reacquaintance with tragedy.

Isabella's older sister Sophia (for whom Isabella had named her
baby) had moved from Ulster County separately from Isabella, but
they reestablished contact in New York City. Now Sophia introduced Isabella to their brother Michael, who had been so cruelly
kidnapped when he was five. In their initial conversation, Michael
gave Isabella startling news: she had met the other victim of the
abduction, their sister Nancy, who had recently died. As Michael
described Nancy, Isabella remembered seeing this woman at Zion
Church who, she now learned, was her sister. Isabella recalled
being struck by the "peculiar feeling of her hand—the bony hard-
ness so just like mine? and yet I could not know she was my sister; and now I see she looked *so* like my mother!" Isabella wept at
this realization, and Sophia and Michael wept with her. "Oh Lord,"
Isabella exclaimed, "what is this slavery, that it can do such dreadful things?"[3] Slavery had turned this family into mourners, and the
atrocities that had become so familiar to Isabella would help explain her choices in the 1830s, when she lived with the Prophet
Matthias.

Between 1828 and 1832 Isabella lived with the Latourette family, even when she and her young son Peter worked for others such as the Perez Whitings. The kindness of the Latourettes, she said, made her feel like one of the family, a sentiment that Peter evidently shared. At the Latourettes', Isabella and Peter were only two of several working-class black residents. Rare but not unique in his lack of racial prejudice, James Latourette was a Canal Street fur merchant, born in 1794. Like the Ulster County Dumonts, he was of French Huguenot descent, with Dutch Reformed connections. Though of comfortable means, the Latourettes' did not let their wealth make them complacent; quite the opposite. The Latourettes were fervent Christians—so ardent that they had rejected the Methodist Church as degenerate—and held religious meetings in their house, as had dissident American Protestants since Anne Hutchinson and the Antinomians challenged Puritan leadership in the 1630s.

These "free meetings," so called because anyone could attend them and speak, were by the early nineteenth century a long-standing American tradition. Free meetings usually assembled in homes, in Latourette's case in an especially designated "upper room," a phrase that resonated with eighteenth-century Methodism, English and American, and seventeenth-century American Puritanism, as well as with the precedent of Jesus and the disciples. Meeting outside churches avoided the issues of denominational exclusion, pew rental, and a regularly ordained clergy, which seemed to perfectionists just so many signs of the corruption of conventional religion.[4]

The Latourettes, having left the regular Methodist Church because of its falling away from the ideals of John Wesley, Methodism's founder, were deeply religious but not at all orthodox. Replicating early Wesleyan practice, they gathered the faithful around them in a tight religious community. Speakers in meeting were encouraged through frequent interjections of "Hallelujah" and "Glory."[5] The Bible was their only text, in accordance with the precepts of Anne Hutchinson, John Wesley, and innumerable other evangelicals. This fellowship, soon dominated by James Latourette, came to be known as the "Holy Club," perhaps in reference to a certain self-righteousness on the part of these ascetics. The name echoes the same mocking terminology applied to the earliest associates of John Wesley in Oxford in 1731.[6]

Gradually, Latourette's sect took on an identity—New York perfectionism—and came to influence a loosely knit group of other bands scattered up the western side of the Hudson River to Albany and across to the west toward Syracuse and Rochester. This became known as the "burnt over district," so called for the spiritual heat generated by the religious fires that burned there in the early nineteenth century.[7] Perfectionism sought to eradicate the corruption of this world, just as John Wesley's Methodism was meant to purify the Anglican Church.

The New York City hub of perfectionism had originated in the Retrenchment Society, a prayer meeting among wealthy married women that Frances Folger had started in 1825 and to which Mrs. Latourette belonged. This free meeting welcomed women from the Presbyterian, Dutch Reformed, Baptist, and Methodist churches on condition that they speak only when moved by the Holy Spirit. Harking back to the ways of the Apostles, Retrenchment Society women repudiated the luxury that would have made their bodies and their houses capitalist trophies. They also adopted an austere diet—no rich foods, tea, or coffee—fasted regularly, and visited the prisons and the poorest district of the city, Five Points, to pray with the prostitutes, criminals, diseased, and homeless people who had gained nothing from the city's booming economy.[8]

The New York perfectionism that Isabella, the Latourettes, Miss Grear, and Frances Folger and her associates shared was only one of a myriad of unorthodox "new light" New York religions like Mormonism and Millerism that were attracting adherents during the dramatic economic and demographic growth that accompanied the completion of the Erie Canal linking the Midwest, via the Great Lakes, to New York City. With a population of more than 200,000 in 1831, New York City (which did not then include Brooklyn, a major city in its own right) was far and away the largest metropolis in the United States.[9] Before the disastrous financial crash of 1837, people of all classes flocked to New York as a burgeoning trade center offering jobs in abundance. If money flowed unevenly and the masses remained poor and wretched, New York's prosperity nevertheless created a considerable class of wealthy merchants who spent freely on whatever struck their fancy.

Some of the rich invested in real estate, and moving away from their offices and warehouses, created fashionable residential neighborhoods uptown (on Bleecker Street, Lafayette Place, Waverly Place, and Irving Place), into and even beyond suburban Bowery Hill (leveled in the early 1830s).[10] Others, like the evangelical Pearl Street businessmen James Latourette, Elijah Pierson, and Arthur Tappan, indulged their tastes for expensive houses but followed the inclinations of their wives and spent on their consciences. In the economic boom of the 1830s, this meant supporting charitable causes in the name of religious philanthropy. Tappan became the country's leading abolitionist by the mid-1830s; Pierson played a central (and tragic) role in the Matthias Kingdom of 1832–34, to which he and Isabella belonged; Latourette was the leading New York perfectionist in the early 1830s. All found ways of transcending the conventional religion of the city's churches.

Latourette and Pierson died without following Tappan—and, indeed, Sojourner Truth some years later—into political reform. But even after Truth had established herself as an antislavery feminist in the 1850s, she and her associates bore the hallmarks of the perfectionism she had accepted in the late 1820s: dressing and living plainly, and listening to "the Spirit"—a voice representing communication and power.[11] Holiness attracted other black women besides Isabella in New York City. In Philadelphia, Rebecca Cox Jackson, a black visionary preacher and later a Shaker eldress, saw a plainly dressed woman walking in the street in 1830 and adopted this simple style of dress as, she wrote, "one ought to do who was aleaving the world, the flesh, and the devil."[12]

IT MIGHT seem puzzling that so poor and hardworking a woman as Isabella would condemn herself for extravagance, but she did. Intangible but crucial was the matter of her children. State law kept them with Dumont, but law does not govern sentiment. Just as Peter had felt that his mother had abandoned him when Dumont sold him away from home, so Isabella probably felt guilt for having moved away from her daughters in Ulster County. She may have seen her pursuit of her own ambitions as a preacher and worker as selfishness. Isabella as a conflicted parent is only visible between the lines of the evidence, but her struggle with the attractions of the flesh is easier to see.

As a slave she was "strong and healthy," according to Gertrude Dumont, "an excellent dancer and a good singer, having a pleasant voice, rich and powerful."[13] Even before leaving Ulster County, she was considered vain, the kind of woman who savored the effect of her attractiveness on others. She made good money as a wage earner and spent freely on personal adornment.[14] In New York she managed to buy furniture and put money in the bank, and she was conscious of living in better circumstances than many others, white and black.

Isabella took pride in fashionable clothing, but the conceit of an improved appearance stirred its own misgivings. Isabella would have known and perhaps shared the disdain with which her middle-class co-religionists regarded flashily dressed working girls and domestic servants. At the same time that plain clothing demonstrated her holiness, it offered her a means of distancing herself from the female lower classes, whose loud dresses announced their lowly status.

Probably more crucial was Isabella's own past: After thirty years in the coarse outfits of a slave, Isabella perhaps saw her free woman's fine clothing as inappropriate, somehow equivalent in decadence to the former ostentation of the ladies of the Retrenchment Society, no matter how disparate their cases.[15] Holiness spoke to her as one who had succumbed to the sin of vanity.

WHILE she lived at the Latourettes', Isabella preached with them in the camp meetings around the city, the most famous of which were in the Westchester County settlements of Croton and Mount Pleasant (which later became known as Sing Sing, then Ossining).[16] During the years 1829–31, a time of revivalist zeal, Isabella established her standing as a powerful and moving preacher. Latourette said that she was remarkable for bringing about conversions, that the effect of her preaching was so "miraculous" that "even learned and respectable people were running after her." She "out-prayed and preached her compeers" and outdrew the celebrated Irish Methodist itinerant, John Newland Maffitt, when they preached together.[17] An eyewitness at one of Maffitt's camp meeting appearances described a scene that Isabella might have caused:

> [Maffitt's] peroration was brilliant as a shower of falling stars, and the effect produced, indescribable. For fifteen minutes before he took his seat, grey-headed men might be seen trembling like leaves in a rushing wind; and beautiful maidens, with jewelled hair, were heard to shriek as if in the presence of a ghost from eternity! All was terror and a tempest of confusion. The altar became crowded to suffocation; but still it could not hold half the mourners. Strong men were stricken down where they stood; and many of both sexes, who fled for safety from their own emotions to the camps, fell down overpowered by the way. Screams for mercy issued from all directions in the surrounding woods, whither those had gone who preferred seeking God in solitude, to the noise and tumult of the altar.[18]

At the peak of his powers in the years when he appeared with Isabella in the early 1830s, Maffitt was one of the nineteenth century's most charismatic preachers, which, considering the brilliance of a field headed by Charles Grandison Finney, is impressive. Maffitt was chaplain to the U.S. Congress in 1841 and over the course of his career was credited with saving more than twenty thousand souls. His shortcomings, too, were legion: In the words of James Mudge, a New England Methodist historian, "his influence was sadly marred by serious defects of character," notably too fond an eye for wealthy, attractive young ladies and a weakness for alcohol. Maffitt died in poverty in 1850.[19]

Inglorious death was the lot of another of Isabella and Latourette's colleagues in holiness, Harriet Livermore. Hardly less celebrated than John Maffitt, Livermore became an unaffiliated itinerant preacher, a self-proclaimed "pilgrim and a stranger," who cut a broad swath in the antebellum era. Livermore came from a far more privileged background than Isabella, but as a colleague of James Latourette, she also moved in the wider community of New York perfectionists. After a long career, during which she addressed the U.S. Congress four times, Livermore died penniless at eighty in 1868.[20]

In the early 1830s, in the world of Maffitt, Livermore, and Latourette, Isabella was at the dawn of her public career. She had the magnetism and asceticism that characterized New York perfectionism, and her physical stature, fervor, eloquence, and singing were making her reputation. Oddly, then, when Isabella first appeared in New York City newspapers, it was neither as preacher nor perfectionist. She attracted notice as part of a religious commune infamous for free love and murder, headed by a fanatic who called himself the Prophet Matthias.

ISABELLA met Matthias through Elijah Pierson, who had been drawn into Isabella's circle through his wife Sarah, a member of the Retrenchment Society, that plain-living band of women around Frances Folger. This band had increased in the mid-1820s, as Mrs. Latourette, Mrs. Ann Folger (Frances Folger's sister-in-law), and Mrs. Pierson brought their husbands into the fold. James Latourette quickly emerged as its leader. The larger, mixed group was still overwhelmingly female, but it was more hierarchical and focused less on plain living and more on sharing the gifts of the Holy Spirit: testifying to their spiritual experiences, praying together, washing each other's feet, fasting, singing hymns, speaking in tongues, shouting, getting happy, clapping, jerking, seeking miracles, and digging for treasure (a fairly common nineteenth-century pursuit that Latourette's people shared with early Mormons).

Miss Grear and Mrs. Latourette introduced Isabella to moral reform by taking her with them to visit the most despised class of female New Yorkers. Isabella did not take well to the work. The difficulty grew out of conflicting assumptions about Isabella's position relative to the ladies and the prostitutes. She did not lump herself with the people at the bottom, poor women and black women who, she knew, were not of her caliber. Such distinctions among the black and the poor would have escaped the notice of wealthy moral reformers. Grear and Latourette probably assumed, with the thoughtlessness that accompanies privilege, that poor, black Isabella would have a special rapport with the downtrodden. This turned out not to be the case.

The one time that Isabella agreed to join a prayer meeting in the slums, the worship was so rowdy that she was knocked down. While Isabella accepted the enthusiasm of the meetings in the Latourettes' house, her tolerance for shouting in distasteful settings had its bounds. She refused to attend prayer meetings with women whose ecstasy turned bruising, although she consented to go pray with and instruct the inmates of Elijah Pierson's Magdalen Asylum on Bowery Hill.[21]

Her distance from the prostitutes did not mean that Isabella saw herself as the equal of the ladies. She knew that in the Holy Club she was associating with people more privileged than she, and from her later recollections it seems that she extended their superior level of education to their attainment of holiness. She reckoned that if they needed to fast for one day to improve their understanding of the things of God, she, who had no education whatever, would need to fast for three.[22]

Elijah Pierson, a leader in the Holy Club, had been the motivating spirit behind the Magdalen Asylum on Bowery Hill. His influence among evangelical, reforming New Yorkers reached its zenith in 1831, when Arthur Tappan joined him in establishing an enlarged Magdalen House of Refuge, a shelter for poor and homeless women.[23]

Born in 1786, Pierson came from a flourishing Presbyterian family of slaveowners in Morristown, New Jersey. He moved to New York City as a young man, went into a business partnership in 1820, and succeeded. In 1822 he married Sarah Stanford, who matched him in religious commitment; both were considered pious and philanthropic. By 1830 he had done well enough in the machinery and patent rights business to accumulate an ample retirement fund of some $70,000.[24]

More recently Pierson had become a perfectionist and acquired a reputation for religious fanaticism. He studied his Bible assiduously, began to see himself as a prophet, and after a divine revelation on a city omnibus on Wall Street in June of 1830, took to calling himself "Elijah the Tishbite." He believed that, like Elijah, the Old Testament prophet in I Kings 17, he would be able to cure illness and banish the awful reality of death.

When his wife Sarah died in 1830 after several months of the Retrenchment Society's strenuous fasting, Pierson tried to pray her back to life. He followed God's advice to the prophet Elijah, seceded from Latourette's congregation, and formed his own church at his home on Bowery Hill, which he called the members of Israel at Mt. Carmel. Pentecostal that he was, he expected the world to end soon in "the great and dreadful day of the Lord."[25]

Isabella met Pierson through Katy, his black servant and fellow perfectionist, with whom she had probably grown friendly in Latourette's Holy Club. Pierson and Isabella quickly recognized each other as kindred souls through a brief, formalized exchange. He asked her if she had been baptized. Her affirmative response, "by the Holy Ghost," established her pentecostal identity. Later, when Katy needed someone to fill her place at Pierson's while she visited her children in Virginia, Isabella became his live-in housekeeper.[26] As with the Latourettes, Isabella had found a co-religionist as well as an employer in Elijah Pierson.

7

In the Kingdom of Matthias

IN MAY 1832, Isabella and the widower Elijah Pierson received a visit from a resplendently dressed figure: Robert Matthews, a Scots-American calling himself "the Prophet Matthias," whose singular manifestations of perfectionism had already created consternation upstate. Sylvester Mills, Pierson's fellow perfectionist Pearl Street merchant, vouched for him. This attractive forty-four-year-old stranger combed his hair and beard to make himself look like the chromo pictures of Jesus. When Isabella met him at the door, she knew immediately from Matthew, Chapter 16, to ask, "Art thou the Christ?" When the visitor answered, "I am," she kissed his feet and burst into tears of joy. Pierson's welcome was equally ecstatic. In the parlor, Isabella, Pierson, and Matthias exchanged their experiences of visions and voices and agreed on everything.[1]

For a while Pierson and Matthias alternated preaching in meetings at Pierson's house, but Pierson—whom Matthias now called John the Baptist—gave up preaching after Matthias said, and his followers believed, that "God don't speak through preachers; he speaks through me, his prophet."[2]

Adept at using the Bible for his own purposes, Matthias had his favorite passages; one was Revelation 10, which he often led the group in reading. Here a mighty angel of the Lord swears "by him

MEMOIRS
OF
MATTHIAS THE PROPHET,
WITH A FULL EXPOSURE OF
HIS ATROCIOUS IMPOSITIONS,
AND OF THE
DEGRADING DELUSIONS OF HIS FOLLOWERS.

PRICE THREE CENTS.

WRITTEN FOR THE NEW YORK SUN.

NEW YORK.
OFFICE OF THE SUN........222 WILLIAM STREET.
1835.

Title page, *Memoirs of Matthias the Prophet* (New York, 1835).
Photo courtesy of the American Antiquarian Society.

that liveth for ever and ever, who created heaven, and the things that therein are, and the earth, and the things that therein are, and the sea, and the things which are therein, that there should be time no longer" (verse 6). To ensure the spread of this imperative, the angel commands that "Thou must prophesy again before many peoples, and nations, and tongues, and kings" (verse 11). New York City was an ideal place to pursue so ambitious a mission.

MATTHIAS'S road to Pierson's house in the spring of 1832 had been irregular and sometimes solitary. An orphan brought up by a poor family in rural Washington County, New York, close to the Vermont border, Robert Matthews had made his living in the prophetic trade of carpentry. As an adult, he had moved his family back and forth between New York City, Washington County, and Albany, pushed and pulled by employment opportunities and the state of his belief. Matthews had become a fervent champion of total abstinence from alcohol and animal food, to the point of taking his two small children into the woods, feeding them on roots and berries for several days, and driving their mother to distraction. Taking heed in 1830 of what he heard as the voice of the Holy Spirit, Matthews began to regard himself as a Jew and renamed himself the Prophet Matthias. He let his beard grow and began to preach an urgent message.

In the name of God, Matthias cried vengeance against the people and the land. Now was the end of the time of the "Gentiles," which meant everyone in America who did not heed his warning, for he, the Prophet Matthias, had been commanded to take possession of the world. Continuing to preach the end of the world and following the lead of the Spirit, he set off to the West. Such journeys were typical. The New Haven perfectionist John Humphrey Noyes some years later followed the Spirit's command to go south. As Sojourner Truth, Isabella would obey a divine command to go east. In the wilderness, Matthias wandered for some months, through New York, Pennsylvania, and New Jersey. Finally he came back around to New York City, where he converted Sylvester Mills, a member of Pierson's Israel at Mt. Carmel Church, who despite his wealth—or perhaps because of it—harbored a notion that his world was about to end. Matthias supplied the date: 9 July 1836.

In the highly competitive world of prophecy in New York City, Matthias began to stand out visually and verbally. Preaching on the Battery that he was the Spirit of Truth, he wore a shiny black

leather cap shaped like a cone, a green frock coat lined with white
or pink satin, a crimson silk sash around his waist, and highly polished Wellington boots outside his trousers.[3]

At the same time that Matthias repudiated the sartorial plainness of the holiness movement from which Mills, Pierson, and
Isabella had come, he placed more emphasis on the Holy Spirit,
especially upon the power he gained as its instrument. He and they
were moving away from holiness's purity to pentecostalism's
power—and from a concentration on the work of Christ to that of
the Holy Spirit.[4] Matthias claimed that after the Spirit of Truth had
disappeared from the earth with the death of Matthias of the New
Testament, he, the Prophet Matthias, possessed the spirits of both
Matthias and Jesus Christ.[5]

As it was for Jesus, so it was for the Prophet Matthias in the
1830s: The Holy Spirit spoke through him, warning that the Day
of Judgment was soon to come. Matthias knew when—in four
years—and thanks to Sylvester Mills's pocketbook, Matthias looked
the part of the prophet. He carried a large, solid gold key that symbolized his power to welcome or expel people from the city of the
New Jerusalem (to be located in western New York); a graduated
rule six feet long marked with the mysterious numbers of the
apocalypse that he would use to mark out boundaries and lots in
the holy city; and a two-edged sword that emblemized the power
of the Spirit to conquer all. His tokens of prophecy included, in
addition, various astrological devices and sacred items of clothing,
all intended to express his godliness and potency.[6] This splendid
wardrobe and Matthias's authoritative demeanor attracted audiences in the streets and churches where he preached.

Although Matthias succeeded in convincing some in the Holy
Club of his divine powers, his seduction left other New York perfectionists cold.

James Latourette attempted to cure Pierson and Isabella of their
fascination. This criticism and an attack on the prophet's person
at Mills's house only strengthened their faith. In October 1832,
Pierson rented a house for Matthias, where he stayed until the
spring of 1833 with Isabella as his housekeeper and material support. She willingly gave him money from her own savings, even
though people she respected considered Matthias an impostor and

told her so. Early in her time with Matthias, Isabella learned both that she had material resources that he needed and that her friends thought giving him money a very bad idea. Leaving him at this point would have been easier than staying, for her decision to stick by him was made against serious opposition and at a clear financial price.[7]

THE MATTHIAS KINGDOM came into being in the summer of 1833, when Mr. and Mrs. Benjamin H. Folger joined Pierson, Isabella, and a few other followers—actually, when all the others moved into the Folgers' 29-acre, Westchester County estate on the Hudson River in Mount Pleasant, also known as Sing Sing. Benjamin and Ann Folger had been friends of the Piersons since 1826 and had attended Latourette's meetings, although Ann Folger had been more attracted than her husband to the Retrenchment Society, which met for several years in their house. She was from a respectable New York City Dutch Reformed family and had been brought up in the church by a pious mother. Very much the lady, Ann Folger was delicately attractive though not quite beautiful. Her soft voice and polished manners conveyed an impression of harmless innocence. Isabella scorned Ann Folger's incompetence, imitating it by fumbling about, then sighing, "Oh, I can't do it."[8]

Benjamin Folger was originally from Hudson, New York, some forty miles north and on the opposite side of the Hudson River from where Isabella had grown up. Like Matthias, Folger had been a poor boy brought up in an adoptive family. But the relatives who took in Folger were rich. From them he received good manners and in 1821 an advantageous situation in business, where his pleasing demeanor and looks stood him in good stead. Besides his hardware importing business, he speculated in real estate.[9]

It took Matthias from the fall of 1832 to the summer of 1833 to bring in the Folgers. They were then staying on the Hudson River for Benjamin's health: perhaps to calm a nervous condition caused by monetary worries, perhaps to escape the cholera that scourged New York City in 1832. The epidemic illustrated New York's extremes of wealth and poverty by striking first and hardest in the poor, Irish parts of the city and taking its toll almost exclusively from among the needy. Matthias and the ministers who preached that cholera was an expression of God's wrath failed to explain why the victims of divine retribution were already the most oppressed.

Isabella, a poor woman, probably knew some who contracted the dread disease in 1832, yet the epidemic figures in her memoir only as Matthias's belief that God was displeased. All in all, the cholera epidemic seems not to have unduly disturbed the members of Matthias's Kingdom. Was cholera too awful to mention? Were they distracted from the life of New York City by the prophet's pronouncements that the world was rushing toward its end? Or did they see the cholera as a prelude to the apocalypse?[10]

The Kingdom of Matthias gained concrete expression in mid-1833, when Pierson and Folger put the Sing Sing estate, now called Zion Hill, and other property in Matthias's name. (Despite Matthias's purported disdain for what he called the institutions of the "Gentiles," Folger, Pierson, and Matthias's transactions were executed according to the letter of the law, with thousands of dollars worth of property painstakingly enumerated in page after page of documentation. Matthias signed himself "Robert Matthias," with flourishes on the Ts and the S.)[11] The community consisted of people of different generations, classes, races, and sexes; Isabella was the only one who was black, but not the only one who was poor.

The other working-class person was Catherine Galloway, the widow of one of Sylvester Mills's servants, who had herself done household labor in Mills's house. In poor health and financial need after her husband's death, Galloway had realized that Isabella had the power to help her. Isabella was willing and brought Catherine to see Ann Folger. Catherine professed a belief that Matthias could restore her health, for like Jesus and the prophet Elijah, he said he could effect miraculous cures. Folger let her come live and work at Zion Hill.[12]

Supposedly everyone belonged to the community on a footing of equality and held everything in common (as in early Christianity), and everyone worked according to physical ability. Nonetheless, a hierarchy that was very reminiscent of the world of the "Gentiles" prevailed. Matthias, called "Father," gave all the orders and sat at the head of the table. He decided when to go to work and when to practice the rituals of the kingdom, such as the communal bathing that he called baptism. No matter when he preached to his followers or how angrily and how long, they were bound to listen. Isabella no longer preached, for Matthias set preaching out of bounds for women.

Matthias had long inflicted corporal punishment on those he controlled. As Robert Matthews he had beaten his wife and children, and as the Prophet Matthias he beat Isabella for the infraction he considered abominable in women: insubordination. On an occasion when she was not feeling well—already the apparent proof that she was possessed by a "sick devil"—she had intervened when Matthias was punishing one of his young sons.[13] Matthias lashed her with his cowhide whip, shouting, "Shall a sick devil undertake to dictate to me?" While in the kingdom he also beat his eighteen-year-old daughter so severely that she bore marks from his whip six weeks later.[14]

Matthias's instincts were patriarchal, literally and figuratively. He did not call the kingdom "the family," but he did insist on being called "Father," and, once he had taken Ann Folger as his "match spirit" (that is, his new wife), he called her "Mother." As Mother she was still a child, for he treated everyone in the household as children, lecturing them for hours, frequently in shrill, harsh anger. Ann Folger described Matthias's power: "We consider[ed] him as God the Father possessing the Holy Ghost, and the power of bestowing it on others; the power also of executing wrath on whom he would. We regarded him as the last trumpet, answering to all the angels of wrath spoken of in the Revelation; that is the executing angels." As the last trumpet, Matthias would bend down, fill his lungs, and shout in a voice loud enough to deafen his hearers temporarily. Ann Folger admitted that "we indeed thought he did cast evil spirits out of us. We were to obey all his commands, and we showed our obedience to him. . . . He had the command of all things in the house."[15]

Inmates in the kingdom dared not act of their own volition, for if they showed independence of mind, Ann Folger said,

> his anger would last a long time, and become very tedious, and he
> would curse us awfully, and threaten us, until we considered ourselves
> lost creatures unless he saved us. He told us he would save us, but we

must get rid of the evil spirits within us, and if we asked for better spirits and deliverance from him he would give them to us. Our obedience extended to all the temporal affairs of the house, and he told us we stood responsible to him for every thing. He claimed the house in which we lived, and he always called it "my house."

Like everyone else in the kingdom, Isabella also was afraid of his censure.[16] The household revolved around Matthias's power, his anger, and obedience to him in all things.[17]

Matthias opposed slavery and would have repudiated the word as applied to his own behavior, but his ideal—submission and obedience to the father in an isolated household cut off from other systems of law or ideology—lay at the core of the institution of chattel slavery. Isabella, the former slave, accepted Matthias's conduct and shared his views, which she said she preferred to those of the churchgoing people and ministers whom she disdained as mere "Christians."[18]

Even with Matthias set above and apart from the rest, the kingdom's egalitarian ideals fell short in practice. Below Matthias were the Folgers and Pierson, members of the commune who among the "Gentiles" had been wealthy and well bred. As time passed and affective ties shifted to make Ann Folger "Mother," she acquired more standing relative to her husband and Pierson. Pierson's age and ill health also weighed against him, ultimately with fatal consequences. Isabella and Catherine occupied a marginal status that was part peer, part servant. Isabella's situation was especially ambiguous. Her race and class disadvantaged her, but she had contributed money and furniture to the kingdom, which gave her a certain standing. Finally, she had a personal fortitude and canniness that gave her more power than the pitiful Catherine.

Though not paid as a servant would be, Isabella was still a black woman with the diminished social stature that came from having been a slave. When the formerly wealthy were about to discuss delicate or weighty matters, it was their habit to send Isabella to do work that would take her out of the room—a practice she disregarded when the kingdom was dissolving and she felt that she must have a say in crucial decisions.[19] Even more important, in a household that included Ann Folger as a pampered lady, was Isabella's ability to work. She was a strong woman who knew how to cook, clean, and launder.

Isabella deferred to Ann but regarded her skeptically. Ann's feelings toward Isabella were also irresolute; Ann was under Matthias's orders to treat Isabella with kindness and respect, yet she found it difficult to deal with this older, black, working woman as a peer. Ann, who never envisioned herself as a worker, approached Isabella more as a highly respected family servant than as an equal.

Ann also used Isabella as an audience and as an erotic object. When the men were away in the city, she would get into Isabella's bed and kiss and embrace her, under the pretext of demonstrating how Matthias showed his affection for "Mother."[20] Isabella later described Ann's caresses without hinting at her own response, but she might well have been reminded of the behavior of her Ulster County mistress, Sally Dumont.

Ann Folger's new status as Matthias's "match spirit" increased Isabella's workload, for now Ann added her prestige as Mother of the kingdom to her inherent exemption from hard work by virtue of being a lady. The sacred honeymoon eroticized the atmosphere and set off chain reactions in a house inhabited by several adults and five or six children, all of whom were twelve or younger.[21] In the manner of young lovers, Ann and Matthias lolled about in bed in the mornings, which meant that not only did Ann do even less housework, but Isabella, who worked in the kitchen, could not get to her other work because they had not had breakfast. When she complained, Matthias told her that she would be furnished with his and Mother's spirits; as they lay in bed, their spirits would be with her, enabling her to do twice the work in half the time.[22] This opportunistic conception of work and love, rather than Matthias's wrath and Ann's fondling, struck Isabella as rank self-indulgence and raised doubts in her mind about the sacredness of such arrangements. As was her way, she guarded her doubts.

The prophet believed that "Gentile law" lost its force in his kingdom, thereby voiding the legal marriage of Ann and Benjamin Folger.[23] As "match spirits," Matthias said, he and Ann were decreed by the Spirit to marry and produce a holy child who would survive the apocalypse. (They did have a girl who seems to have stayed with the Folgers after the kingdom collapsed. The record of the child's ultimate destiny is unclear.)[24] After Ann and Matthias's Zion Hill marriage ceremony, Isabella thought that Benjamin Folger looked like a dog that had been dragged through the gutter.[25] Matthias attempted to heal Folger's hurt by finding him a match spirit, perhaps Catherine Galloway, perhaps his own daughter, Isabella Laisdell, who was married to a working-class Englishman.

In the ostensibly egalitarian kingdom, Catherine's lower-class origins made her available to rich Benjamin as a sexual partner but less attractive to him as a match spirit than Matthias's beautiful eighteen-year-old daughter. Catherine tried to disregard the class difference between herself and Benjamin; she thought she had a claim on him because he had slept with her several times. Isabella discerned the class dynamics underlying Benjamin's intimacy with Catherine, seeing that he treated Catherine as a mere "hack," not as a wife, a pattern of intimacy common between gentlemen and servants in the world of the "Gentiles." When Matthias offered his daughter Isabella, living in Albany, Benjamin accepted immediately and without regard to the desires of either Catherine or the daughter. Benjamin went up to Albany and brought Isabella Laisdell back to Zion Hill, seducing or raping her on the way.[26]

The only two members of the kingdom now without sexual partners were Pierson and Isabella. Both regretted being left out. Isabella said later that she avoided the "particular pollution" of the kingdom mainly through force of "circumstances," and she evidently would have welcomed a match spirit of her own, whether or not she accepted the common assumption that her race, age (she was then in her late thirties), and class rendered her ineligible.[27]

Elijah Pierson died after a series of seizures in August 1834. His copulatory gestures and cries of Ann Folger's name left no doubt that he died a sexually frustrated man.[28] Like his wife, who had died in 1830, Pierson received no medical attention during the last weeks of his illness. His body, his comrades believed, held an evil spirit that had to be mortified in order for him to recover. Matthias regarded illness as a devil in the body, manifestation of the presence of evil spirits. A complete distrust of doctors and medicine was part of the kingdom's health regimen, which followed Matthias's earlier precepts: exercise, which here meant work in the house and on the farm, fresh fruit and vegetables, little meat, no alcohol, and frequent cold baths.[29]

After Pierson died in 1834 and the kingdom began to unravel in earnest, the one person who stood fast was the one who had been a slave. Accused of murdering Pierson, Matthias dithered over what to do about the accusation and where to go. The Folgers reconciled and returned to Latourette, who scolded them for backsliding, a serious Methodist failing. They gave Isabella $25 in lieu of wages, then accused her of trying to poison them.

Isabella did not hesitate. She stood ready to testify on Matthias's behalf at his trial for Pierson's murder. She visited John Dumont to ask for his advice and engaged herself a lawyer. She approached her Ulster County and New York City employers for certificates of character. Dumont, A. Bruyn Hasbrouck, John Rutzer, and Perez Whiting all came through for her. Only James Latourette, reproaching her for leaving his Holy Club for Matthias, withheld his reference.[30] These certificates stood her in good stead when the story was all over the newspapers in 1835. Traveling to Morristown, she explained herself to Pierson's family. She advised an uncertain Matthias on which lawyer would best represent him in court. When Catherine Galloway fell on hard times once more, Isabella gave her money and enlisted her support against the Folgers.

Through all this confusion, Isabella remained loyal to Matthias, with whom she made plans to take the kingdom into the wilderness. She handed over every cent she had to Matthias, reckoning, perhaps, that he needed or deserved it more than she. She followed Matthias when he went back to his wife in Albany without her. Then Isabella took the Folgers to court for slander and won $125 in damages, thereby vindicating her reputation as a trustworthy person and cook.[31]

Pierson's death had brought the Matthias Kingdom under the scrutiny of the New York City press, which soon picked up on village gossip regarding sexual improprieties. Matthias's 1835 trial in Westchester County on the charge of poisoning Pierson generated whole columns of front-page press coverage; three books came out of the affair, one of which, by the immigrant English Free Thinker and deist Gilbert Vale, has remained a rich source for information about Isabella, Latourette, and Matthias.

In Isabella, Vale discerned "a peculiar and marked character." He portrayed her as the energetic, intelligent, commonsensical person who later became so effective as a feminist abolitionist in the 1850s. Greatly impressed by her vigor and "considerable shrewdness," he hypothesized that after the Matthias Kingdom collapsed, she wanted nothing more than to clear the air of doubt lingering about her reputation by telling "the *whole truth*."[32]

Yet Vale—who believed in no prophets and sought to exempt Isabella as much as possible from the folly of Matthias—drew two uneasy conclusions about her: She had continued to give Matthias money even after the commune broke up and it was plain to others that he was a charlatan; and she was very good at keeping her own counsel. When she expressed her views, Vale said, she was usually correct, but "she is not communicative, and if circumstances did not prompt her to tell all she knows, it would be difficult to get at it."[33] The riddle of Isabella's loyalty to Matthias endures, and Vale's strategy of portraying her as a skeptical observer remains tempting, even though such an analysis runs counter to the evidence of her devotion to Matthias's person and his theology, which was very much her own.

A CHASM seems still to separate the strong, canny person who would create the legendary Sojourner Truth from the woman who stayed with a scoundrel who beat her up, suppressed her preaching, took her money, and made her do his housework for nothing, who lay abed with another man's wife and proclaimed that his spirit was helping with the floors and the laundry. How could the woman who could outpreach John Maffitt submit to being bossed about by Matthias and fondled by Ann Folger?

Placing Isabella somehow outside the Matthias madness—highlighting her strength, stressing her independence, and discounting her vulnerabilities—has been the strategy of those who focus on the Sojourner Truth figure who became a heroine. These biographers want her to have a single, essential identity, unchanged over time. But the 1830s were not the 1840s or 1850s, and in 1833 Isabella was not many years out of a slavery calculated to make her believe that brutality must be a natural component of her life.

Although she impressed others with her strength, in the 1830s another vulnerable and diminished part of her seems to have felt at home when being treated badly. She was sundered in these early years, when she was a woman growing strong yet still wounded by her past. She was attracted to the power that Matthias manifested on her behalf and against her: He *was* brutal toward her, but, like John Dumont, he also seemed to care for her. Matthias made Isabella feel that she was loved, even if that mixed-up, divine-carnal love stopped short of genital sexual contact. Lack of sexual relations with Matthias does not mean that Isabella was immune to the kingdom's rampant sexuality. Neighbors in Sing Sing gossiped that Matthias slept with all the women at Zion Hill and saved black Isabella for Sundays. Even if this were not literally true, there is little doubt that a potent erotic current ran between Isabella and Matthias.[34]

Less than a decade away from slavery, Isabella was not one smooth whole. In New York City she was yearning for family as well as religion, and in the Kingdom of Matthias, she found both. The synthetic family around Matthias resembled the one she had grown up in over her sixteen years with the Dumonts: abusive but familiar. She was still in need of assurance, still in need of family.

During her New York years, Isabella repeatedly traveled upstate to keep in touch with her children and with John Dumont, the closest she had to a father, and he continued to advise and ground her. She seems never again to have seen her husband Thomas, who died in the county poorhouse not long after emancipation, but she regularly visited her other family. In addition to Dumont, who had moved to Dutchess County across the Hudson River between Poughkeepsie and Hyde Park, these included her daughters, who were living nearby.[35] The quest for family would persist longer than her time in the city and state of New York, but she grew nonetheless in inner strength over the years. Never again would her recreated families be as noxious as the Kingdom of Matthias.

IN 1835, Matthias was acquitted of the charge of murdering Pierson through poisoning, for it was far from certain that Pierson had been poisoned at all; Matthias did, however, serve four months in

prison for assault on his daughter, whom he had whipped for dis-
obedience, and for contempt of court. While he was imprisoned,
a New York City theater ran a comedy entitled *Matthias the
Prophet*. When Matthias regained his freedom, he went briefly to
Albany, where Isabella caught up with him, but then he went west
alone.[36]

Isabella would have accompanied Matthias had he let her, for
she remained attached to him and faithful to his tenets. While he
wandered about the West, she returned to household labor for the
family of Perez Whiting (probably fellow perfectionists), who had
employed her before she joined the Matthias Kingdom in Sing
Sing. When Matthias died in 1841—after having met and failed to
impress his fellow prophet, Joseph Smith of the Mormons—Isabella
was struggling to survive in the hard economic times that had followed the Panic of 1837 and worrying about her son Peter, whom
she had left in the city while she lived in the Matthias Kingdom
in Zion Hill.[37]

8

Isabella's
New York City

Of her life in the years between the breakup of the Matthias commune in the mid-1830s and her decision to leave New York in 1843, Sojourner Truth says very little in the *Narrative*. That little consists mostly of anxieties regarding her son Peter, who had worried her from the time he returned from Alabama badly mauled physically and psychologically. Surviving in the city as a poor, single, working parent was a full-time occupation, for dealing with Peter consumed an enormous amount of Isabella's time and mental energy. Yet in light of her subsequent fame as an abolitionist, Isabella's absence from the budding antislavery movement during the years when New York City was its center is striking.

During the Matthias years, the moral reformers Isabella had met in New York City became abolitionists. Elijah Pierson, whose death at Zion Hill precipitated the breakup of the Kingdom of Matthias, had been a founder of the New York Magdalen Society (successor to his Magdalen House of Refuge) and a pillar of the American Tract Society alongside Arthur Tappan. Tappan, with his brother Lewis, was New York's leading evangelical reformer in the 1820s and 1830s, and he was New York City's principal white friend of the Negro.

The absence of Arthur Tappan's name from the *Narrative of So-*

journer Truth emphasizes her distance in the 1830s from organized temperance, sabbath-keeping, and antislavery. Tappan, born in Northampton, Massachusetts, in 1786, was not a religious perfectionist in the come-outer sense of Isabella, Latourette, Pierson, and Matthias. Tappan stayed with his New York Presbyterian church, living simply in homes in New York and New Haven, not mansions, but imposing enough in their quality and size to bespeak wealth behind their plainness. In the late 1820s, Tappan had not yet become an abolitionist; saving prostitutes, distributing Bibles and religious tracts to New York's poor, and fostering temperance and sabbatarianism delineated his conception of doing good in the world.

Tappan's ideas about what needed to be fixed broadened in the 1830s. During the years when Isabella was living with Pierson, Matthias, and the Folgers in New York and at Zion Hill and had nothing to say about racial issues, Tappan was starting to do what he could to ameliorate the condition of the free people of color in the North, who were nearly everywhere and nearly always despised. In the wake of the abolition of slavery in the early nineteenth century, persecution and exclusion of blacks became the rule in the North, whether in small country villages or big cities like Philadelphia and New York, which in the 1830s and 1840s held the largest concentrations of African Americans in the United States.

As local public services such as streetcars and public schools were first being established in places like New York, they operated in ways meant to humiliate people of color. Black parents, their children barred from the newly organized public schools, had to set up their own private schools with the assistance of their friends. Streetcars set aside for whites refused to take black passengers, and in no public accommodations could black New Yorkers count on being served.

During Isabella's years in New York City, insult constantly fouled the lives of the black poor, and even educated and respectable colored gentlemen ran up against bigotry on a regular basis. The Reverend Samuel Cornish, publisher of New York's black newspaper, the *Colored American,* and a member of the executive board of the American Anti-Slavery Society, was refused a cup of tea in a restaurant patronized by the editors and agents of the American Bible Society, the Tract Society, and the workers who put out the *New York Evangelist,* on the excuse that the "customers would not put up with it."

Another upstanding African American, Thomas Van Rensalaer, was assaulted for having the "presumption" even to enter a similar downstairs lunchroom. James McCune Smith, a medical doctor trained in Scotland, was not allowed to enter the New York Academy of Medicine even after his credentials were made known. In 1853, Smith and Charles B. Ray were expelled from the World Temperance Convention because of their race.[1]

On the personal and political levels, northern black people's transition from slavery to freedom was dogged by violent assault and legal harassment. From the halls of state legislatures to the streets where small boys yelled "nigger" and threw stones, African Americans faced a campaign of denigration that gave the Declaration of Independence a hollow ring. In Connecticut, New York, Pennsylvania, and North Carolina, poor white men gained the vote as wealthy black men lost it. The Jacksonian era of the common man, actually the era of the common *white* man, turned black history into a narrative of struggle to delete the word "white" from rights recognized by the state. In the wake of the Civil War the legal battle was won, giving blacks the right to public accommodations on a non-discriminatory basis. But even in the late 1860s, when officially sanctioned segregation and disfranchisement ended in the North, discriminatory habits held on.

Arthur Tappan saw this and began to focus on the oppression of the African Americans around him in the mid-1830s. In 1833 he underwrote organization of the Phoenix Society, an improvement society for young black men. Its leaders included Samuel Cornish, whose salary as agent of the society Tappan paid. Tappan also attempted, without success, to found a school for blacks in New Haven.[2]

Tappan soon joined forces with William Lloyd Garrison of Boston, who had founded the antislavery *Liberator* in 1831. As an abolitionist, Tappan angered southern slaveholders, who purportedly offered a $50,000 bounty for his head. To this information he is reported to have replied: "If that sum is placed in the

New York Bank, I may possibly think of giving myself up."[3]

Tappan and Garrison were two of the founders of the American Anti-Slavery Society in New York in 1833, at a meeting in Phoenix Hall that narrowly escaped being mobbed by New Yorkers who disliked blacks enough to resent any opposition to slavery. Blacks and abolitionists did not elude the mob the following year. In 1834 a mob that became increasingly better organized and violent over the course of several days viciously attacked the Anti-Slavery Society's Fourth of July commemoration, black homes and churches, and Lewis Tappan's house. This antiblack and anti-abolition outbreak was the worst of the violence in New York's "year of riots."[4]

Isabella (working as a servant and still known simply by her first name, sometimes shortened to Isabel or Bell) was not involved. It is possible but unlikely that she was aware of the Tappan brothers' evolution from evangelical moral reform into antislavery. In any case, no evidence exists from the 1830s or later reminiscences that their paths ever crossed, even though their interests would subsequently intersect.

The *Narrative of Sojourner Truth* also passes in silence over the biggest local news story of 1835: the inferno that destroyed much of New York City on the bitterly cold night of December 16. The fire raged through the business district at the southern tip of Manhattan, inflicting damage on the businesses of Isabella's surviving associates, Benjamin Folger and James Latourette. Flames were visible from Ridgewood, New Jersey, and the glow could be seen from as far south as Cranbury, in the middle of the state.

The tabloid *New York Sun* issued a special edition on the fire that showed a map of the loss and described the "grim compendium—the hideous skeleton as it were, of the mammoth destroyer as he now lies upon the ground:—South street is a pile of ruins from Wall street to Coenties slip; Front street lies in ruins throughout the same distance; Water street lies in the same state for the same extent. Pearl street is levelled with the earth from Wall street to Coenties alley, where the flames were stopped by the blowing up of a building with powder." The fire burned for a day and a half, and smoldered for months afterwards, destroying about 650 buildings and property worth $15 million.[5]

If one were of an apocalyptic turn of mind and had spent years with a man like Matthias who preached that the world was soon coming to an end, this fire might present a perfect example of prophetic catastrophe. But the conflagration occurred in December, not in the spring season of Pentecost, when the Holy Spirit spoke to Isabella most urgently. Her son Peter—rather than anti-slavery organizations, mobs, and fires—is the subject of Isabella's memoir dealing with her years in New York City after Matthias.

PETER was about seven years old when Isabella brought him with her to New York City and Miss Grear helped find him work. According to the *Narrative*, Peter was a "tall, well-formed, active lad, of quick perceptions, mild and cheerful in his disposition, with much that was open, generous and winning about him, but with little power to withstand temptation." The boy had been something of a troublemaker before leaving Ulster County: Gertrude Dumont recalled that "no one could do anything with him, and everybody expected he would land in State Prison." She also added, with a slaveholder's logic, that Peter "went"—not was sold and transported—to Alabama.[6] Securing him employment did not prove difficult, but from the beginning Peter found it hard to hold a job. Employed as a groom, he pawned his livery and used the money for gambling.

Perhaps his mother reckoned that Peter need not be limited to the jobs she could aspire to and that he needed more schooling to prepare him for interesting work. At any rate, one of her wealthy women friends agreed that Peter was "so smart, he ought to have an education, if any one ought," and paid his tuition at a school of navigation. Peter cut classes to go dancing. Time and again he was picked up for petty theft and loitering, but his mother and her influential friends always got him out of trouble. Finally, in 1839, Isabella decided that he would have to accept the consequences of his misdeeds, and she refused to come to his aid.[7]

For some time Peter had been telling the police that he was "Peter Williams," a name borne by two illustrious figures, father and son, that would have given him, perhaps, a more elevated standing in his own eyes and more respect from others. Peter Williams, Sr., had been the slave of the John Street Methodist

Church, where he served as its sexton. With proceeds from his tobacco and funeral businesses he had purchased his freedom in
1796. One of New York's leading black Methodists, Williams was
a founder of Zion Church in the same year he made himself a free
man. His son, Peter Williams, Jr., whose name Peter Van Wagener
was borrowing, had been ordained as an Episcopal priest in 1826
and led St. Phillip's African Church. Among St. Phillips's congre-
gants were some of New York's most prominent African Americans: James McCune Smith, Alexander Crummell, Charles L.
Reason, and George T. Downing (Truth's later colleague in advocating votes for women).

The younger Peter Williams was active in black civic affairs as
an opponent of the white-led movement to colonize free black
Americans outside of the United States and was a founder of several public institutions: the first black newspaper in the United
States, the New York *Freedom's Journal*, in 1827; the black convention movement, which beginning in 1830 annually brought together concerned black men from around the country to discuss
the situation of the race; the Phoenix Society in 1833; and the
American Anti-Slavery Society that same year. The mob that terrorized blacks and abolitionists in July 1834 burned down St.
Phillip's Church and rectory and made Williams and his family
homeless.[8]

When Isabella determined to let her son stew for a while in the
hands of the authorities, he asked the police to summon the real
Reverend Peter Williams, Jr., who, it turned out, knew what to do
with a young man with a penchant for trouble in the city. Williams
arranged for Peter to join the crew of a Nantucket whaling vessel—
a common fate for boys and men, black, white, and red, who ran
afoul of the local authorities. Williams told Isabella—who had
already considered sending her son to sea to straighten him out—
what many early nineteenth-century adults believed about whaling: that it was a school of hard knocks and tight discipline that
would quickly shape up a young miscreant. It would be in everyone's interest, he said, for Peter to get away from all-too-familiar
temptations. As a recruiting agent, Peter Williams would have received a cash bounty for Peter's employment.

Peter, now eighteen years old, shipped out of Nantucket on the

Zone in 1839 under a captain named Hiller, joining the legions of black men who found a better opportunity in seafaring than on the land. Between the end of the eighteenth century and the Civil War, seafaring was one of the three most common occupations for northern black men (farming and household service were the other two), and whaling was one of their specialties. Whaling crews were as close to racially egalitarian as possible in any American institution of the time. For their pay whalemen received a "lay," or share of the net proceeds of the sale of whale products, minus expenses incurred, which meant that wages depended on the success of the trip. A very lucky man might take as much as $1,000 from a voyage, but around $200 was more usual, even for voyages as lengthy as Peter's, which lasted more than three years.[9]

According to Peter's first letter to his mother, dated 17 October 1840, life on the *Zone* (which is transcribed as the "Done" in the *Narrative*) was not to his liking. He writes of "troubles and hardships" and of having been punished severely for trying to keep other people out of trouble. In his second letter, dated 22 March 1841, Peter again speaks of having "very hard luck." By his fifth and last letter (the third and fourth are not reprinted in the *Narrative*), his luck had turned, and he was hoping to make some money out of the voyage.

In his first two letters, Peter asks after his sisters and cousins and gives news of the death near Tahiti of a shipmate who also used to live with the Latourettes. In the last letter Peter is discouraged by his mother's silence, which, in her *Narrative*, she does not explain. Did she ask someone write to him for her, but her letters were lost? Did she not write? What went through her mind as she reprinted Peter's plea to hear from her, nine years after he wrote, hoping, she said, that someone would have news of him?

Peter said he would be home in another fifteen months. Truth recalled his promises to "do better," and his hope, as expressed in his first letter, that she and everyone else he had hurt would "forgive me for all that I have done." Having left New York City in the summer of 1839, Peter disappeared from his mother's life with this last letter in September 1841, but not from her thoughts. Not until the early 1870s did she find ease over his fate, evidently after hearing from his spirit.[10]

PETER WILLIAMS, JR., and Isabella had not been acquainted before her son's mishaps brought them together, and she seems not to have kept in touch with the man she termed her son's "benefactor" after Peter's departure.[11] If not for her son, Peter Williams and the rest of black New York that figures in the histories would seem divorced completely from Isabella's own experience. She seems to have existed in a world entirely separate from that of black male institutions like the Phoenix Society, from the fledgling antislavery movement that men also dominated, from the people, virtually all men, who appear in the pages of the *Colored American* in the 1830s and 1840s. After she went off with Matthias, she was even absent from black churches, also led by men, though women provided the great bulk of their support. Her distance from all this, which initially seems a mystery, becomes, on a second look, altogether comprehensible.

Although black New Yorkers were discriminated against and tended to live in a few poor wards of the city, there was no district of solid black residence, as there would be in twentieth-century Harlem and Brooklyn. Antebellum New York City lay entirely south of what is now 42nd Street, and it was overwhelmingly white. In 1830, New York County (Manhattan) was 7.1 percent black, and Kings County (Brooklyn) 9.8 percent. The largest proportion of blacks in the area was in Queens County, which was 13.1 percent black.[12] Blacks and whites lived together all over the city: in poor and middling districts, they might be renters in the same house or boarders in the same pitiful apartment. They also lived together in wealthy houses, where, like Isabella, blacks worked as live-in household help.[13]

Lacking in the 1830s and 1840s a clearly defined geographical base and the habits of thought and association that come from long segregation, black people in New York City did not form a "black community." They were not yet a people bound by their own institutions and living in homogeneous neighborhoods. What we can identify in retrospect is less a black community than a few educated black New Yorker men who enter the historical record through written documents. Active in civic life, men like David Ruggles and the Reverends Samuel E. Cornish, James W. C. Pennington, and Henry Highland Garnet wrote and published their views on the politics of the day and were eager supporters of Arthur Tappan's undertakings. They also formed their own organizations, in which they pursued literate culture, prayed together, and paid for decent burials. They protested against the loss of equal male suffrage in the 1820s and the injustices and indignities that the city's prevailing racial prejudice made their everyday portion.

David Ruggles, a Lispenard Street grocer and bookseller, enters the annals of black New York history as an abolitionist. In 1834 he had been the twenty-four-year-old organizer (with Henry Highland Garnet) of the Garrison Literary and Benevolent Association.[14] Sharing the concerns of Peter Williams, Jr., for boys like Isabella's son Peter, Ruggles published a pamphlet citing the danger of their "being led into idle and licentious habits by the allurements of vice which surround them on every side."[15] He countered the temptations of evil by operating an informal employment agency and setting up a bookstore in his grocery to satisfy young men's "mental appetites." As the main agent of the Vigilance Society, he moved the reading room to the society's offices in the late 1830s.[16]

UNTIL Ruggles's eyesight began to fail in the early 1840s, he remained at the forefront of the city's antislavery forces. The head of the Vigilance Society, he was the key figure in New York City's underground railroad and took care of fugitive slaves from the South such as Frederick Douglass and his fiancée, Anna Murray, in 1838.[17] In 1842, the antislavery author and editor of the New York *National Anti-Slavery Standard*, Lydia Maria Child, suggested that Ruggles move to her base, Northampton, Massachusetts, where he soon joined the Northampton Association and met Sojourner Truth.[18] Acquaintance with Ruggles in Massachusetts in the 1840s and exchanges about her son with the Reverend Peter Williams in 1839 were her closest encounters with New York's prominent black men.

These notable men, who have become synonymous with the history of black New York, were for the most part ministers, and they held their own views about what was and was not appropriate in religion and in women. They would have been embarrassed by Isabella, who lived with the white prophets and cultists who were so common a feature of the era. Notable black men worried about the oppression of all the black people in New York City, but they held traditional ideas about women's proper place. Women were to be beautiful, modest, soft, tasteful, quiet, and chaste, the qualities that defined ladyhood à la Ann Folger, but that were impossible to cultivate without time, money, and the protection of men of authority. Had the men who wrote in the columns of the *Colored American* been aware of Isabella's existence, they would have been appalled by the figure of this powerful, middle-aged, unlettered preaching woman from the country.[19]

Her religious unorthodoxy would have struck the leading colored men as something to be hidden rather than prized, lest her lack of respectability feed the fires of racist stereotype that such men saw as part of what was keeping the race down. Prominent black ministers and citizens also would have deplored Isabella's lack of interest in abolitionism, for they often railed against their contemporaries who gave insufficient support to the large and noble causes of political activism.

Women like Isabella, who lived with their employers and shared their views, women who remained outside of what would later be called "the black community," mostly disappear from history's view. One example is to be found in the person of Catherine Ferguson, a "Christian philanthropist," who died in New York City in 1854 at about seventy-five (though estimations of the ages of older women were notoriously unreliable). Like Isabella, Ferguson was born a slave of a New York owner and was separated from her mother by sale. Also like Isabella, she never learned to read. Ferguson founded one of the first Sunday Schools in New York City, and she ran a prayer meeting at her house for more than forty years. She also raised forty-eight orphans—black and white. Known for her "sensible chat" and "pious discourse," Ferguson supported herself and her foster children as a baker, but she was remembered more for her generosity than for her business acumen.[20]

For the most part, unseen holy women like Ferguson and Isabella, who performed household labor and were known more for piety than for wealth or agitation, served as targets of criticism. The educated black abolitionist Martin Delany, for instance, berated blacks satisfied to live as servants. His views appeared in the

columns of the Rochester *North Star,* which he and Frederick
Douglass co-edited.[21]

Delany and other up-and-coming black young men ached to see
the race exert its manhood by going into business and becoming
financially independent. Here, they thought, lay the route to respect from a wider American population, so busily persecuting
them in every conceivable manner. Although later in life Isabella
would, in a sense, go into business and become more or less financially independent, her ways out of humiliation were not those
of Martin Delany or other leading black men.

Mental orientation as well as ideals of gender divided leading
African Americans from Isabella. They took their cues from the
public realm, from politics and business, while she heeded the
voice of the Holy Spirit. As men, they moved earlier into the larger
world. In the 1830s and 1840s, the imperatives of politics drove
educated, urban black men—later they would call themselves "representative men"—and the upstanding, middle-class black women
lecturers who would join them on the antislavery lecture circuit.
For this minority of urban black people most noted in historical
accounts, public life held much attraction. History, however, has
ignored an untold number of women for whom the politics of race
did not supply meaning to life.

We know from the published autobiographies of nineteenth-
century black preaching women like Jarena Lee, Zilpha Elaw, Rebecca Cox Jackson, Julia Foote, Sister Tilghman, and a woman
known simply as Elizabeth, that the life of the spirit attracted
other women besides Isabella. The black and white women who
were itinerant preachers were unconstrained and outspoken, and
as the nineteenth century unfolded, they moved farther from the
evolving ideal of femininity we know as Victorian, which effaced
the existence of women so deeply autonomous and independent
of mortal men.

The developing historiography of black Americans further ob-
scured the existence of preaching women, because black history
traces the struggle against white racism, and because that struggle
was not the paramount mission of black preaching women. Their
invisibility is a part of the general effacement of preaching women,
who are just now being rediscovered. Numbering about eighty, the

prominent women preachers before the Civil War heralded the
abolitionist and feminist women who pioneered in public speaking in the early nineteenth century.[22]

Nearly everything we know of preaching women comes from
what they themselves published, which means that while Isabella
was an itinerant preacher and not yet an abolitionist or a feminist,
what we know about her comes primarily from her *Narrative*. At
least there *is* a *Narrative*, so that something about her early life
can be perceived. But much is missing, and many questions remain: Where was she living and what was she doing during the
grinding hard times of the late 1830s and early 1840s, when men
like Arthur Tappan were becoming abolitionists and going broke?
She says that she continued to live with the Perez Whitings in
Canal Street, her faithful employers with whom she had lived before and after Matthias. She may well have returned to the congregation of James Latourette and stayed until his death in 1841.

WHY, on 1 June 1843, did Isabella quit New York and become "Sojourner Truth"? In the depression that followed the Panic of 1837,
she, like other poor people, was working hard and making very little money. In her *Narrative* she says that life in the city appeared
to her as a "great drama," no more than "one great system of rob-
bery and wrong." She chastised herself for depriving poor men of
the half dollar that one of her employers gave her to have snow
cleared from the steps and sidewalks by clearing them herself, and
she hated herself for being "unfeeling, selfish and wicked." The
material hardship that she was witnessing, and that she felt she
was contributing to, intensified her holiness convictions. She absolutely had to flee this sinful city.

Isabella's pentecostalism shines through her description of her
departure. She was "called in spirit" on 1 June—which in 1843 was
the day of Pentecost. Pentecost since 1827 had held a special importance in her beliefs, and the Holy Spirit spoke to her dramat-
ically. Explaining her decision, she mentions the role of the
"Spirit" twice, in phrasing that echoes the emphasis on the Holy
Spirit that had pervaded the communities of James Latourette
and the Prophet Matthias. Isabella's rebirth in 1843 as Sojourner

was a second adventist reworking of a Methodist style of sanctification.

Drawing on imagery and narrative from Genesis, she said that she was "fleeing" a "wicked city," a "second Sodom," a destruction that she saw in biblical imagery of fire and brimstone. As she departed, she dared not look back for fear that, like Lot's wife fleeing Sodom, she would be turned to a pillar of salt at the sight of the city in flames. In the story told in Genesis, Sodom was one of two ancient Palestinian cities (the other was Gomorrah) that the Lord destroyed for their sinfulness in an inferno of burning sulphur. At the time of the destruction, Lot was a sojourner in Sodom, meaning that though his immediate family was with him, he was a stranger without established family and tribal ties. Two angels of the Lord warned Lot: "Escape for thy life; look not behind thee, neither stay thou in all the plain; escape to the mountain, lest thou be consumed" (verse 17). Then the Lord overthrew the cities and their evil inhabitants. The next morning, Lot and his family were at a safe distance from the devastation. Abraham looked down on the plain and "lo, the smoke of the country went up as the smoke of a furnace" (verse 28).

Isabella told her employer, Mrs. Perez Whiting, only an hour before her departure that she must leave the city to go east, where the Spirit called her. (She said that she kept her departure a secret from her children and friends, because faced with her determination to leave, they would have raised a distressing ruckus. Two months later, she had someone write from Connecticut to inform them of the motives for her departure.) She must travel and lecture under a new name: No longer Isabella, she was now "Sojourner," a name that carried many layers of meaning.[23]

On one level, "Sojourner Truth" means itinerant preacher, for a sojourner is someone not at home, and truth is what preachers impart. She saw her mission as lecturing to the people, testifying and exhorting them to "embrace Jesus, and refrain from sin."[24] But there is much more to both names.

When Isabella became Sojourner Truth in 1843, she was not merely appropriating the title of her erstwhile spiritual leader, the Prophet Matthias, who had called himself the "Spirit of Truth." The Spirit of Truth was also the Paraclete, the Holy Spirit as conceived in the Gospel of John, who, sent by God the Father and Jesus the Son, comes to convince people of sin and judgment (John 16:7–16). She was taking a last name that designates her role as preacher.

Isabella had a long-standing preoccupation with truth. As a girl she had been beaten and sexually abused, as an enslaved worker her word had been subject to disbelief, and as a litigant reclaiming her honesty, she was liable to be doubted in situations of the utmost seriousness.

By 1843 she had twice been to court over matters of enormous familial and material importance. In 1828, in order to regain custody of her son Peter, she had to convince an Ulster County judge that she was actually her son's mother. Seven years later in Westchester County, New York, she had sued Benjamin and Ann Folger for libel after they had accused her of poisoning. Gilbert Vale's 1835 book presenting Isabella's side of the story of the Matthias Kingdom bears a long subtitle ending with *"Containing the Whole Truth—and Nothing But the Truth,"* and repeatedly insists on her desire to present "the *Truth,*" "the *truth,*" "the whole truth," "the *whole truth.*"[25] In both cases Isabella prevailed, but the experiences would have reinforced her anxiety over the integrity of her word. Taken together, these experiences virtually determined the choice of her new name.

WHILE "Truth" raises a host of issues regarding knowledge, representation, and communication, Isabella's new first name, "Sojourner," speaks to the question of impermanence. "Sojourner" conveys more than itinerancy, for it imparts the image of a person in a home, with connotations of a temporary stay—home being another of Isabella's and Sojourner Truth's preoccupations. In the mid-1820s, Isabella and her husband Thomas were disappointed not to have their own home as cottagers. The failed dream of being able to save enough to buy "a little home for herself, in her advancing age" was one of her grievances against New York City on the eve of her departure. The *Narrative* ends with further evocations of home, with Sojourner Truth's seeking a home in the Northampton Association, and, after its dissolution, her hoping to raise money for her own home through the sale of the *Narrative* itself.[26]

The Negro spiritual "Steal Away," ending with the line "I ain't got long to stay here," provides a further clue to meanings of "Sojourner" and an explanation for the urgency of her flight in 1843. A sojourner does not have long to stay here, in this instance because the world was coming to an end with Jesus' second coming—the second advent. In the little time left before Sojourner Truth would be living with Jesus, she was on a "pilgrimage," telling people to come to Jesus while there was still time.[27]

Convinced that the end was imminent, Truth required few material goods: She carried only two York shillings—the equivalent of 25 cents—and belongings that fit inside a pillow case. She was acting on millennial beliefs that she had held at least since the 1830s, and she was leaving New York City in the midst of the nineteenth century's greatest millenarian moment.[28]

II

Sojourner Truth, A Life

9

Among the Millerites

SOJOURNER TRUTH'S choice of 1843 as the year of her rebirth was no less meaningful than her leaving on Pentecost or her new name. She left precisely at the height of the second adventist movement known as Millerism. Some fifty thousand Millerites in the Northeast expected the world to end in the Jewish year that began in 1843. Another million or so, like Sojourner Truth, were expectant without necessarily agreeing with Miller's precise apocalyptic dates: first 21 March 1843 to 21 March 1844, and then 22 October 1844.[1]

"Father" William Miller, born in 1782, was a farmer from Washington County, New York, the northeastern county where Robert Matthews, later the Prophet Matthias, grew up. Miller's thought closely paralleled and perhaps inspired that of his neighbor Matthews. In any case, Miller was one of legions of nineteenth-century Americans—indeed, of Christians over the centuries—called dispensationalists, who made calculations about the end of time based on the numbers cited in the Book of Daniel. Dispensationalists believe that the salvation and perdition of millions are at stake in their dating, for to be caught un-saved on the Day of Judgment is to burn in hell forever. Their mission is to convert as many people as possible before the end of time.[2]

Although Miller's date for the second advent ultimately extended to the fall of 1844, the constituency of the New York Millerite newspaper, the *Midnight Cry*, initially expected the end by
mid-1843. In late December 1842, Millerites were greeting the
New Year certain that they would "not see another before we see
the Son of Man coming in the cloud of heaven."[3] In the winter and
spring of 1843, they were counting disasters: earthquakes in the
American Midwest, terrible storms and shipwrecks, hard times in
Pennsylvania, starvation in Scotland, the federal government's
lack of money, and even terrible loss of life (due to war) in China.[4]

By April 1843, the *Midnight Cry* was disparaging the present as
"the age of debauchery—insatiate lust, and bold-faced, reckless,
desperate debauchery."[5] A Millerite conference in Hartford, Connecticut, heard brethren declare that *"Pecuniary distress among
all classes is* MUCH GREATER *than at any previous time."*[6] In May,
the paper's editor, Joshua Himes, proclaimed to his readers that
"we are determined to live in the daily expectation of meeting
Christ."

By mid-May, Millerite strongholds on Long Island were setting
up camp meetings to take place in early June, and the *Midnight
Cry* was at a high pitch of expectation. Himes expressed his in-
tention to publish a double number on 8 June, "Providence
permitting," and he ran a notice of another Long Island camp
meeting to take place, "the Lord permitting."[7] On 8 June itself
Himes confessed that "A large portion of our subscribers have paid
only to the present number. If they wish still to receive the paper,
they are requested to forward the money *now*." Even so, he expected to publish no more than six additional months. Toward the
end of June, the *Midnight Cry* proclaimed that *"There are none of
the prophetic periods as we understand them that extend beyond
the year 1843."*[8]

THE NEW woman Sojourner Truth took to the road in the peak
of this Millerite anticipation, and the impulse and imagery surrounding her mission also affected others in New York and New
England. Many dropped their usual vocations to take up itinerant
preaching, including Lucy Maria Hersey, a schoolteacher who

preached a "call to repentance," and Luther Boutelle, a shoe-
maker who, like Truth, set out on foot with "one penny and the
promise of God" to preach of the approach of end time. Although
the city of Babylon, which figures in Revelation, appeared more
often in second advent diction, an unnamed Philadelphia Millerite,
like Sojourner Truth, spoke of fleeing Sodom before the day of destruction.[9] A hymn from Joshua Himes's Millerite hymnbook, the
Millennial Harp, put the sentiments of these itinerants to music:

> Here o'er the earth as a stranger I roam,
>   Here is no rest—is no rest;
> Here as a pilgrim I wander alone,
>   Yet I am blest—I am blest.
> For I look forward to that glorious day
>   When sin and sorrow will vanish away,
> My heart doth leap while I hear Jesus say,
>   "There, there is rest—there is rest."[10]

In racial terms, the Millerite movement resembled the company
that Truth usually kept, being mostly white, but heterogeneous.
People of all sorts—rich and poor, educated and untutored, black
and white—flocked to Millerite gatherings. Nameless black people
appear in reports of Millerite camp meetings, and three black men
were sufficiently prominent (although Truth was not) to be known
by name: the Reverends Charles Bowles and John W. Lewis, and
the layman William E. Foy, who had visions such as those of Ellen
White, the Maine Millerite who later became the prophetess of the
Seventh-Day Adventist Church. Lewis was designated as head of
second advent work among African Americans in the spring of
1843.[11]

Millennialism appealed to black Americans throughout the
nineteenth century, not merely in 1843, for the starkness of racial
injustice made the need for God's judgment all the more imperative. In 1828 a slave in Southampton County, Virginia, Nathaniel
Turner, heard "a loud noise in the heavens, and the Spirit instantly
appeared to me and said the Serpent was loosened." The Spirit told
Turner that he should take up the yoke that Christ had borne for
the sins of man and lead the fight against the Serpent; echoing the

language of Matthew 19:30, Turner testified that the time was nigh when "the first should be last and the last should be first." In 1831, Turner led the South's largest slave insurrection.

In Boston in 1829, a free man, David Walker, warned white Americans of divine retribution for their oppression of blacks in his searing *Walker's Appeal:* "O Americans! Americans!! I call God—I call angels—I call men, to witness, that your DESTRUCTION *is at hand,* and will be speedily consummated unless you REPENT."[12]

Thousands, perhaps millions of white Americans also believed they were living in end time—that the Day of Judgment was imminent—but Americans whose collective past and present included the iniquity of slavery gave their second adventism a collective dimension grounded in that awful institution. Repeatedly during the nineteenth century, African Americans seized upon the millennial theme in Christianity, with its deep concern with vindication, especially as expressed in the Book of Daniel.[13]

IN THE Millerite stronghold of Long Island, her first destination, Sojourner Truth immediately encountered ready-made settings for her preaching. Millerites in New York, New England, and the upper Midwest, where the movement flourished, were holding scores of camp meetings in 1842–44: at least thirty-one in 1842, forty in 1843, and fifty-four in 1844.[14] To get their meetings going, Millerites needed fiery speakers who could attract and hold an audience, which explains in part why Truth was so welcome to preach. Camp meeting organizers worried about turnout. A successful meeting in Williamsburg, Long Island (now part of Brooklyn), fell apart when competing preachers, including perhaps Truth, pulled away some of the Millerites.[15]

In the camp meeting on 12 June in Hempstead (also now in Brooklyn), the turnout was at first disappointing: The only people there were a few curiosity seekers. By evening some Millerites turned up, and a black man spoke first, followed by two white women. The man may have been William Hodges, who had given up his grocery business to join the Millerites.[16] After this inauspicious start, the week-long meeting eventually attracted two thousand second adventists—a small turnout for Millerites at the time.[17]

Truth was not entirely certain whether she was a Millerite or not. In the winter of 1842–43, before her departure from New York City, she had attended at least one of a series of lectures that Miller gave in the Millerites' building at the corner of Catherine and Madison Streets.[18] She became convinced that the world was soon to end, but she was not persuaded by Miller's system of dating. And with good reason, for even Miller himself was reluctant to specify the date as closely as some of his followers wished. Although acceptance of the Jewish year 1843 (for Miller, March 1843–March 1844) came to be a near test of faith among Millerites, one prominent figure in the movement resisted the setting of dates: N. N. Whiting of Long Island, a scholar of ancient languages who may have been related to Isabella's employers in New York City, the Perez Whitings.[19]

I suspect that Truth was closer to the Millerites in June 1843 than she indicated when she dictated her *Narrative* in the late 1840s. Millerites having acquired a reputation for folly in the wake of the Great Disappointment of 1844, by 1849 she may have marked her distance from the Millerites. But others, including many who identified themselves as Millerites, saw her as one of them. However strict a Millerite she may have been, it was with the Millerite message that she began the process of making the woman born Isabella into a symbol called "Sojourner Truth." What she stood for then was the need to come to Jesus before the second advent, before the end of the world.

Truth joined fellow itinerant preachers Zilpha Elaw (who was black) and Harriet Livermore (white) in the conviction that they were living in end time. Elaw exhorted her followers to make themselves ready for the "midnight cry": "Mark, I beseech you, the signs of the times they are awfully portentous."[20] Livermore warned of "a day of trouble—of alarm—of tempest—of great fears— and of great frosts—of sore famines—wars—pestilences—noisome beasts—awful delusions! and horrid desolations."[21] Many others, including abolitionists, also believed they were living in end time. Angelina Grimké, a white abolitionist then living in New Jersey with her husband, Theodore Weld, spoke of the time as five minutes to midnight, just that close to the end of the world. Gerrit Smith, another well-known abolitionist who would welcome Sojourner Truth and Harriet Tubman to his home in later years, sub-scribed to the *Midnight Cry*.[22]

Truth's preaching expressed her ambivalence toward the doc-trine of the Millerites who welcomed her so warmly. As she was addressing their camp and prayer meetings, they would ask her, "Oh, don't you believe the Lord is coming?" She would reply with a certain evasiveness: "I believe the Lord is as near as he can be, and not be it." Truth was speaking through the pentecostal Book of Luke (17:21), which quotes Jesus as saying, "the Kingdom of God is within you." There are many meanings here: The Kingdom of God is inside believers, among believers, or within but just beyond their grasp.[23]

Only after an outburst of fanaticism, which perhaps reminded Truth of the prostitutes of the Magdalen Asylum who knocked her down and tore her dress, was Truth certain that she was not a Mil-lerite.[24] The incident that made up her mind was most likely the infamous Stepney, Connecticut, camp meeting near Bridgeport in mid-September 1843. At Stepney, John Starkweather, a graduate of Andover Theological Seminary with a reputation for extremism, whipped the crowd into a frenzy. Starkweather paced the aisles of the meeting waving a tree branch and crying, "Hallelujah!" and "Glory!" at the top of his lungs.

Such interjections were not unusual among Millerites or Methodists, but Starkweather went further: He preached that no one who held to the things of this world could be saved, and he singled out members of the meeting as "sealed" for eternal damna-tion. In the name of the Spirit of God, he so agitated the crowd that hysterical Millerites shed whatever symbolized their vanity, whether clothing, long hair, jewelry, even false teeth.

Disgusted by the frenzy, Truth "mounted a stump and called out, 'Hear! Hear!' " to the deeply agitated Millerites. Gathering some of the people around her, she addressed them as "children" and asked why they were carrying on so. "Are you not commanded to 'watch and pray'?" she demanded. "You are neither watching nor praying." Like a mother speaking to her babies, she invited them to return to their tents, watch, and pray quietly, "for the Lord would not come to such a scene of confusion." Taking the advice of the

"good sister," the Millerites who heard her regained their composure.[25]

Then Truth returned to the rest of the meeting where Starkweather and the other ministers were, she thought, irresponsibly
roiling the people. She addressed the preachers as well as the people:

Here you are talking about being "changed in the twinkling of an
eye." If the Lord should come, he'd change you to *nothing!* for there
is nothing to you.

You seem to be expecting to go to some parlor *away up* somewhere,
and when the wicked have been burnt, you are coming back to walk
in triumph over their ashes—this is to be your New Jerusalem!! Now
I can't see any thing so very *nice* in that, coming back to such *a muss*
[her word] as that will be, a world covered with the ashes of the
wicked! Besides, if the Lord comes and burns—as you say he will—I
am not going away; *I* am going to stay here and *stand the fire*, like
Shadrach, Meshach, and Abednego! And Jesus will walk with me
through the fire, and keep me from harm. Nothing belonging to God
can burn, any more than God himself; such shall have no need to go
away to escape the fire! No *I* shall remain. Do you tell me that God's
children *can't stand fire?* [And her manner and tone spoke louder than
words, saying,] It is *absurd* to think so![26]

Truth had help in reintroducing a sense of proportion at Stepney. Leading Millerite preachers in attendance were equally exasperated and embarrassed by the *"fanaticism"* of the "disgraceful
scene." They had seen nothing so shameful, they said, since the
"impiety and fanaticism" of the Kingdom of Matthias.[27] One of the
movement's main leaders, Charles Fitch, seized the lectern, declaring that all this carrying on was "of the devil," and that the
fanatics must leave. Indeed, Starkweather came under intense
criticism for inducing fanaticism and hysteria, although there was
no formal Millerite organization from which to expel him. Truth
may have concluded that this loss of self-control made Millerites
different from her, but other prominent Millerites also drew a line
between fanatics and themselves.[28]

Millerite ministers in Connecticut admired Truth's thinking and the very fact that she was willing to argue with them and contest their monopoly on Christian wisdom. She had, they said, "the lever of truth, that God helps her to pry where but few can." She still believed the tenets that she had held when she belonged to the Kingdom of Matthias in the 1830s, except that she no longer needed a superior in insight. She saw God as an "all-powerful, all pervading spirit" who spoke to her directly, as a voice in her head or in the scriptures. (Harriet Tubman, too, heard God's voice speaking to her directly, telling her what to do and where to go.)[29] Truth distrusted any mediation between herself and God, whether trained and paid ministers, anyone who presumed to interpret the Bible for her, or even the Apostles who had recorded God's message.

Truth examined the scriptures by hearing them, and she preferred children rather than adults as readers. Children, she said, would reread the same passage as many times as she requested without adding comment, but adults began to explain when she asked for repetition: "giving her their version of it and in this way, they tried her feelings exceedingly. In consequence of this, she ceased to ask adult persons to read the Bible to her." Hearing without comment, "she was enabled to see what her own mind could make out of the record, and that, she said, was what she wanted, and not what others thought it to mean."[30]

Truth believed that the voice of the Holy Spirit within her carried an authority commensurate with scripture. The "spirit of truth" spoke in the scripture, she concluded, but she considered the Bible a mixture of God's words and the ideas of those who had written it. Millerites recognized her views on divine revelation as "one among the many proofs of her energy and independence of character."[31]

MILLERITES in Connecticut gave Truth the addresses of people in western Massachusetts who would welcome her. And so she proceeded up the Connecticut River valley to Chicopee and Springfield, where Millerites continued to invite her into their homes and meetings.[32] They recommended Truth to other second adventists because they did not mind a certain level of heterodoxy and "often found at their meetings many singular people" who did not agree with them entirely. They appreciated her "commanding figure and dignified manner" and her "singular and sometimes uncouth modes of expression," which they never ridiculed. She became a "great favorite," adored for her "remarkable gift in prayer, and still more remarkable talent for singing." Already Sojourner Truth was becoming known for the gifts that we still associate with her name: "the aptness and point of her remarks, frequently illustrated by figures the most original and expressive."[33]

IN THE late fall, when New England's cold prohibited travel by foot and outdoor meetings, the woman now known as Sojourner Truth ended her first season of pilgrimage. In search of a quiet place for the winter, she considered three possible refuges: Friendly Millerites who had sheltered her in Springfield and asked her to stay on with them; Enfield, Connecticut, Shakers (whose full name, the United Society of Believers in Christ's Second Appearing, expressed their millennial, pentecostal convictions); and the transcendentalists of the Fruitlands settlement at Harvard, Massachusetts, which Bronson Alcott (father of the author Louisa May Alcott) was just starting in 1843, although it was to fail six months later for lack of members.[34]

In light of Truth's preference for communal living, Millerite friends in Springfield recommended a fourth alternative: a cooperative community in Northampton, Massachusetts, where she did go and where opened the third great chapter in her life.[35] After thirty years in slavery, fifteen years of making herself free through the power of the Holy Spirit, Sojourner Truth now launched the career of antislavery feminism for which she is known to this day.

10

Northampton

MILLERITE second adventists knew enough about the world they saw ending to steer Truth to the utopian Northampton Association for Education and Industry. The people in the Northampton Association were not second adventists; they were counting on the world to last long enough for them to cure its savagery and injustice.[1] They were starting on a small scale, with the manufacture of silk under enlightened principles. Surely this would ultimately reform the global political economy.

In mid-1843, the commune consisted of thirty men, twenty-six women, and forty-six children, plus six townswomen hired to work in the silk room. Intellectual exchange was its greatest pride, based in a library, reading room, and more or less formal lectures from illustrious visitors. Lecturers included the most prominent of American reformers: William Lloyd Garrison, president of the American Anti-Slavery Society and editor of the Boston *Liberator;* Frederick Douglass, who in the Northampton years was just starting a long and illustrious career as a journalist and statesman; Wendell Phillips, Boston Brahmin pillar of antislavery and labor reform before and after the Civil War; as well as the health evangelist Sylvester Graham, who lived in Northampton.

Intellectual enrichment was one thing, physical comfort another. Northampton Association residents took their baths in the river. Even sympathizers saw the community's living conditions as rough and tactfully praised its "simplicity."[2]

When Truth first saw the huge stone building that doubled as factory and dormitory, she "did not fall in love at first sight." The place looked so primitive that she agreed only reluctantly to stay even one night.

But meeting the leaders of the Northampton Association gave Truth pause; the sight, she said, of "accomplished, literary and refined persons" living so simply and enduring such privation suspended her negative judgment, and led her to remain. Over time she became so attached to the place and its way that the community, which she thought consisted of "some of the 'choicest spirits of the age,' " became her professed home. No other place, she concluded, would have offered her the same "equality of feeling," "liberty of thought and speech," and "largeness of soul."[3]

THE Northampton Association of Education and Industry began during the nineteenth century's greatest utopian moment; one-fifth of the 270 utopian communities founded in the United States between 1787 and 1919 were begun between 1842 and 1848.[4] During this period the proto-socialist thought of Henri Saint-Simon, Charles Fourier, and Robert Owen inspired intentional communities (what we now call communes) meant to improve the future of mankind. Little utopias sprang up in Russia (where Fyodor Dostoyevsky joined a socialist commune in 1846), Romania, France, and England, as well as in the United States. Ralph Waldo Emerson remarked that in those days, there was "hardly a reading man but carried a draft of a new community in his waistcoat pocket."[5] Massachusetts produced several utopian communities in the 1840s, the best known of which were Hopedale and Brook Farm.

The Northampton project grew from a strong center, out of William Lloyd Garrison's conversations with his brother-in-law, George W. Benson. Benson, a lawyer-turned-businessman from Brooklyn, Connecticut, belonged to an abolitionist family. His father had been a founder of the Providence, Rhode Island, anti-

Mill building of the Northampton Association, Florence, Massachusetts.
Photo courtesy of Forbes Library, Northampton, Massachusetts.

slavery society, and his sister, Helen, had married Garrison in 1834. Benson was in the thick of an incident that in 1833 exposed the racial intolerance of supporters of colonization, who often passed themselves off as moderate abolitionists. This was the Prudence Crandall affair.

Prudence Crandall, a Quaker teacher, opened a school for girls in Canterbury, Connecticut, six miles from Brooklyn, in 1831. The following year, Crandall admitted a well-known tri-racial girl, so light-skinned that she could pass for white, whose father was a prosperous Canterbury farmer. This seemingly innocuous act provoked deep outrage among the parents of the other students. As the parents threatened to withdraw their daughters, Crandall decided to expel them and open a school that would serve only black girls. At the prospect of a school for blacks, a local colonizationist mobilized even greater opposition, which intensified after the passage in May 1833 of a "black law" that prohibited blacks from coming into Connecticut.

Crandall endured two trials in Brooklyn, the county seat, and was finally freed on a technicality. Her school and her twenty well-mannered black scholars were so constantly terrorized that the harassment forced her to close down in 1834. The ordeal marked a watershed in the evolution of the antislavery movement. Moderate opposition to slavery had meant support for the removal—"colonization"—of American blacks in Africa. But Crandall's attackers, self-professed stalwarts of the American Colonization Society, now revealed themselves as extreme negrophobes.

After the Prudence Crandall affair, colonization looked more like racism than forbearance in opposition to slavery. The affair also increased the prestige of radicals like Garrison, who had supported Crandall throughout her persecution by official Connecticut. It sealed the antiracist sentiments of her supporters around Canterbury and Brooklyn, including George Benson.[6] Benson soon moved to Northampton, where he and his family spent the 1840s.

In 1841, after the silk boom of the mid-1830s and bust of the late 1830s, Benson, Samuel L. Hill (a Quaker-turned-Baptist also from Brooklyn, Connecticut), and two others bought the bankrupt Northampton Silk Company along Mill River in what became Florence, Massachusetts, two and a half miles from Northampton. The property included a fully outfitted large brick factory building that was four stories high and measured 120 by 40 feet, plus several other industrial outbuildings and six dwelling houses on 420 acres of land, situated on the 27-feet falls of the Mill River.[7]

THE LOFTY principles of the Northampton Association began with a rejection of the current state of the American political economy that was reminiscent of Fourier's criticism of civilization.[8] According to the organizers of the Association,

> Life is with some a mere round of frivolous occupations or vicious enjoyments, with most a hard struggle for the bare means of subsistence. The former are exempted from productive labour while they enjoy its fruits: upon the latter it is imposed as a task with unreasonable severity and with inadequate compensation. The one class is tempted to self-indulgence, pride, and oppressions: The other is debased by ignorance and crime, by the conflict of passions and interests, by moral pollution, and by positive want and starvation.[9]

This conflict appeared in much of the literature of economic reform throughout the balance of the nineteenth century, in the writ-

George W. Benson, one of the founders of the
Northampton Association of Education and Industry,
in a daguerreotype from about 1845. Photo courtesy
of the American Antiquarian Society.

ing of the Enlightenment-inspired utopians, Karl Marx and
Friedrich Engels, and of the late nineteenth-century American visionary, Henry George. The Northampton community, proposing
itself as an object lesson of remedy, took as its first principle of in-
corporation that all people have the duty to perform productive
work and the right to the fruits of their labor. Competition was
deemed an evil; cooperation, in the interest of women's rights, freedom of expression, liberal education, and the abolition of slavery,
a good.[10]

Although animated by many of Fourier's ideals, such as har-
monizing social and economic relations—in Fourier's words, "har-
monism" and "harmonic utopia"—the Northampton Association
was not a Fourierist community. It did not hold property in com-

mon or attempt to supplant existing family arrangements. According to Garrison, it was organized "by religious men, upon
anti-slavery ground."[11] The need to heal the class conflicts of the
larger society, the worst of which was slavery, was one of the
Northampton Association's basic tenets. Its prevailing religious
sentiment was tolerant and of a decidedly antislavery bent; members were critical of orthodox religion, and, like Sojourner Truth,
condemned a paid ministry. Appropriate to such unorthodox religious sentiments, the Northampton Association generated a non-
denominational free meeting that later became the Florence Free
Congregational Society, where Truth was an invited speaker.[12] But
religion was only a small part of the Association's ideology, for the
many abolitionists in the community took women's equality as a
given and supported temperance, vegetarianism, and peace.

The Association's unusual intellectual and ideological attractions brought in so many people that housing quickly ran short.
While a few of the community's leading families (including the
Bensons) lived in houses of their own, most were put on the top
floor of the factory, which served as a cramped boarding house.
One former member recalled that the "quarters were rude and
plain, and the fact that the members were willing to submit to the
many inconveniences, and to forego all luxuries and many of the
comforts to which they had been accustomed, showed how dear
to their hearts was the cause they had espoused."[13]

At its peak in 1844–45, the Association had some 210 members
from eight states (98 from Massachusetts, 88 from Connecticut)
and two foreign countries.[14] Able-bodied adults worked ten hours
a day; children also worked, but fewer hours, according to age and
strength. All adult workers received 6 cents per hour, and they
paid 50 cents a week for board and lodging.[15] The Association operated a highly regarded school that accepted black children (one,
from New Bedford, was the grandson of the prominent black
Bostonian sea captain Paul Cuffee) and children who were non-
residents for $100 per year.[16]

The Association's refreshingly good-natured egalitarianism gratified members and guests. Frederick Douglass visited in 1843, on
the edge of his career as a leading abolitionist and the foremost
black man of the nineteenth century. He recalled that the "place

and the people struck me as the most democratic I had ever met. It was a place to extinguish all aristocratic pretensions. There was no high, no low, no masters, no servants, no white, no black. I, however, felt myself in very high society." Douglass, like Truth, was enthralled by the lack of class and racial stratification. He listed the upper-class people he met there who were "yet fraternizing with the humblest members of the association." (Douglass was evidently not aware that the Association had voted to pay a woman $1.50 per week to do housework.)[17]

The community held two main goals: to create a non-competitive, open-minded, intellectually stimulating place in which to live and work; and to realize a profit from the manufacture of silk. The former goal quickly overshadowed the latter, and members interested in financial well-being started to peel off as early as 1842. A January 1843 amendment to the constitution that gave all members, whether or not they owned stock, equal say in the debt-ridden enterprise fatally undermined its finances. Another innovation, "mutual criticism," encouraged more forthright critique than the society could manage amicably. Samuel L. Hill, one of the founders who stuck to the community to the bitter end, nonetheless resented the "*taunts* & unkind *insinuations*" and "unjust accusations of my fellows."[18] Chronic debt and the eventual withdrawal of nearly all of the founders led to the dissolution of the community in November 1846.[19]

DURING the Northampton Association's days as a commune, Sojourner Truth seems to have fit in easily. Here there was no hanky-panky as in the Kingdom of Matthias, no elevating of "Father" and "Mother" out of the ranks of labor. Truth worked in the laundry and complained when others gave her too many clothes to wash or items that were too dirty. She was one of the more memorable characters—at least in retrospect—and former associates memorialized her with varying amounts of imagination. George R. Stetson, George Benson's nephew, who had joined the Association with his family in 1843 when he was six years old, recalled Truth many years later and in the light of her subsequent fame.

Stetson remembered her as an African of possibly royal stock who bore tribal markings, "a conspicuous figure during the anti-slavery controversy," who was "accustomed to speak and some-times to sing." He quoted Truth as having once remarked that "three thirds of the people are wrong." When someone noted that that accounted for everyone, she replied, "I am sorry, as I had hoped there were a few left." When a boy fell off the dam into the river, he was lucky enough to fall into a small but deep pool, the only place he could escape serious injury. Truth said, "If the Devil made him fall the Lord had a fixed place for him to light in." Singing, working, or speaking, Truth commanded attention, hav-ing "a tall imposing figure, a strong voice, and a ready wit."[20]

The Northampton Association provided Truth's opening to the reformers of antislavery feminism. One of these was James Boyle, another was Giles Stebbins. Boyle was a Methodist minister about Truth's age who had been born Catholic in Ontario. He had been a New Haven perfectionist with John Humphrey Noyes in the mid-1830s, had broken with Noyes, become a manual worker in Newark, New Jersey, then, in the early 1840s, took up antislavery socialism, which brought him to Northampton.[21] Stebbins, from central Massachusetts, was twenty years younger than Truth and did not enroll as a member. He came only to study, and stayed for a year. Truth, Boyle, and Stebbins would share their belief in abo-litionism, woman suffrage, and spiritualism in the decades to come.[22]

There were other black residents, including David Ruggles, for-merly of New York City, and Basil Dorsey, a young fugitive who arrived in 1844.[23] Dorsey has fallen out of history, but three of the black people who were at the Northampton Association became historical figures: Truth; Ruggles; and the occasional visitor, Dou-glass, who left the fullest direct testimony.

11

Douglass, Ruggles, and Family

SOJOURNER TRUTH had something in common with each of the other prominent black people associated with the Northampton Association: with David Ruggles, it was New York City; with Frederick Douglass, slavery and, to a certain extent, Methodism. In the late 1820s and early 1830s, both Douglass and Truth had become Methodists, but Methodists of very different persuasions. Douglass encountered Methodism in Baltimore, where he attended an African Methodist Episcopal (AME) church and Sabbath school. This experience reinforced his allegiance both to the written word and to urban, preacher-centered orthodoxy.

Douglass was licensed to preach in the AME church in about 1840 in New Bedford, and had he not turned his gift as a speaker toward the struggle against slavery, he might well have enjoyed a career in the ministry. Truth, on the other hand, was an itinerant preacher who, as a woman, could never have become an AME minister, even had her religion been more conventional. Conventional it was not, and twentieth-century people who are unfamiliar with pentecostalism are tempted to see her reliance on the power of the Holy Spirit as a manifestation of her African, rather than her perfectionist heritage. But Douglass, though also African-American, had little in common with Truth beyond their race.

Frederick Douglass daguerreotype, ca. 1847. Photo courtesy of the
National Portrait Gallery, Smithsonian Institution.

Frederick Douglass's first meeting with Truth occurred at
Northampton, as Douglass was charting a course into freedom di-
vergent from hers. Like many other fugitive slaves, Douglass associated illiteracy with enslavement, and strove to complete his
emancipation through the acquisition of fluency—elegance, in his
case—in reading and writing. He saw himself as a statesman-in-the-
making and modeled his comportment on the well-educated antislavery leaders with whom he worked.

Though some twenty years younger than Truth, Douglass patronized her industry and amiability, calling her one of the community's most useful members "in its day of small things." What

most galled Douglass was Truth's lack of sympathy with his own means of personal rebirth. While Douglass was schooling himself to "speak and act like a person of cultivation and refinement," Truth, he said, "seemed to feel it her duty to trip me up in my speeches and to ridicule my efforts." Douglass saw Truth as "a genuine specimen of the uncultured [N]egro," who "cared very little for elegance of speech or refinement of manners."

For all his condescension, Douglass grasped the key to Truth's impending success among white reformers, the qualities that made her memorable and were so widely described in print. Truth, Douglass said, was a "strange compound of wit and wisdom, of wild enthusiasm and flint-like common sense," who "seemed to please herself and others best when she put her ideas in the oddest forms." "Her quaint speeches," he noted, "easily gave her an audience."[1] Testimonials from the decades that followed corroborate his insight. Truth's persona, her seeming utter differentness, proved irresistibly entertaining to white reformers. Over the years after 1850 they usually tried to show her otherness through the use of what they thought was Negro dialect, and they dwelled at length on descriptions of her body.

DOUGLASS was more respectful toward the other black New Yorker at Northampton. Five years earlier, as one of New York's leading abolitionists and head of the Vigilance Society, David Ruggles had arranged the New York–New Bedford stage of Douglass's flight from slavery. Douglass found Ruggles at Northampton a figure of "sterling sense and worth."

Ruggles had arrived in Massachusetts in 1842, blind, ill, and destitute, but had subsequently cured himself of his unspecified illness, though not of his blindness. In the process he learned the theory and practice of water cure and set up Northampton's first water-cure establishment.

Water cure, or hydropathy, was one of many interrelated reforms that flourished in the mid-nineteenth century, although the benefits of clean water had been recognized earlier. John Wesley's eighteenth-century *Primitive Physic* advocated cold water as a cure for disease, and in the 1830s Sylvester Graham had included it in the list of practices he recommended to remedy disease and foster health: temperance, a vegetarian diet, regular exercise, fresh air, non-restricting clothing, sexual moderation, and frequent bathing. In the United States, water cure was most closely associated with temperance, which meant abstinence not merely from alcohol but also from coffee, tea, and tobacco. The people who frequented water-cure establishments tended to embrace other reforms, notably women's rights. Water-cure spas, like the one in Dansville, New York, sometimes functioned as feminist refuges from the ravages of activism.

In 1840, the first American water-cure establishment appeared in New York City, modeled on Vincenz Priessnitz's Gräfenberg spa in the mountains of Silesia. Employing a series of cold water baths, drips, and wraps, and the drinking of lots of water, water cure eschewed drugs but offered a comprehensive system of prevention and healing that appealed to reformers as natural and gentle. Water cure could be practiced at home, provided one had access to abundant clean water—not to be taken for granted at a time when indoor plumbing and pure city water were not commonly available. More often patients journeyed to water-cure establishments, such as the one David Ruggles set up in Northampton in 1846.[2]

Ruggles's own Northampton Water Cure was the first in its vicinity, and it succeeded even though he screened his clients: Everyone had to apply in writing, allowing him to discourage those he could not help. Hopeless cases may have been few, for he recommended water cure as appropriate for the treatment of a wide variety of ailments: "headache, tendency of the blood to the head, cold extremities, general and nervous debility, bronchitis, pulmonary affection, liver complaint, jaundice, acute or chronic inflammation of the bowels, piles, dyspepsia, general debility, nervous and spinal affectations, inflammatory and chronic rheumatism, neuralgia, sciatica, lame limbs, paralysis, fevers, salt rheum, scrofulous and erysipelas humors." Stays at Ruggles's establishment, where patients had to supply their own blankets and linen, cost $5.50–$8.50 per week, at the low end of the price range. At the time, one visit to a regular (allopathic) physician usually cost at least $5.00.[3]

From January 1846 to December 1849, Ruggles operated the

Northampton Water Cure in the "old mill house" in Northampton. He had outfitted it through purchases at the Northampton Association store of graham flour, sugar, yards and yards of cotton cloth, nails, saws, frames, one door latch, butts and screws, linseed oil, carpet binding, soap, bed ticking, and lamp wicking and oil, among other supplies.[4]

A fugitive notation in the store ledger raises intriguing romantic possibilities: "1 shawl for Elizabeth Gedney," $2.50, and $1.25 for "1/2 dozen tumblers."[5] Elizabeth Gedney was Sojourner Truth's twenty-one-year-old daughter (named for Truth's mother), one of three who were with her in Northampton during 1843–45. But if David Ruggles planned to marry Truth's daughter Elizabeth, nothing came of it, not in 1846 or later.[6] His business fortunes, too, declined after his modest establishment faced fancier competition in the late 1840s. Had he not died on the day after Christmas 1849, he would have gone bankrupt in 1850.

THE LISTING of Sojourner Truth's daughters—if daughters they all were—in the Northampton Association store ledger is full of mystery. Elizabeth and Sophia definitely were daughters, born in about 1825 and 1826. But the name "Jane" appears nowhere else in the sources surrounding Truth; she may have been Truth's elusive second child, or she may have been a granddaughter or niece. For lack of guidance, I will speak of her as a daughter, acknowledging that the sole clue to her identity consists of a single notation of her name in a store ledger.

Truth appears in the ledger as "Sojourner"—the only patron at the community store mentioned with only one name—as well as "Isabel" and "Isabella," "Van Wagner" and "Van Wagnen," and, once, as "Mrs. Sojourner."[7] Her daughters also appear under several titles. Elizabeth, Sophia, and Jane are each mentioned as "Van Wagner," "Van Wagnen," and "Gedney." The names "Van Wagner" and "Van Wagnen" establish the relationship between Truth and her daughters; but "Gedney," the name of the family of Truth's Ulster County, mistress, Sally Dumont, implies a deeper, longer-standing, and more complicated attachment between the two families.

To the thorny employer-employee relationship that Truth mentions in the story of the illegal sale of her son to Alabama and her children's indentures (only vaguely cited) must now be added a voluntary identification. The keeper of the store ledger at the Northampton Association, after all, had no independent source for the daughters' identification. Sojourner Truth's daughters must have decided on their own to perpetuate the link with the Gedneys, who appear in the *Narrative of Sojourner Truth* as little more than spoiled, rich white people.

Just as the sources do not permit any further understanding of David Ruggles's purchase of an expensive shawl for Sojourner Truth's daughter Elizabeth, so they are silent on the tangled feelings that Truth and her daughters harbored about each other and toward the Gedneys. The *Narrative of Sojourner Truth* was written while Truth was at Northampton, but it gives no sign of the presence of Elizabeth, Sophia, and Jane, says nothing about their sense of self as expressed in their names. The daughters inexplicably remain shrouded in the *Narrative*, and the section on Northampton is no exception.

Peter is the only one of Truth's children whose history and character are visible in the *Narrative*. This may be because he was the source of his mother's greatest anguish, or because he was male and by that token his experiences seemed to merit recording. Twin conventions of biography—according to which the family of the protagonist does not appear and the black American acts against a backdrop of white racism—may also be reinforcing one another. Or the daughters may have been figures whom Truth thought best to leave beyond the autobiography's ken. Silence was the easiest means of avoiding misgivings about how little she had been able to do for her daughters, and Truth says nothing; Olive Gilbert, speaking in circumlocution, impugns both the daughters' morals and the mother's care.

Gilbert tells Truth's readers that Truth's children have not benefitted from the salutary atmosphere of a proper home, in which she could "instill into the opening minds of her children those principles of virtue, and that love of purity, truth and benevolence, which must ever form the foundation of a life of usefulness and happiness." Gilbert recognizes that part of the blame lies at the door of slavery and indenture. Isabella was unable to make her children a home while she was enslaved or immediately after her emancipation, when her wages were too small to afford a home together.

After their own emancipation, the daughters were still indentured to various members of the Dumont-Gedney-Waring family. During this time, Gilbert says, Truth's children were "scattered, and eminently exposed to the temptations of the adversary, with few, if any, fixed principles to sustain them." But lack of freedom is only part of the explanation that Gilbert sees for the daughters' corruption.

Gilbert also blames Truth herself for neglecting, even in difficult circumstances, to inculcate strong moral values in her children. Bringing them up properly was "far beyond [Truth's] power or means, in more senses than one," states Gilbert, who, while recognizing the challenge of child rearing in slavery, does not wish to "shield any one [i.e., Truth] from merited rebuke!" Gilbert judges Truth a failed parent and the shortcomings of her children the product of parental disregard. She describes Truth's children as disreputable, but in the late 1840s they were adults, and Gilbert thought them old enough to take responsibility for their own failings. "If they now suffer themselves to be drawn by temptation into the paths of the destroyer," that is their own sin, for which they will ultimately pay.[8]

For Gilbert, and perhaps also for Truth, the lack of a home, with all its Victorian connotations of shelter from a cruel and heartless world—a haven of femininity in a sea of masculine predation—explained much of the weakness in Truth's family life. From a farther vantage point, however, the absence of Truth's daughters from her life story can be recognized as the familiar shroud of silence around black women who, for lack of protection, become sexual prey. Unwilling to focus on women who had not been shielded from predatory men or who were possibly unchaste, Gilbert and Truth made a commonplace erasure of the most vulnerable and least visible people in American history.[9]

12

The *Narrative of Sojourner Truth*

THE NORTHAMPTON ASSOCIATION dissolved in late 1846, having uplifted only a tiny part of its world. Truth stayed on, first trying to make her own way, then lodging with the Bensons, who had withdrawn from the Association in 1845 and bought a nearby cotton mill. Although she was with people who cared for her, Truth was impatient with her situation and longed, once again, for her own home. The success of Frederick Douglass's 1845 autobiography, the *Narrative of the Life of Frederick Douglass, An American Slave*, which sold 4,500 copies in less than six months, doubtless suggested a means of affording a house of her own.[1] A year after Douglass published, Truth began dictating her autobiography to Olive Gilbert.

Of Gilbert, I know little: She was born in 1801 and died in 1884. Well educated and well read, she belonged to the Northampton Association in 1845–46, and after the Civil War she was still living in the Northampton environs. Gilbert's original connection to the Association came through the Bensons, her neighbors in Connecticut, more exactly through George and Helen's spinster sister Sarah. Sarah lived with the Bensons in Northampton and, like Olive Gilbert, never married. Gilbert was also friendly with Helen and her husband William Lloyd Garrison, and spent time with them in Boston.[2] Although the sources are virtually silent about Prudence Crandall's female supporters, Gilbert undoubtedly was involved in her Connecticut neighbor's defense, which closely engaged the Benson family.

Between the commencement of Truth's narrative and its completion three years later, Gilbert spent more than two years in Daviess County in northwestern Kentucky, probably as a governess.[3] Otherwise, the outline of Olive Gilbert's life is unclear. The joint project provides nearly all the extant information about her, some of which can be glimpsed only between the lines.

Like Truth, Gilbert may have been attracted to Millerism in 1843–44, for the *Narrative* contains a great deal of material, sympathetically presented, on Truth's experiences with the Millerites. Instead of a description of Truth's stay in the Northampton Association, for instance, the section on 1843–49 concerns Truth's en-

Before buying her own house on Park Street, Sojourner Truth lived with the Benson family in this house on Maine Street, Florence (Northampton), Massachusetts. Photo courtesy of the American Antiquarian Society.

counter with hostile young men at a Millerite camp meeting in the spring of 1844. As one of the rare depictions of Truth's preaching by someone who had often heard her preach and sing, Gilbert's report of this episode deserves a closer look.

During 1844, Millerite meetings were frequently subject to ridicule and disruption, as was the case for a nighttime camp meeting near Northampton.[4] A mob of rowdy young men burst into the services, terrifying the worshippers and threatening to burn down the tents. Truth's first impulse was to hide behind a trunk, thinking, "I am the only colored person here, and on me, probably, their wicked mischief will fall first, and perhaps fatally." But as the ruffians were shaking the tent, she had a little talk with herself in biblical terms:

> Shall I run away and hide from the Devil? Me, a servant of the living God? Have I not faith enough to go out and quell that mob, when I know it is written—"One shall chase a thousand, and two put ten thousand to flight"? I know there are not a thousand here; and I know I am a servant of the living God. I'll go to the rescue, and the Lord shall go with and protect me.[5]

As when she defied the rich and powerful of Ulster County over the sale of her son, Truth's religious faith gave her strength: "I felt as if I had *three hearts!* and that they were so large, my body could hardly hold them!" Thus emboldened, she urged other Millerites to help her face down the attackers. They declined, and she left the tent alone, walked to a high place, and began singing in what Gilbert terms "her most fervid manner, with all the strength of her most powerful voice, the hymn on the resurrection of Christ":

> It was early in the morning—it was early in the morning,
>   Just at the break of day—
> When he rose—when he rose—when he rose,
>   And went to heaven on a cloud.[6]

This was one of Truth's favorites, and Gilbert remarks that "All who have ever heard her sing this hymn will probably remember it as long as they remember her. The hymn, the tune, the style, are each too closely associated with to be easily separated from herself, and when sung in one of her most animated moods, in the open air, with the utmost strength of her most powerful voice, must have been truly thrilling." Truth would sing the same hymn on her deathbed, forty years later.

Fulfilling a requirement of spiritual autobiography, Truth pacified the unbelievers; she preached and sang to them for the better part of an hour.[7] Her sermon began with a metaphor of the second advent's Judgment Day: "Well, there are two congregations on this ground. It is written that there shall be a separation, and the sheep shall be separated from the goats. The other preachers have the sheep, *I* have the goats. And I have a few sheep among my goats, but they are *very* ragged." The crowd laughed and settled in to be entertained.

Truth grew weary, wanted to stop preaching, but her audience would not let her go. She addressed them as "children," as she had the fanatical Connecticut Millerites: "I have talked and sung to you, as you asked me; and now I have a request to make of you: will you grant it?" She would sing one more song if they would leave in peace afterwards; she had to ask them three times. Long after the demise of Millerite camp meetings, Truth would repeat her song:

> I bless the Lord I've got my seal—to-day and to-day—
> To slay Goliath in the field—to-day and to-day—
> The good old way is a righteous way,
> I mean to take the kingdom in the good old way.

Running back to the main road, the roughnecks frightened the other Millerites but created no further trouble. Truth had assuaged their angry spirits and saved the meeting.[8]

The twenty pages of the *Narrative of Sojourner Truth* dedicated to her time with the Millerites contain none of the internal strains of other parts of the story. Elsewhere, Gilbert the abolitionist is often at odds with Truth the autobiographer. The abolitionist presses Truth to provide examples of the iniquities of slavery, which Truth delivers and Gilbert amplifies, but which must be tacked on to Truth's own, more enigmatic story.[9] And toward the end of the book, Gilbert addresses Truth rather than the reader,

NARRATIVE

OF

SOJOURNER TRUTH,

A

NORTHERN SLAVE,

EMANCIPATED FROM BODILY SERVITUDE BY THE STATE OF
NEW YORK, IN 1828.

WITH A PORTRAIT.

' SWEET is the virgin honey, though the wild bee store it in a reed
And bright the jewelled band that circleth an Ethiop's arm;
Pure are the grains of gold in the turbid stream of the Ganges;
And fair the living flowers that spring from the dull cold sod.
Wherefore, thou gentle student, bend thine ear to my speech,
For I also am as thou art; our hearts can commune together;
To meanest matters will I stoop, for mean is the lot of mortal;
I will rise to noblest themes, for the soul hath a heritage of glory.'

BOSTON:
PRINTED FOR THE AUTHOR.
1850.

Green paper cover of the first, 1850, edition of the *Narrative of
Sojourner Truth*, 128 pages, 7 3/4″ x 5″. Photo courtesy of the
Sophia Smith Collection, Smith College.

admonishing her to revise her harsh judgment of the Bensons.

Gilbert comes close to calling Truth paranoid, and, returning her address to the reader, builds a case for the purchase of the *Narrative* based on Truth's and her daughters' own deficiencies. The daughters are too sinful and foolish to care for their mother in the old age that is now upon her, and the mother has wasted her money on the likes of the Prophet Matthias.[10]

NARRATIVE

OF

Sojourner Truth.

HER BIRTH AND PARENTAGE.

THE subject of this biography, Sojourner Truth, as she now calls herself, but whose name originally was Isabella, was the daughter of James and Betsey, slaves of one Col. Ardinburgh, Hurley, Ulster County, N. Y. Sojourner does not know in what year she was born, but knows she was liberated under the act of 1817, which freed all slaves who were forty years old and upward. Ten thousand slaves were then set at liberty. Those under forty years of age were retained in servitude ten years longer, when all were emancipated.

Col. Ardinburgh belonged to that class of people called Low Dutch.

Of her first master, she can give no account, as she must have been a mere infant when he died; and she with her parents and some ten or twelve other fellow human chattels, became the legal property of his son, Charles Ardinburgh. She distinctly remembers hearing her father and mother say that their lot was a fortunate one, as Master Charles was the best of the family,—being, comparatively speaking, a kind master to his slaves.

James and Betsey having, by their faithfulness, docility, and respectful behaviour, won his particular regard,

18

The opening page of Olive Gilbert's 1850 *Narrative of Sojourner Truth.*

Whether or not Gilbert shared Truth's second adventism, together they produced a narrative that is strikingly spiritual. This emphasis on the evolution of Truth's faith and her religious experiences—including the long episode in which she pacifies rowdies at the camp meeting—has made the *Narrative of Sojourner Truth* difficult for readers to fit into the more familiar southern drama of slavery, with its contest between virtuous slave and cruel master.

To this day, the *Narrative of Sojourner Truth* remains outside the canon of ex-slave narratives. It ends, not with indictment, but with the Christian forgiveness of a slaveholder, on the occasion of

This engraving purports to come from a photograph of Truth as Isabella, though no such photograph was ever taken. This drawing, by an unknown artist, is from imagination and appears in all editions of the *Narrative of Sojourner Truth*.

Truth's 1849 visit to her oldest daughter, Diana, who had remained with John Dumont in Dutchess County, New York. These last two pages of the *Narrative* are about Dumont, not hardworking Diana, and they convey Truth's satisfaction that he had come to see that slavery was wrong. She closes with exultation: "A slaveholding master turned to a brother! Poor old man, may the Lord bless him, and all slaveholders partake of his spirit!" Phrases too tender for an antislavery message in the decade of discord before the Civil War![11]

The *Narrative of Sojourner Truth* marks a turning point in the biography of Sojourner Truth—her first step into deliberate representation of self. In her interviews with Gilbert Vale in 1835, Isabella had sought only to vindicate herself as a vulnerable member of a suspect community. The *Narrative* makes her a person worth reading about in her own right.

HAVING furnished a writer, Truth's Northampton connections also found her a printer. The most illustrious of Northampton's visitors, William Lloyd Garrison, was editor of the Boston *Liberator* and president of the American Anti-Slavery Society, which had already published Frederick Douglass's narrative. Garrison put Truth in touch with his own printer, George Brown Yerrinton.

Truth had met Garrison in the fall of 1843, when the Garrison family paid an extended visit to the Bensons, and she probably saw him again in July 1848, when Garrison accepted David Ruggles's offer of free treatment at his Northampton Water Cure.[12] Yerrinton, originally from Providence, was a Free Thinker (like Gilbert Vale) whose ties to progressive causes and publications dated back to the 1820s.[13] He printed Truth's *Narrative* on credit, and the debt weighed heavily on Truth until she was able to repay it fully in the early 1850s. Having paid for the printing, Truth, rather than Yerrinton, is the publisher of her book. It is unclear why the plates remained for the time being in the possession of one of Truth's Northampton Association colleagues turned spiritualist-physician in New York, James Boyle, but he later gave them to her and made possible the editions of the 1850s, 1870s, and 1880s.[14]

In 1850, Truth's publishing herself was not unusual, for the line between publisher and printer was only then becoming established, and the functions of printing, distributing, and selling books were not always distinct. Acting as her own distributer and bookseller, Truth was well within the bounds of ordinary practice. More unusual, though, was the cheapness of her book: 25 cents per copy for a 128-page, 7 3/4-by-5-inch, soft-covered edition. She kept the price low, perhaps to encourage purchase, for sales of the *Narrative* were to be her means of paying off the mortgage on her new house. An advertisement for Truth's *Narrative* appeared in the *Liberator* in May 1850 with a blurb from Garrison: "This is a most interesting Narrative of a most remarkable and highly meritorious woman, the sale of which is to be for her exclusive benefit. We commend it to all the friends of the colored people."[15] Once the *Narrative* was printed, Truth had the means to fulfill her dream. For the first time in her life, she acquired a home of her own.

We cannot know what went wrong between Truth and the Bensons, but her preference in 1843 for wintering in an intentional community over prolonging her stay in a private home makes a

Sojourner Truth's house, Park Street, Florence (Northampton),
Massachusetts. Photo courtesy of the American Antiquarian Society.

statement: When she had a choice, she preferred being one among many to one among a few. She resisted situations in which she was "just like one of the family" and dependent strictly on her hosts. In the event, Truth had no choice but to find new lodging. George Benson's cotton mill failed, and the family moved to Long Island.[16]

Meanwhile, Northampton Association stalwart Samuel Hill and his brother-in-law acquired the property that had belonged to the Association and were selling it to various former members. Truth took out a $300 mortgage from Hill, bought a house on Park Street, across from the cemetery, and made it her home until the mid-1850s.

The world did not yet know her exclusively as "Sojourner Truth," for her 1850 deed names her as "Isabella Vanwagner . . . sometimes called 'Sojourner Truth' "; the 1854 deed omits "Truth" entirely. Although her identity wavered between that of working-class New Yorker and itinerant preacher, one thing was clear. In 1854, she discharged the mortgage and, at last, owned her own house free and clear.[17] She was about fifty-seven years old.

IN LATE middle age, Sojourner Truth emerges from her *Narrative* as a complex individual, a mixture of brightness and shadow. She is a woman of "native enthusiasm," with the "energy of a naturally powerful mind—the fearlessness and child-like simplicity of one untrammelled by education or conventional customs." Her character is pure, her adherence to principle unflinching. She is a singing evangelist whose religion is joyous, optimistic, and "at times ecstatic. Her trust is in God, and from him she looks for good, and not evil. She feels that 'perfect love casteth out fear.' " But her faith consorts with foreboding.

Apparently facing the twilight of her years, Truth has "set suspicion to guard the door of her heart," allowing it "to be aroused by too slight causes." She magnifies the "phantoms of her fears into gigantic proportions." Olive Gilbert presents a figure of fervor and enthusiasm, but also one of apprehension and distrust.[18] Fervor and enthusiasm were what her audiences would see as she became famous as an abolitionist.

13

Networks of Antislavery Feminism

IN EACH of the three great chapters of Sojourner Truth's life—slavery, evangelism, and antislavery feminism—she built networks of human contact. These networks sustained her materially and spiritually, steadily broadening her horizons.

Her first network, in Ulster County, had consisted of her enslaved family, owners, and employers, most enduringly of her children and the wealthy whites in the extended family of Warings and Gedneys around John and Sally Dumont, all people she related to more or less, for better or for worse, as family. The second network spun out of perfectionist Methodism and second adventism, beginning with the Ulster County Methodists and extending through the Grears to New York City, where Truth lived with the Latourettes, Piersons, Folgers, the Prophet Matthias, and the Whitings, before finally joining the Millerites. Millerites formed her bridge to the Northampton Association and her third network—abolitionists, feminists, and spiritualists, her associates for the rest of her life.

This third network eventually encompassed the leading intellects of American reform. It spread out from the Benson family, with whom Truth lived in Northampton, to Sarah Benson's close friend Olive Gilbert, Truth's amanuensis, and Helen Benson's husband, William Lloyd Garrison. The Garrisons opened to Truth a far-flung antislavery community that included Isaac and Amy Post of Rochester, New York. Despite her disgruntlements upon leaving the Benson household, Truth did not forfeit the friendship or the causes of the Benson-Garrison clan. The year 1850 found her not at the beginning of her retirement, as Gilbert had written at the end of the *Narrative,* but on the brink of a new career.

The evolution of the evangelist Sojourner Truth into the antislavery feminist Sojourner Truth had begun well before publication of the *Narrative.* In the fall of 1844, Truth gave her first antislavery speech in Northampton. In May 1845, she spoke to the annual meeting of the American Anti-Slavery Society in New York City, identified in the *National Anti-Slavery Standard* only as "a colored woman who had been a slave, but more recently resident of Northampton, Mass." Truth's remarks, according to the *Standard,* were full of "good sense and strong feeling."[1]

I cannot track completely Truth's antislavery and women's rights appearances, for reporters did not invariably consider her worth identifying by name, or even mentioning at all. She doubtless attended and addressed many meetings without notice between 1845 and 1850. I do know for certain that she attended and addressed a large women's rights meeting in Worcester, Massachusetts, in 1850—the first such meeting of national scope in the United States. This Worcester meeting was an immediate successor of the pioneering Seneca Falls, New York, women's convention of 1848 organized by Elizabeth Cady Stanton, Lucretia Mott, and others—including the Rochester abolitionist Amy Post, who would play so large a role in Truth's later life.

Women had been publicly vindicating their rights as women, as workers, and as blacks in the United States since the Scotswoman Frances Wright lectured in New York City in the late 1820s and the African American Maria Stewart spoke in Boston in the early 1830s. But women as speakers before mixed, or "promiscuous" audiences of women and men were rare, even when the subject was evangelical and the tradition—as in the case of women itinerant preachers—centuries older. Women lecturers like Angelina Grimké and Abby Kelley caused a sensation when they joined the antislavery circuit in the 1830s, since critics opposed women's right to advocate anything in public.

By 1840, the issue of women as leaders in abolitionism had split the American movement, with Garrisonians like Frederick Douglass and Abby Kelley defending women's rights, and less radical men, especially Arthur and Lewis Tappan, leaving the American Anti-Slavery Society on this and other grounds. The Tappans' unwillingness to mix antislavery with other reforms, such as women's rights, is probably the main reason they do not appear in the *Narrative of Sojourner Truth*. The rival society set up by the Tappans and their supporters withered, while the Garrisonian American Anti-Slavery Society flourished. After 1840, in the fashion of excommunicators, the Garrisonians pretended that the Tappans did not exist, despite their crucial early role in abolitionism.

Garrison firmly supported the 1850 women's rights meeting in Worcester and may have suggested that Douglass and Truth speak. According to a newspaper report, Truth "uttered some truths that told well," although her skin was dark and her outward appearance "uncomely." Truth spoke primarily as a preacher: "She said Woman set the world wrong by eating the forbidden fruit, and now she was going to set it right. She said Goodness never had any beginning; it was from everlasting, and could never die. But Evil had a beginning, and must have an end. She expressed great reverence for God, and faith that he will bring about his own purposes and plans."

In her concluding remarks, Lucretia Mott, a leader of the convention, mentioned Truth by name as "the poor woman who had grown up under the curse of Slavery," and repeated Truth's formulation of the finite nature of evil and the everlasting quality of good.[2] Truth's other early reported antislavery speech in 1850, at the annual meeting of the Rhode Island Anti-Slavery Society in Providence, in November, was also vague on antislavery politics. While the men, Frederick Douglass, Charles C. Burleigh, and Charles Lenox Remond, damned the Fugitive Slave Act for hours and demanded Garrison's version of disunion—"No union with slaveholders!"—Truth was reported as brief and hesitant: "she had been a slave, and was not now entirely free. She did not know anything about politics—could not read the newspapers—but thanked God that the law was made—that the worst had come to worst; but the best must come to best."³

TRUTH'S first tour on the antislavery and women's rights circuit in the winter of 1851 came at Garrison's behest. He invited her to accompany him and his dear friend, the radical British Member of Parliament George Thompson, on a trip into western New York. Thirteen years later, Truth recollected that Garrison had suggested the trip as a means of repaying her debt to her printer, George Yerrinton, an obligation that weighed heavily on her mind. "Every cent I could obtain went to pay it," she recalled. Garrison said, "I am going with George Thompson on a lecturing tour—Come with us, and you will have a good chance to dispose of your book." Lacking money for traveling expenses, Truth demurred; Garrison then offered to defray them for her. She signed on.

Truth's first antislavery traveling companion, George Thompson, at right, with Wendell Phillips and William Lloyd Garrison, Boston, ca. December 1850. Photo courtesy of the Trustees of the Boston Public Library.

When Truth arrived at the first stop on the tour—Springfield, Massachusetts—Garrison was not there. Having fallen ill, he was at home in Boston. Not only was he not in Springfield as arranged, he had failed to alert Truth of his indisposition. Cast adrift in Thompson's hotel, she mustered the courage to ask for his room. Once she found Thompson, "He received & seated me with as much courtesy and cordiality as if I had been the highest lady in the land . . . if I would go with himself and Mr. [George] Putnam it would be all the same." When Truth revealed her pecuniary embarrassment, Thompson offered to redeem Garrison's pledge. " 'I'll bear your expenses Sojourner' said [Thompson], 'leave with us!' And so I went. He accompanied me to the cars [the train] and carried my bag."

Truth was touched by Thompson's lack of the racial prejudice that marred white American relations with blacks: "At the Hotel tables he seated me beside himself & never seemed to know that I was poor and a black woman." Thompson also advertised her presence at their joint appearances: " 'Sojourner Truth has a narrative of her life—'Tis very interesting. Buy largely[,] friends!' " Truth praised Thompson as a "Good man! genuine gentleman! God bless George Thompson! the most kind hearted friend of my race."[4]

Perhaps Garrison's absence was a blessing to Truth. As fellow travelers, these three would be spending countless hours together, but Garrison and Thompson had been fast friends for eighteen years. Garrison named his first child, born in 1836, for Thompson, and they remained in close contact until well after the Civil War. Truth would have been the outsider in their company.

Thompson's reform convictions ran deep. He supported Chartism and other workers' causes in Britain, opposed the Corn Laws that increased the cost of bread for the British poor, and advocated the abolition of slavery in the West Indies. During his 1834–35 visit to the United States, he had aroused such intense pro-slavery opposition that he had been forced to flee for his life. He was mobbed in New York City for criticizing American slavery and associating with African Americans on a footing of equality. A mob in Boston failed to put its hands on Thompson, but paraded his host, William Lloyd Garrison, through the streets with a rope around his neck.

Fifteen years later, Thompson returned a somewhat mellower Member of Parliament from London who advanced a still unpopular but now better organized cause. His eight-month stay in late 1850 and early 1851 succeeded all around, although his presence was still incendiary.

Garrison and Thompson saw eye to eye and scrutinized politics eagerly and knowingly. Their conversations in 1850–51 surely dissected at great length the personalities and issues of the Compromise of 1850, which preserved the Union in the midst of severe sectional tensions over the extension of slavery into the vast area seized from Mexico. Garrison and Thompson were on the moral and intellectual leading edge. But more and more northerners were finding it impossible to ignore slavery after the war with Mexico and the annexation of Texas in the mid-1840s, as southern slaveholders threatened to fill the West with their Negroes.

The Compromise of 1850 reinforced the Garrisonians' call for northern secession from the slaveholding South and opened a decade of intense sectional conflict over slavery and its political repercussions: fugitive slaves, the Kansas-Nebraska Territory, the creation of antislavery political parties, the Dred Scott decision, and John Brown's raid. These sensations were still to come when Thompson and Truth set out together.

ARRIVING in Rochester in early 1851, Thompson and Truth stayed with former Quakers who had a long history in antislavery and women's rights reform: Amy and Isaac Post. The Posts would remain among Truth's lifelong friends, housing her for long visits and writing often. Extraordinary among nineteenth-century white Americans for their lack of racial prejudice, the Posts were intimate friends and correspondents of several other black abolitionists who stayed with them over the years: Frederick Douglass, who became their neighbor in Rochester; Harriet Jacobs, the author of an 1861 fugitive slave narrative, *Incidents in the Life of a Slave Girl;* and Garrison's young and gossipy assistant on the *Liberator* in Boston, William C. Nell.

Originally from Long Island, the Posts were about the same age as Truth; Isaac was born in 1798 in Westbury, Amy in 1802 in Jeri-

cho (both towns about fifteen miles east of Queens). They moved
to Rochester in 1836, where Isaac left farming to become a drug-
gist. Amy was a founder of the Western New York Anti-Slavery Society in 1843, and both were true radicals. The Posts ultimately had
to decide between their politics and their religion. They chose abolition, and withdrew from their Quaker meeting in 1845. Amy was
also a feminist, helping to organize the Seneca Falls meeting that
in 1848 inaugurated the nineteenth-century struggle for women's
rights.[5]

TRUTH was based with the Posts throughout the winter of 1851,
as she went around selling her books at meetings with Thompson
in western New York and Ohio. In the spring, she moved on to
Salem, a strong antislavery community in northeastern Ohio. There
she stayed with Marius and Emily Robinson, who, like the Posts,
were old and committed Garrisonians. Originally from Dalton,
Massachusetts, Marius Robinson had taught in the Cherokee Nation (then located in Georgia) and in Alabama before enrolling as
a student at Lane Theological Seminary in Cincinnati. Lane was
headed by Lyman Beecher, the father of Harriet Beecher Stowe,
and was the home of an early concentration of abolitionists, the
"Lane rebels" of 1834, whose best-known figure was Theodore
Weld. Weld married the pioneer antislavery lecturer Angelina
Grimké, and together they compiled the 1839 documentary indictment of slavery, *American Slavery As It Is.*

   While in Cincinnati, Robinson had lived his antislavery principles by teaching in a school for black children, where he met
Emily Rakestraw, a fellow teacher. As one of the Lane rebels,
Robinson withdrew from Lane when Beecher attempted to squelch
talk of abolition, but he did not move on to Oberlin College with
Weld and the other rebels. Instead, Emily and Marius married in
1836, and Marius became an agent—traveling lecturer—of the
American Anti-Slavery Society in Ohio. He paid a price for his
principles: In early 1837 he fell victim to a pro-slavery mob that
beat and tarred him.

   Robinson made one further tour under the auspices of the
American Anti-Slavery Society in the second half of 1837, then he

resigned his agency and took up farming. In early 1851, as Truth was entering the western antislavery arena for the first time, Robinson was president of the Western Anti-Slavery Society, which encompassed western New York and Pennsylvania, Ohio, Indiana, and Michigan.[6]

The Robinsons had moved to Salem only in April 1851, when Marius had hesitantly agreed, despite lack of experience in journalism, to become the editor—Emily the publishing agent—of the only antislavery paper west of the Alleghenies, the Salem *Anti-Slavery Bugle*. A clarion of temperance and women's rights as well as antislavery, the *Bugle* preached Garrison's peace and anticlerical convictions. During the Robinsons' eight years, the paper achieved a very respectable circulation of 1,400.[7]

The *Bugle* regularly covered feminist gatherings. In March 1851, it began running a call for the second annual Ohio women's rights convention, to meet in Akron in May. The call reached out to "all the friends of Reform, in whatever department engaged," and mentioned by name several evils that invitees regularly denounced: slavery, war, intemperance, and sensuality.[8] In answer to the call, hundreds of reform-minded women and men turned up for women's rights on a hot day at the beginning of a southern Ohio summer. Among them was Sojourner Truth.

14

Akron, 1851

THE Ohio Woman's Rights Convention, now so closely associated with Sojourner Truth, convened in the Stone Church in Akron at 10:00 A.M. on 28 May 1851. The stifling church was packed, so crowded that Jane Swisshelm—the prickly, nationally recognized editor of her own newspaper, the Pittsburgh *Saturday Visiter*—had to push her way in. The only place left for her to sit was on the steps of the pulpit.[1]

Presiding was Frances Dana Gage, a writer from McConnellsville whose work had appeared regularly in the *Saturday Visiter* since 1849. They were an odd pair: Gage tall and earnest, Swisshelm tiny and vain. They had clashed often over the true meaning of women's rights. Gage insisted on women's complete equality with men, filling her essays with hardworking, poor women who toiled in adverse circumstances, while Swisshelm savored differences between the sexes as expressed in the genteel middle class.

Swisshelm preferred to imagine the existence of a "great law of nature, which says he [the man] is the stronger, and owes her [the woman] assistance." She cherished "all the beautiful amenities of life, which make it proper for a woman to receive one kind of attentions from the other sex, and repay them with another."[2] She

Frances Dana Gage daguerreotype. Photo courtesy of J. B. Devol.

dedicated many a column inch to dress and congratulated the women at Akron on their appearance. She had expected feminists to "dress and behave like frights," but was delighted to find the women there "attired with peculiar elegance and taste." Women's cause was strengthened, Swisshelm thought, because many speakers "would have been singled out in any drawing-room as a specimen of female loveliness."[3] Women's outward appearance was not one of Frances Dana Gage's vital concerns.

Swisshelm and Gage also disagreed fundamentally on whether issues of slavery and race had a place in their movement, even whether African Americans belonged in women's rights meetings at all. Gage said yes, emphatically, but Swisshelm said no, for her concept of women's rights extended only to rights denied women like herself. Swisshelm had no interest in poor and black women's most pressing concerns; those were not women's issues, even if they were uppermost in other women's minds.

Swisshelm criticized the 1850 women's rights meeting in Worcester, where Douglass and Truth had spoken, for "the introduction of the color question. The convention was not called to discuss the rights of color; and we think it was altogether irrelevant and unwise to introduce the question."[4] She saw the women's rights movement as a small boat in choppy waters that "*may* carry woman into a safe harbor, but it is not strong enough to bear the additional weight of all the colored men in creation." Colored men, not women. Swisshelm was not very concerned with black women: "As for colored women," she wrote, "all the interest they have in this reform is *as women.* All it can do for them is to raise them to the level of men of their own class." She was just as indifferent to poor whites: "We only claim for a white wood-sawyer's wife that she is as good as a white wood-sawyer—a blacksmith's mother is as good as a blacksmith. . . ."[5]

Swisshelm's conservatism met keen contestation from other feminist abolitionists, even in her own pages. Parker Pillsbury noted in the *Saturday Visiter* that the mere presence of black speakers at the Worcester women's rights convention in 1850 had not made race an issue. He contended nonetheless that the existence of race within questions of sex must be acknowledged: "That *any* woman has rights, will scarcely be believed. But that *colored* women have rights, would never have been thought of, without a specific declaration."[6] Doubtless other feminists shared Swisshelm's aversion to race matters in women's rights conventions, but she by no means spoke for a dominant constituency.

Exhorting women to unite in a bloodless revolution for their rights, Gage's keynote compared the drive for women's rights with the American conquest of the West. This self-confident speech so stirred Marius Robinson that he printed it in its entirety in the *Bugle*. The opening speech was Gage's main contribution, for the novelty of trying to chair a lively meeting required all her attention.[7] Other women picked up where she left off.

Emma Coe, an experienced lecturer on women's history and greatness, took to the floor repeatedly with "brilliant" speeches that "thrilled the audience." Swisshelm's interventions were also numerous, though less trenchant; a neophyte speaker, she found it difficult to clarify her points. (One reporter said: "Mrs. Swisshelm is an odd genius. She lives amid opposition, and seems to have a constitutional tendency to antagonize.")[8] Coe and most of the others who spoke were more radical than Swisshelm, who continually sought—in vain—to water down the resolutions and insist that men's intentions toward women were noble. From opposing positions and in contrasting styles, Coe and Swisshelm dominated the debate, though many other able women like Sarah Coates and Mary Ann Johnson also played spirited roles.[9]

At one point in the discussion, several men spoke up; then another man suggested that men should not speak, for this was a women's convention. Mary Ann Johnson defended men's right to participate. This was a women's *rights* convention, she said, and whoever supported women's rights was welcome to take part. During the second day's deliberations, according to Robinson's report in the *Bugle*, "Remarks upon the subject of the education and condition of women were made by Mrs. Coe, Sojourner Truth and Rev. Geo. Schlosser and Miss Coates."[10]

Marius Robinson's editorial expressed the general view of the meeting, a satisfaction that

> [t]he business of the Convention was principally conducted by the women, as will be seen by a reference to the list of officers.—The manner in which they acquitted themselves, must, we think have convinced the most skeptical—not of the propriety or rightfulness merely, of the participation of both sexes in deliberative bodies; but of its very great advantages in facilitating business and sustaining interest and decorum.

Others praised the convention's female "army of talent."[11] "[This] meeting has never been surpassed or equalled in point of talent and importance," the *Liberator* concluded; "no person could have attended this Convention, and then said that woman was unqualified to sustain an equal position with man."[12]

A much later report would attribute a dominant role to Sojourner Truth. In fact she was only one of several self-possessed, competent, and experienced antislavery feminists who conducted this meeting so boldly—and with the support of the men who were there. Her remarks did not bring the meeting to a halt or even change its course, but they engrossed the audience. Her friend and host, Marius Robinson, was used to her way of speaking and was also serving as secretary of the convention. He printed his report of her whole address:

One of the most unique and interesting speeches of the Convention was made by Sojourner Truth, an emancipated slave. It is impossible to transfer it to paper, or convey any adequate idea of the effect it produced upon the audience. Those only can appreciate it who saw her powerful form, her whole-souled, earnest gestures, and listened to her strong and truthful tones. She came forward to the platform and addressing the President said with great simplicity:

May I say a few words? Receiving an affirmative answer, she proceeded; I want to say a few words about this matter. I am a woman's rights. I have as much muscle as any man, and can do as much work as any man. I have plowed and reaped and husked and chopped and mowed, and can any man do more than that? I have heard much about the sexes being equal; I can carry as much as any man, and can eat as much too, if I can get it. I am as strong as any man that is now. As for intellect, all I can say is, if a woman have a pint and man a quart— why cant she have her little pint full? You need not be afraid to give us our rights for fear we will take too much,—for we cant take more than our pint'll hold. The poor men seem to be all in confusion, and dont know what to do. Why children, if you have woman's rights give it to her and you will feel better. You will have your own rights, and they wont be so much trouble. I cant read, but I can hear. I have heard the bible and have learned that Eve caused man to sin. Well if woman upset the world, do give her a chance to set it right side up again. The lady has spoken about Jesus, how he never spurned woman from him, and she was right. When Lazarus died, Mary and Martha came to him with faith and love and besought him to raise their brother. And Jesus wept—and Lazarus came forth. And how came Jesus into the world? Through God who created him and woman who bore him. Man, where is your part? But the women are coming up blessed by God and a few of the men are coming up with them. But man is in a tight place, the poor slave is on him, woman is coming on him, and he is surely between a hawk and a buzzard.[13]

Robinson introduces Truth as an ex-slave, but without the use of dialect or other rhetorical techniques to emphasize her blackness. He characterizes her in expressions that would reappear often in Truth imagery: power, soul, earnestness, and gesture. Truth is simple and honest, in an implicit contrast with speakers who had mastered the conventions of public declamation. Robinson has Truth moving forward to speak, as though she had been sitting or standing somewhere away from the front of the church. According to Robinson, Truth did not seize the floor, she asked permission to speak; and as though doubting her right, she announces that her intervention will be brief.

In Robinson's report, Truth addresses three aspects of women's identity: work, mind, and biblical precept. She demands rights for women by virtue of her own physical equality with men. Her experience as a worker validates her claim, and the work in question, as well as the criterion for equality—muscular strength—are masculine. She does not mention her household work: the laundry, cooking, and cleaning that she had been doing in New York and Northampton, and that she would have contributed to the families, such as the Bensons, Posts, and Robinsons, with whom she stayed for extended periods.

Her examples come from her time in rural slavery, and her work is the work of the farm, which even in the industrializing 1850s Americans saw as the symbol of their economy. Along with masses of other Americans, including other rural women, she idealizes farm work as the embodiment of real work.[14] She enumerates the stages of production (plowing, reaping, husking, weeding, and mowing), transportation (carrying), and consumption (eating)

of crops that sustain life. At every step, she is the bodily equal of
a farming man.

Turning from the body to the mind, Truth pulls away from personal experience to concede that "woman's" (not necessarily her
own) mental capacity may not measure up to man's. As if to reinforce sexual difference, she switches to feminine metaphor and em-
ploys measures associated with cooking—pints rather than bushels.
Employing the sarcasm for which she would become famous, Truth
allots to man a quart of intellect and to woman a pint, physical mea-
surements that are virtually craniometric. Knowledge and rights,
she insists, are not a zero-sum game. As women are in physique
or essence smaller than men, they cannot take "too much."

She belittles men who are completely perplexed by women's demands. As though confusion were an illness demanding a cure,
Truth prescribes a remedy: Grant women the rights that men are
wrongfully withholding. She insinuates that rights are like bur-
densome objects, or perhaps bowels, which can be moved without
causing deprivation or crisis.

Having used pints and quarts to mock the American pretense
that intelligence can be measured quantitatively, Truth turns from
mental capacity to her own knowledge. She enters the argument
over the Bible as a basis for or against women's rights, confident
of the soundness of her wisdom. Hearing but not reading, she
knows the Bible better than over-educated ministers who blame
Eve for sin. Even if Eve caused original sin, which Truth doubts,
the story of Adam and Eve is no place to look for the meaning of
the Bible's role for women. Look not in Genesis, but in the New
Testament, in John and Luke, for the story of Lazarus, Mary and
Martha, and Jesus.[15] Americans should heed the example of Jesus,
who respected women and took pity on two sisters who beseeched
him to return their brother to life. The story of the resurrection of
Lazarus also reinforces the class dimension of Truth's message, for
poor Lazarus stood opposite Dives, the rich man. A dead Dives
goes to hell, while dead Lazarus lies in the bosom of Abraham.[16]

Going to the synoptic gospels for Jesus' lineage, Truth demonstrates further biblical authority. What are the origins of the
greatest man of all? she asks. God and woman, she answers. She
compares man's absence from the creation of the saviour to man's

role in the present antislavery and women's rights agitation. Assimilating "man" to pro-slavery and antifeminist white men, Truth casts this character as peripheral, passive, and doomed. The poor slave and blessed woman together consign white men to torment in the beak and talons of predators and consumers of carrion. Only a few (white) men are on their way to regeneration through women's rights; presumably others may reform and save themselves from the birds of prey.

MARIUS ROBINSON presented Truth's words in standard English, though he mentioned the impossibility of capturing all her dimensions in print. A novice journalist, he was too innocent of convention to dwell on Truth's body. He says nothing of laughter as an audience response.

The reporter for the Boston *Liberator* similarly confessed to the inadequacy of words: "Sojourner Truth spoke in her own peculiar style, showing that she was a match for most men. She had ploughed, hoed, dug, and could eat as much, if she could get it." Then the *Liberator* report adds a comment that would practically become standard: "The power and wit of this remarkable woman convulsed the audience with laughter."[17]

Throughout the 1850s, audiences responded to Truth's speaking with amusement, which jars our sensibility. Had we been there, would laughter have been our response? From this vantage point it is not possible to know. Our response, a century and a half later, is closer to awe than to jest.

A reading of reports of Sojourner Truth's speeches, including the one at Akron in 1851, shows clearly that she was saying what needed to be said, sometimes indignantly. But her manner of speaking undercut the intensity of her language. To capture and hold her audience, she communicated her meaning on several different levels at once, accompanying sharp comments with nonverbal messages: winks and smiles provoking the "laughter" so often reported. This complex medley of tough talk and humorous delivery generated diverse estimates of her character, as the depictions by Harriet Beecher Stowe and Frances Dana Gage would later attest. The humor was shrewd, for it allowed her to get away

with sharp criticism, but it permitted some of her hearers to ignore her meaning. Even today, when Truth can symbolize the
angry black woman for most in her audience, others can see her
as a kind of pet.

Truth's multiple meanings cannot be reconciled. Part of what
makes us laugh is incongruity, here of words and gestures. With
the passage of time, too, a change in Truth's relative status has altered her audience's response. Today, Truth is a highly respected
figure; her stature equals that of her constituents. In the deeply
white-supremacist mid-nineteenth century, by contrast, her white
comrades in reform would have seen themselves as her superiors,
and laughter has long functioned as a means of reinforcing hierarchical relations. If the laughter that Truth prompted annoyed
her, she did not allow her chagrin to be committed to writing.

CONTRARY to legend, Truth had not braved a hostile white crowd,
for the crowd was friendly. She had not stopped a malicious male
attack on women, for the men supported women's rights. Nor had
she saved a mass of cowering white women, for the women spoke
with confidence. But Truth did see her presence in the meeting as
a rousing success. Writing to her friend Amy Post, she said she had
met "plenty of kind friends just like you & they gave me so many
kind invitations I hardly knew which to accept of first." The convention also fulfilled Truth's expectations in a second respect: "I
sold a good many books at the Convention and have thus far been
greatly prospered."[18]

In 1851, Truth was pleased to have made numerous valuable
contacts and fulfilled her bookselling mission. She was anxious to
pay off her $500 debt to her printer, and by late summer she had
sent Garrison at least $50. Women's rights conventions repre-
sented a golden opportunity to sell the *Narrative* and reduce a debt
that included precious dollars spent for shipping books from
Boston.[19]

IN THOSE days, Truth seldom addressed the political questions
of the time, preferring to speak the lessons of the Bible as a woman

who had been a slave. Others, however, including other women, found national politics alarming in the wake of the Compromise of 1850. One convinced crusader was Harriet Beecher Stowe, who had been writing professionally since the mid-1830s. The shocking revision of the Fugitive Slave Act and the death of one of her children galvanized Stowe into writing her first novel, which became the nineteenth century's most famous American work of fiction: *Uncle Tom's Cabin: or, Life Among the Lowly*.

The 1851–52 serial publication of *Uncle Tom's Cabin* in Gamaliel Bailey's moderate, antislavery Washington *National Era* proved wildly successful, and when the book appeared in March 1852, its sensational reception transformed Stowe's career. Breaking sales records throughout the world, the book sold 10,000 copies on the first week of publication, 300,000 in its first year.[20] *Uncle Tom's Cabin* made Stowe highly sought after—and Sojourner Truth became one of the seekers.

Truth's personal appearances created a lively market for the *Narrative of Sojourner Truth* in audiences she could reach directly, but her obscurity blocked the way to a wider public. To gain a greater readership, she needed the endorsement of notables. Garrison had helped Truth along by introducing the first edition of her book in 1850, but when Truth parsed the politics of the literary marketplace a few years later, the testimony of the world's most famous author promised to deliver higher visibility and more sales of her own *Narrative* than reliance on face-to-face appeals and Garrison's earnest authentication.

In 1853, Truth seized the initiative. Joining the legions of authors and publishers seeking advantageous "puffs," she journeyed to Andover, Massachusetts, and asked Stowe directly for a puff, which she received. As Stowe wrote it out by hand, the blurb began like this:

The following narrative may be relied upon as in all respects true & faithful, & it is in some points more remarkable & interesting than many narratives of the kind which have abounded in late years.

It is the history of a mind of no common energy & power whose struggles with the darkness & ignorance of slavery have a peculiar interest. The truths of Christianity seem to have come to her almost by a separate revelation & seem to verify the beautiful words of scripture "I will bring the blind by a way that they knew not, I will make darkness light before them & crooked things straight."[21]

Stowe's puff surely boosted Truth's sales. More importantly, this encounter began a literary relationship that portended far greater notice for Truth than any blurb could generate. But not right away.

15

Vengeance and Womanhood

THE DESPERATE decade of the 1850s saw "the Slave Power" everywhere ascendant. The fearsome proof—the punitive, massively cruel Fugitive Slave Act—turned the whole country into the enemy of black people. Danger was palpable, humiliation officially sanctioned, the threat of abduction real. Each fugitive recaptured was literally a person who, they knew, "could be me."

Daniel Webster, the engineer of the Compromise of 1850, a man anathema to abolitionists, had included a strengthening of the eighteenth-century federal fugitive slave law to garner the support of southern representatives in Congress. Tailored to the interests of powerful southerners, the Fugitive Slave Act meant to do black people harm. A slaveholder needed only to swear that a particular black person was his slave, and federally appointed commissioners and marshals would seize the purported fugitive. Marshals could draft any citizen into the capture of the designated runaway, and whoever who did not cooperate was liable to incarceration and thousands of dollars in fines.

The fugitive's redress was circumscribed. His or her testimony was not admissible in court, and he or she lacked the right to trial by jury. When the captive was sent into slavery, the commissioner received $10; when the captive was set free, the commissioner received only $5.

Even before President Millard Fillmore signed the act into law in the fall of 1850, blacks throughout the North assembled to discuss their response. In Boston, the fugitive abolitionist Samuel Ringgold Ward announced that blacks no longer owed allegiance to their country—it was time to exercise the "right of Revolution." In New York City and Elmira, New York, crowded meetings denounced the federal government and vowed defiance. In Philadelphia, the free-born black abolitionist Robert Purvis, long a Garrisonian stalwart, swore that if "any wretch enter my dwelling, any pale-faced spectre among ye, to execute this law on me or mine, I'll seek his life, I'll shed his blood." Douglass's abolitionist colleague in Pittsburgh, Martin Delany, now a physician, amplified Purvis:

> If any man approached [my] house in search of a slave—I care not who he may be, whether constable, or sheriff, magistrate or even judge of the Supreme Court—nay let it be President Millard Fillmore surrounded by his cabinet and his bodyguard, with the Declaration of Independence waving above his head as his banner, and the constitution of his country upon his breast as his shield—if he crosses the threshold of my door, and I do not lay him a lifeless corpse at my feet, I hope the grave may refuse my body a resting place, and righteous heaven my spirit a home. O, no! He cannot enter that house and we both live.

Again in Boston, even the great and prudent black statesman Frederick Douglass uttered sanguinary threats: "We must be prepared ... to see the streets of Boston running with blood. . . ."[1]

Beyond anguished talk, blacks in Ohio and Pennsylvania organized vigilante groups, as in Christiana, Pennsylvania, where a slaveholder attempting to recapture several fugitives paid with his life, and U.S. Marines tried in vain to enforce the law. In these frightful circumstances, blacks warned their fellows to keep firearms close at hand.

Successful and failed efforts to foil the recapture of blacks claimed as fugitives occurred with awful regularity. When a fugitive called Shadrach was rescued in Boston in 1851, his liberators were put on trial. In the famous "Jerry rescue," Jerry McHenry was saved in Syracuse, New York, and again his rescuers were tried but acquitted. Harriet Tubman led the successful rescue in Troy, New York, of a fugitive about to be returned to southern slavery in 1860.[2] The rescues went down in history, but the legions of kidnappings were not the stuff of legend.

Rescues were not enough to make the United States feel safe for black people. Martin Delany called a convention in 1854 on black emigration out of the United States. A women's rights man, Delany invited women as well as men. For the first time in a Negro convention, women represented one-third of the delegates in 1854, having hitherto been barred or only barely tolerated. The convention advocated flight.

Thousands of fugitives, including Harriet Tubman, escaped to Canada. Even Delany, who was free, retreated north for safety's sake. He advocated emigration out of hopelessness: Blacks were too completely oppressed in the United States to remain secure within its boundaries, even within North America. In 1859, he and a colleague traveled to what is now Nigeria to arrange for African-American settlement.[3]

IN THESE agitated times, when fear and anger dogged her people, Sojourner Truth's itinerary did not include the Negro conventions so dominated by men. Her lecture circuit usually took her from nearly all-white antislavery meetings to nearly all-white women's rights meetings and back. Yet in tandem with her fellow blacks, her message grew broader, deeper, and sharper. She moved from a recitation of her own experience in slavery—now a quarter century and more behind her—to a condemnation of American slavery as an institution and of white people as a whole. She grew increasingly angry, and while contriving not to alienate her audiences, she let her anger show.

Her audiences preferred not to grapple with all she had to say. Speaking in biblical code and lacing her remarks with humor, she made it easy for them to gloss over her wrath and millenarian conviction that a day of reckoning was at hand. Yet her words were angry in the 1850s, as she anticipated the time when black people would take their revenge against white people generally. She said "white people"—not "slaveholders" or "white southerners," or any narrower subset of the guilty.

As this decade of crisis opened, Truth was still relatively obscure, known only to black and white radicals. Among them she appeared frequently. On 8 September 1853, Truth spoke at a women's rights convention in New York City, on the heels of a temperance gathering of the very same people. As usual with feminist or antislavery meetings in New York City, the audience included a good number of hostile rowdies, people Truth knew to handle in the language of the Prophet Matthias: "It is not good for me to come and draw forth a spirit, to see what kind of spirit people are of? I see that some of you have got the spirit of a goose, and some have got the spirit of a snake."

She said she felt at home in the city and described herself as a "citizen" of New York, a term that became inappropriate in a few years, when the United States Supreme Court, in the Dred Scott decision of 1857, declared Americans of African descent ineligible for citizenship. But now, in 1853, she said that she knew "a little mite" about women's rights and wanted "to throw in my little mite, to keep the scales a-movin'."[4]

Weighing the federal government's meanness, Truth compared Congress unfavorably to the king in the Old Testament Book of Esther. Truth's metaphor works on two levels. She speaks of Esther as a woman, but Esther is not merely a woman, she is also a Jew. Threatened as a group, the Jews stand in for Truth's own oppressed people.

Most Americans of Truth's generation—including William Lloyd Garrison and Abraham Lincoln—so often reread their Bibles that they knew them practically by heart. They would recall the whole story when Truth mentioned its main character, Esther; they would know that Esther became queen when the Persian king Ahasuerus (or Xerxes I, ruled 486–465 BCE) dismissed his previous queen, Vashti, for refusing to exhibit her charms to his carousing men. Truth knew, and her audience knew, that the Book of Esther begins with an alarming feminine challenge to patriarchy.[5]

They would know, too, that Esther was a beautiful Jewish woman passing for Gentile who learns that the king's favorite courtier, Haman, wanted to have all the Jews killed and their property plundered, because the Jew Mordecai would not bow down to him. Esther screws up her courage and risks her life when she speaks to the king without being summoned. The king, luckily, is well disposed to hear her request. Twice he says to her: "What wilt thou, queen Esther? and what is thy request? it shall be even given to thee to the half of the kingdom" (Esther 5:3, 7:2). Truth contrasted Ahasuerus' generosity with Congress's niggardliness toward women.

Esther tells the king that his prickly favorite, Haman, plans to kill all the Jews, which would mean killing her as well. Outraged, the king reverses the order and invites the Jews to attack their would-be assailants. The Book of Esther culminates on a note of triumph: "Thus the Jews smote all their enemies with the stroke of the sword, and slaughter, and destruction, and did what they would unto those that hated them." Several verses enumerate the carnage, a triumph celebrated annually as the festival of Purim.[6]

Truth's message cut two ways, against whites and against men. The slaughter of the enemies of the Jews warns whites. But speaking as a woman, she underlines the gender of the enemies of the Jews: "I do not want any man to be killed, but I am sorry to see them so short minded. But we'll have our rights; see if we don't; and you can't stop us from them; see if you can. You may hiss as much as you like, but it is comin'."[7]

KILLING one's enemies was Truth's message for whites. But to "my people, a poor, down-trodden race," she had other things to say. She preached uplift—cleanliness and economic independence—not vengeance. At a black church in New York City in December 1853, she began, as usual, with a song and a recitation of the brutality of her enslavement. Then she mocked white people's inability to keep New York City clean:

> Now the white people have taken it in hand, the dirt lies in the streets till it gets too thick, and flies all around into the shops and people's eyes and then they sift water all over it, and make it into mud, and that's what they do over and over again, without ever dreaming of such an easy thing as taking it away. In the course of time it becomes too

thick, and too big a nuisance and then they go to work right straight off with picks and crow bars, and pull up the stones, above the dirt, and then go on again! (Laughter.)[8]

Convinced the Negro race had improved over the last fifty years, she demanded further improvement. New York City blacks could better themselves, not by staying in the city, but by going into the field to sharecrop for the Pennsylvania farmers who had cried out to her for "good men and women." On farms the colored people would prosper in the fullness of time and become self-reliant. Decades later escape from the city and farming as a route to independence would again engage her thought.

The Fourth of July 1854 found Truth back before white audiences, speaking at an Independence Day celebration in Framingham, Massachusetts. She spoke after a white abolitionist from Virginia described his ordeal in jail. This experience, he said, helped him appreciate the sufferings of blacks. Truth agreed. "White folks should sometimes feel the prick," she said, eliciting "laughter and cheers." Despite such merriment, her message, as recorded by the secretary of the meeting (her printer, George Brown Yerrinton), was severe and anguished:

> God would yet execute his judgments upon the white people for their oppression and cruelty. She had often asked white people why God should have more mercy on Anglo-Saxons than on Africans, but they had never given her any answer; the reason was, they [white people] hadn't got it to give. (Laughter.) Why did the white people hate the blacks? Were they [white people] not as good as they were brought up? They [black people] were a great deal better than the white people had brought them up. (Cheers.) The white people owed the colored race a big debt, and if they paid it all back, they wouldn't have anything left for seed. (Laughter.) All they could do was to repent, and have the debt forgiven them.

Abolitionists were fond of implicating orthodox Christianity in the moral economy of slavery. The regular ministry and conventional churches tolerated slavers and slavery, they said, and Truth picked up this theme. The proceeds of the sale of slave children, she says, paid for the training of ministers of the gospel.

Then she returns to a question that haunts Americans still: Why did white people hate blacks so much? If whites were not able to answer her question now, she threatens, "they would have to answer it before God."

Speaking through the Bible, Truth declares that "Even the blood of one man, Abel, did not call from the ground in vain." In both the Old and New Testaments, Abel stands for the righteous who are killed for their faithfulness, and "the blood of Abel" is a call for vengeance. In Genesis 4:12, the Lord curses Cain: "When thou tillest the ground, it shall not henceforth yield unto thee her strength; a fugitive and a vagabond shalt thou be in the earth."

Truth calls down the curse of Cain on white Americans. She imagines a day when whites shall cry, like Cain, "My punishment is greater than I can bear" (4:13). She speaks straightforwardly: "The promises of Scripture were all for the black people, and God would recompense them for all their sufferings in this world." To the masses of Americans who carried their Bibles in their heads, "recompense" plainly conveyed vengeance as well as salvation.[9]

Delivered straight, these lines would never have elicited cheers and applause from her mostly white audiences. She spoke of sinful whites and vengeful blacks, but her humor let her listeners exempt themselves. They did not hear wrath against whites, but against the advocates of slavery. It is understandable, no doubt, that Truth's audiences, who wanted so much to love this old black woman who had been a slave, found it difficult to fathom the depths of her bitterness.

BY THE late 1850s, Truth was a big enough draw to convene a series of meetings on her own in Indiana. After the third of these meetings in 1858, a group of Democrats (i.e., men soft on slavery) led by one T. W. Strain, challenged her authenticity as a woman, knowing that much of her appeal lay in her uniqueness as a former slavewoman condemning the evils of slavery.[10] According to the report, which neglects the content of Truth's speech, the proslavery sympathizers made no attempt to break up the meeting during her remarks. At the close, however, they prevented adjournment, claiming her voice was that of a man. The charge was irrelevant to the issue of slavery. Her opponents were hoping to subvert her performance by exposing her as a sexual impostor.

Denying the womanliness of women speaking in public was a familiar ploy. Hostile audiences questioned the sexual identity of American women preachers like Harriet Livermore, of lecturers like the antislavery poet Frances Ellen Watkins Harper, and of actresses like Rachel, the great French tragedian.[11] The challenge was to the woman's authenticity. A similar challenge, to his authenticity as a former slave, prompted well-spoken Frederick Douglass to write his first autobiography. Truth had long understood the worth of her authenticity as a former slave and used testimonies from Garrison and Stowe as advertisements. She claimed special insight into slavery for having herself been enslaved.

The charge that Truth was a man polarized the meeting between pro- and antislavery factions. The pro-slavery band insisted that Truth step aside and show her breast to the women in the audience, who would report on her sex. The antislavery faction was "surprised and indignant at such ruffianly surmise and treatment." The result was "confusion and uproar." Americans were obsessed with sexual identity, with manhood in particular.

When a boisterous voice vote corroborated the doubt over her sex, Truth responded with a tongue-lashing that shamed her questioners and impugned their manhood:

> Sojourner told them that her breasts had suckled many a white babe, to the exclusion of her own offspring; that some of those white babies had grown to man's estate; that, although they had suckled her colored breasts, they were, in her estimation, far more manly than they (her persecutors) appeared to be; and she quietly asked them, as she disrobed her bosom, if they, too, wished to suck! In vindication of her truthfulness, she told them that she would show her breast to the whole congregation; that it was not to her shame that she uncovered her breast before them, but to their shame.[12]

Truth's counterattack turned on the tensions between infancy and adulthood, black motherhood and white motherhood, and the madonna-whore imagery of the bare female breast. The potency of her assault depended on the mingling of all those elements. Although black motherhood was discounted, she claimed that the

slaveowning babies she had suckled had grown into better men—
be they slaveholders or not—than those before her whose masculinity she maligned. To bare a mother's breast, no matter what
its color, was not shameful, she insisted, exhibiting her own to men
as well as to women. By inviting her critics to suck, she infantilized
them. She unmanned them.

Truth had turned the challenge upside down. Her skillful re-
making employed the all-too-common exhibition of an undressed
black body, with its resonance of the slave auction that undressed
women for sale. What had been intended as degradation became
a triumph of embodied rhetoric. This speech act (together with
"ar'n't I a woman?") is at the heart of the current symbolism of
Sojourner Truth. In it, the image of her older woman's black body,
a body that transcends shame through hardship, defeats the juve-
nile pricks of philistines.[13]

The display of a sensitive part of Truth's body raises the para-
dox of her sexuality: On the one hand, black women over the centuries have been considered degraded and unclean, as oversexed
Jezebels, or at least sexualized objects. Even among abolitionist
friends, the sexual vulnerability of slavewomen was a main theme.
For friend or foe, in racist stereotype and antislavery ideology, rampant sexuality clings to the figure of the black woman.

On the other hand, sexuality never appears as part of Truth's
persona. She remained spotless, with what a friend termed an
"unimpeachable moral character."[14] Truth's closest approach to
carnal themes came with the exhibition of her breast, which en-
trained everything connected with sexuality without her naming
it. Her words, instead, relate to motherhood and suckling. She
shames the white men who taunt her by patronizing and belittling
them, not by making them into rapists.

This asexual approach might threaten to turn Truth into the
other stereotypical black woman figure in American culture, the
mammy. Truth avoided the mammy snare through disinterest in
the needs of white children and young white women. When Truth
spoke to white women, she spoke as an equal, not as a mammy—
no mean feat considering the strength of stereotype.

It helped that Truth was an older woman during the career that
made her famous, and that she spent her time alone, with her

grown children, or with other older women. As Sojourner Truth, she lived mostly among women, as what we would now term a "woman–identified" woman. Even on the lecture circuit, she rarely traveled with men, preferring above all to travel alone.[15] Given the difficulty that other black women have encountered trying to avoid Jezebel or mammy stereotypes, Truth deserves recognition for her ability (in our times and her own) to avoid completely these stereotypes of over-sexuality and public motherhood.[16]

Truth said that she showed her mother's breast "in vindication of her truthfulness," but this truth concerned her sexual identity, not necessarily her experience as a slave. The *Narrative of Sojourner Truth* does not mention her nursing her owners' children, which is not surprising. As a young woman she lived with the Dumonts, whose daughter was not much younger than she. Wet nursing by slaves was far more prevalent in the plantation South than Dutch New York, and Truth's claim that "her breasts had suckled many a white babe, to the exclusion of her own offspring," evoked her symbolic history as a slave mother rather than her own actual experience.

Truth functioned as a former slave on the lecture circuit, and by the late 1850s this connoted a southern rather than a northern setting. As an authentic representative of slavery, Truth in performance was refashioning herself as a southerner. In her later years she tampered further with her past, routinely claiming to have been enslaved for forty, not thirty, years. This revision most likely replicated the biblical experience of the children of Israel in their forty years of bondage.

The Indiana breast-baring has been recounted compulsively since it became well known through the 1870s editions of the *Narrative of Sojourner Truth*. The editions after 1875 reprinted an edited version of a letter that describes the incident, sent to Truth by her abolitionist friend Parker Pillsbury after the Civil War. The version in the *Narrative* includes the sentence explaining that two young men attempted to shield Truth from the audience as she showed her breast, but the sentence that follows has been excised. It reads: "One of the Democrats present cried out, 'Why, it does look like an old sow's teat.' "[17]

The deletion is not surprising in a book dedicated to preserving Truth's legend, for this puerile little comment undercuts the magnificent gesture that plays on the drama of the black body revealed for inspection and the hatefulness of the domestic slave trade. The need to edit Truth's history was not lost on Truth and her Battle Creek neighbor and friend, Frances Titus, as they put together the 1875 edition of the *Narrative*. A boyishly irreverent comment no longer tarnished the pathos of the symbolic slave mother's body.

16

Spiritualism

SOJOURNER TRUTH, itinerant preacher, stayed on the road in the 1850s. We have seen her in antislavery and women's rights meetings; she also embraced a new religion on the American landscape: spiritualism. Or rather, she embraced the people who were spiritualists. Alongside scores of assorted other reformers, she made the rounds of the quarterly and yearly Meetings of the newly formed, spiritualist Progressive Friends, from Longwood, Pennsylvania, to Waterloo, New York, and Battle Creek, Michigan. Truth had a very good time through the three-day founding of the Longwood Meeting of the Progressive Friends in May 1853.

A mixture of revival, picnic, sing-along, and séance, Progressive Friends' Meetings regularly reunited Truth's new extended family. Isaac and Amy Post; Ruth and Joseph Dugdale of Chester County, Pennsylvania; Giles Stebbins; and feminist abolitionists such as Frances Dana Gage, William Lloyd Garrison, and Parker Pillsbury all put in regular appearances on this circuit of spiritualism.[1]

For Truth, the Posts played a vital role. At first she appreciated them more for their racial tolerance than their spiritualist beliefs— for her, a by-product rather than the central feature of their radicalism. They vindicated the slave and demanded women's rights, though they also attended séances, heeded spirit voices, and formed new religious organizations.

Amy and Isaac Post's long journey from Quakerism into spiritualism began decades earlier. They had left orthodox Quakerism along with Elias Hicks, who was Amy's cousin. Hicks had separated from orthodox Quakers in 1827 in a spirit of holiness reminiscent of his contemporary, James Latourette, who at the same time was leaving Methodism. Hicksite Quakers sought a return to the primitive simplicity and freedom of conscience of the seventeenth-century Quakerism of George Fox and William Penn. Between 1827 and the late 1840s, however, Hicksite Quakers, like orthodox Quakers, grew conservative and intolerant of the abolitionists in their midst. The Hicksite leadership tried to censor antislavery talk and quash any combination in reform with non-Quakers. In response, antislavery Quakers withdrew to form their own free meetings, open to all, Quaker and non-Quaker.

They called their new Meetings "Progressive Friends," or "Congregational Friends," or "Friends of Human Progress," and exchanged visits, speakers, and letters. Progressive Friends advocated freedom of conscience, speech, and action. They believed in nonviolence (a Garrisonian as well as a Quaker tenet), and they supported the abolition of slavery and the equality of women.[2] They also communicated with spirits, a practice they explained in the imagery of a force only recently discovered: electricity.

Spiritualism in its various guises fascinated hundreds of thousands of reform-minded Americans in the 1850s, Harriet Beecher Stowe among them. Its most sensational aspects—séances and spirit visitations—appeared in 1848, with the spirit rappings of the Fox sisters in Hydesville, New York, not far from Rochester. But spiritualism also had a more rational side, one inspired by the thought of the eighteenth-century Swedish scholar, Emanuel Swedenborg.

Swedenborg taught that the spirit of God and the spirits of people could not be separated; he united nature and spirituality. His philosophy also blurred boundaries between the living and the dead, the physical and the supernatural. Doing away with original sin, Swedenborg put the responsibility for salvation in the hands of people, a responsibility that appealed to reformers.

Perhaps what attracted adherents most was Swedenborgianism's synthesis of liberal religion and science. Giles Stebbins, Truth's friend from Northampton and one who would remain close for the rest of her life, said that "[m]odern spiritualism makes the future life real and near, binding it to this by the strong ties of eternal law and undying human love, and gives us a natural religion and a spiritual philosophy, rational, inspiring, and enlarging." Stebbins also revealed a side of spiritualism akin to Truth's pentecostalism. Spiritualism, he said, duplicated primitive Christianity in manifestations that pentecostals called the gifts of the Holy Spirit: healing through the laying on of hands, prophecy, and speaking in tongues.[3]

In a certain sense, spiritualism was comfortable for Truth, for the Holy Spirit had figured prominently in her religion—as in the religion of Quakers—for thirty years. But what characterized spiritualism was less its pentecostal strains than its Quaker pacifism. An optimistic and tolerant faith of individualism and autonomy, spiritualism turned its followers more toward the spirits of the dead than toward Jesus the saviour; this was perfectionist in a way new to Sojourner Truth.

American spiritualism's leading intellectual, Andrew Jackson Davis, had his own brand of millennialism, 180 degrees from the baleful warnings of Father Miller and his followers. Millerites cried, "Wo! Wo! Wo!" and warned Americans to repent before it was too late. Davis's "Harmonial Philosophy" predicted the end of the era of ignorance, superstition, fanaticism, and intolerance, and the dawning of a new and golden age. All sorts of slavery were dying, Davis said, for "spiritual intercourse" proved that

> all men shall ultimately be joined into one Brotherhood, their interests shall be pure and reciprocal; their customs shall be just and harmonious; they shall be as one Body, animated by Universal Love and governed by pure Wisdom. Man's future is glowing with a beautiful radiance.[4]

Many spiritualists were intent on hearing from the dead. According to spiritualist authors such as Isaac Post and Andrew Jackson Davis, the dead inspired their writings. While in a trance, Davis dictated the *Great Harmonia*, which plagiarized Swedenborg yet became the Bible of American spiritualism and prompted the name—"Harmonia"—of the intentional community near Battle Creek that Sojourner Truth joined in 1857. In his trance-induced *Voices from the Spirit World, Being Communications from Many Spirits, by the Hand of Isaac Post, Medium* (1852), Post presented the posthumous views of Swedenborg, George Washington, Thomas Jefferson, and Benjamin Franklin, as well as other great men who spoke through him as a "writing medium."[5]

Truth, like Garrison, had been initially skeptical of communication with the dead. Only years later did she grow less suspicious of spirits, even coming to see her father's spirit as a protector. Her conversion to spiritualism took place over the course of a decade.

When Truth first attended a séance in Rochester in 1851 with Amy Post and another nationally respected feminist, Elizabeth Lukins, she made fun of the proceedings. This séance was not very satisfactory, but Truth's presence made the experience "very rich and piquant" for Lukins: Truth's "matter-of-fact simple minded manner of seeking intercourse with spirits, was amusing beyond description. The sounds were faint and low, and given at long intervals, although a complete circle was formed around the table.— Sojourner stuck to the belief they could be better heard on the table, and while she listened with all her soul, part of the time with her ear on the floor, called out very unceremoniously, 'come spirit, hop up here on the table, and see if you cant make a louder noise.' "[6] In séances, as in secular meetings during the 1850s, Truth's role was often to interrupt earnest proceedings with irreverence.

Lukins came to know Truth better during her extended visit to Rochester in 1851. There Lukins recognized the quality that made Truth memorable in antislavery and women's rights settings, her *"great strong* character." Lukins marveled at Truth's ability to overcome the disabilities of a life in slavery and, at the age of sixty-five (Truth was actually about fifty-four years old) enter the arena of reform "with an energy, and overwhelming power that we might look for in vain among the most highly civilized and enlightened."

Lukins saw even more than power in Truth: "Her heart is as soft and loving as a child's, her soul as strong and fixed as the everlasting rocks, and her moral sense has something like inspiration

or divination." Truth knew how to puncture prevarication and pretense; "simple and artless as she herself is, her eye will see your
heart and apprehend your motives, almost like God's.—Nothing
could be more characteristic than her name!—*truth* indeed seems
to have taken refuge and by *sojourning* for a season in the person
of this poor untaught, unknown slave, and her perfect originality
is shown in the choice of it."[7]

This "poor untaught" woman had in fact become quite sophis-
ticated through long association with well-educated people. This
did not deter Lukins from drawing a flawed connection between
Truth's illiteracy and her wisdom, as would others during Truth's
long public career: "It seems as though ignorance had been the
shield to guard her rare intuitions, her great pure heart and strong
individuality from any worldly taint."[8] This desire to see Truth as
natural and uncorrupted, an exotic among middle-class white
Americans, fed the fascination that sustained Truth's attractiveness
as a truth-telling entertainer.

PROGRESSIVE FRIENDS were too tolerant to seek the millennial
settling of scores so central to Truth's beliefs. But in the 1850s, she
was not yet ready to renounce the division of the saved from the
damned promised after the end of time. While Truth spoke of
vengeance—of Queen Esther and the blood of Abel—spiritualists
jettisoned the idea of a Day of Judgment, of permanent confine-
ment in a heaven or hell.

Spiritualism's transcendence of sin and anger spilled over into
antislavery politics, mellowing abolitionists' opposition to the slave
power and its minions in the U.S. Congress. Many an antislavery
conference in the 1850s turned into a spiritualist "experience-
meeting." Amy Post's friend Lucy Colman recalled one such meeting in Michigan, in which abolitionists preached that "now the
spirits would, without doubt, bring about the emancipation of the
race."[9] Tough-minded spiritualists like Post and Colman were
able to heed the attraction of spiritualism without forfeiting their
outrage against slavery and the political economy that supported
it. But the staunchest abolitionists guarded their radicalism by
keeping spiritualism secondary to reform.

IN 1857, a year after Truth's first visit to Battle Creek for the Yearly Meeting of the Michigan Progressive Friends, she moved to the newly founded community of Harmonia, six miles west of Battle Creek. Selling the little house in Massachusetts that had symbolized the realization of a dream, she joined a racially mixed community of Progressive Friends, spiritualists all. Truth still preached revenge against slavers and bigots while she lived among peaceably minded spiritualists. But at that point in her life, residence among kind-hearted, unprejudiced, educated people was probably more important to her than a perfect meeting of the minds and, as they would add, of the spirits.

Unfortunately, Truth's life in this period is shrouded in mystery. The sources do not permit us an understanding of how she reached her decision to move from Northampton, and they tell us little of Harmonia. It seems never to have thrived, despite the efforts of Truth's neighbors Mary and Reynolds Cornell. The Cornells, friends of the Posts, had envisioned a community built around the integrated progressive school they ran in the 1850s and into the 1860s. We do know that Truth's daughters Diana and Elizabeth were with her in Harmonia, and that their sons, James Caldwell and Samuel Banks, traveled with her as companions and amanuenses. By 1860, Truth had left her house in Harmonia to her daughter Sophia and moved into Battle Creek.[10]

III

Sojourner Truth,
A Symbol

17

The "Libyan Sibyl"

How LONG might Sojourner Truth have traveled the lecture circuit in relative obscurity had the Civil War not arrived to transform her identity? The war altered everything.

With Lincoln's Preliminary Emancipation Proclamation of September 1862 and the acceptance of black men into the Union Army, black people suddenly rose in the national consciousness. As the Civil War became a crusade against slavery, a curious northern reading public clamored for information about black Americans. The subject of "the Negro" exploded in the popular press.

Into this clamor, Sojourner Truth and Harriet Beecher Stowe once again stepped together, this time in an article by Stowe entitled "Sojourner Truth, the Libyan Sibyl," in the April 1863 *Atlantic Monthly*. By then, Truth and Stowe had spiritualism in common, and Stowe's essay bears its traces. Outside of a shared religion, their lives had otherwise grown farther apart in the decade between Truth's 1853 visit to Stowe at Andover and the publication of "Sojourner Truth, the Libyan Sibyl." Truth remained confined rather obscurely to the world of reform, while Stowe had become a very important public figure, truly a star worldwide.

While Truth made the rounds of women's rights and antislavery meetings, a pretty much taken for granted figure who spoke

Carte-de-visite of Harriet Beecher Stowe and her brother Henry Ward Beecher by Jeremiah Gurney. Photo courtesy of the Gernsheim Collection, Harry Ransom Humanities Research Center, University of Texas at Austin.

and sold books bearing Stowe's blurb, Stowe built on *Uncle Tom's Cabin* with a second antislavery novel, *Dred, or a Tale of the Dismal Swamp*, published in 1856. A complicated tale of an aborted slave revolt, *Dred* features a Truth-like, Christian mother figure named Milly who talks Dred out of insurrection and converts him to non-violence.[1] While no match commercially for *Uncle Tom's Cabin*, *Dred* was by no means a flop. Stowe's regular readership, now estimated at 150,000 on both sides of the Atlantic, pulled it along. *Dred* made her $20,000 in royalties, half in the United States and half in Great Britain.[2]

During the 1850s, Stowe's prosperity matched her fame.[3] While Truth's style of life remained modest, Stowe joined fashionable society, traveling as a celebrity and meeting others of equal renown. Scrambling to pay for her little house in Northampton and then in Harmonia was Truth's main financial responsibility, while Stowe underwrote an international style of life that included multiple elegant residences. Stowe spent lavishly on houses—she furnished her Andover house grandly and built and furnished an Italianate-Tudor mansion that she called "Oakholm" in Hartford, Connecticut.

By 1863, when Stowe published "Sojourner Truth, the Libyan Sibyl" for a likely payment of $200, she had adjusted her lifestyle to prosperity and consequently was always in need of funds. She was writing quickly about marketable subjects, and the market rather than political conviction drove the endeavor.[4] She had never been a radical abolitionist, and her advocacy of women's rights went not much deeper. After her two early antislavery novels, Stowe turned away from slavery and toward themes she discovered in her three trips to Europe in 1853, 1856–57, and 1859. Her later writing presented an idealized portrait of her native New England in books that became primers on how tastefully to live the good life.[5]

Like other fashionable Americans in the 1850s, Stowe now wintered in Rome, where she associated with the right people—notably the hub of the American colony, the expatriate Boston Brahmin sculptor William Wetmore Story, who would play a central role in "Sojourner Truth, the Libyan Sibyl." Story introduced Stowe to his friends, including the prominent British novelist Elizabeth Gaskell.

At breakfast at the Storys' Palazzo Barbarini, Stowe told Gaskell Sojourner Truth stories in dialect. Gaskell's response was not recorded, but Story was so enchanted by Stowe's impersonation of Truth's "ringing barytone" that he asked her repeatedly to do Truth for his friends.[6]

STOWE begins "Sojourner Truth, the Libyan Sibyl" by describing Truth's 1853 visit to Andover. Stowe contrasts Truth, "a sort of self-appointed agency," with her houseguests, "several eminent clergymen," who include her brother, Henry Ward Beecher, the foremost preacher in the country. News of Truth's arrival is brought upstairs (presumably by a servant) to Stowe, indicating that Truth is not an invited guest. When Stowe comes downstairs, Truth rises to meet her. As in most nineteenth-century descriptions of blacks in the popular media, Stowe's begins with an inspection of Truth's body, which is described as tall and spare, the physique of "a full-blooded African." Stowe terms Truth a fine "specimen of the torrid zone," and compares her with "The Negro Woman at the Fountain" by the acclaimed (now forgotten) Victorian sculptor Richard Cumberworth. Stowe calls Truth "a living, breathing impersonation" of a work of art, and carries this theme through the essay.[7]

In "The Libyan Sibyl," Stowe and her family appear as people of culture who appreciate Sojourner Truth as a primitive objet d'art and source of entertainment. Stowe emphasizes Truth's Africanness and otherness, quoting her in Negro dialect and praising her naivete. Mining the vein that had produced her black characters in *Uncle Tom's Cabin,* Stowe makes Truth into a sort of quaint and innocent exotic who has little to say about slavery beyond the chronicle of her own experience. Stowe's Truth disdains feminism. She wonders what women want, and says, " '[e]f women want any rights more 'n dey 's got, why don't dey jus' *take 'em,* an' not be talkin' about it?' " The "chief delight" of this Truth, who is far more preacher than radical, is "to talk of 'glory' and sing hymns."[8]

Stowe's admiration for Truth emerges clearly: Stowe the spiritualist speaks of Truth's "strong sphere," and compares her ability to mesmerize an audience with that of Rachel, the fascinating star of the Comédie Française.⁹ Yet Stowe mixes her admiration with distancing, condescension, and error. In a piece nine pages long, Stowe uses the words "Africa" or "African" six times, "Libyan" seven times, "Ethiopian" once, "Egypt" once, "native" three times, and terms for exotic locales ("torrid zones," "desert") six times. Through force of repetition, she depicts herself and her guests as a neutral American audience and Truth as a denizen of the desert on display in the exhibition hall of Stowe's parlor.¹⁰

Among Stowe's eminent clergymen, Truth—a native of Ulster County, New York, with its Catskill Mountains and freezing winters, and a resident of New York City for more than a decade and a half—becomes an untamed foreigner. Stowe imagines Truth as a creature from the Sahara, and compares her to "[Truth's] own native palm trees, waving alone in the desert."¹¹

Truth's grandson, James Caldwell, who had accompanied her, emerges from Stowe's pages endowed with less veneration. Stowe introduces him, like Truth, as an African "specimen," but Caldwell plays the sort of role that recalls the minstrel shows so popular throughout the North. Caldwell, Stowe says, was a "little black Puck," who was "grinning and showing his glistening white teeth in a state of perpetual merriment."¹²

"The Libyan Sibyl" relates some of Truth's early history, including her tragic childhood, her parents' piteous grief for their children who had been sold, and Truth's self-emancipation from John Dumont. Stowe calls Truth's Dutch Reformed employers, the Van Wagenens, Quakers.

The essay quotes Truth liberally in dialect, as in this excerpt, in which Stowe presents Truth describing her initial encounter with the Methodists of Ulster County. As was conventional in dialect narrative, Stowe frames Truth's remarks by quoting herself in literary English that emphasizes the hierarchy that sets the author above her subject: "But, Sojourner, had you never been told about Jesus Christ?"¹³ Truth answers in dialect so shallow that it serves only to set her apart from her educated audience:

No, honey. I had n't heerd no preachin'—been to no meetin'. Nobody had n't told me. I'd kind o' heerd of Jesus, but thought he was like

Gineral Lafayette, or some o' them. But one night there was a Methodist meetin' somewhere in our parts, an' I went; an' they got up an' begun for to tell der 'speriences: an' de fust one begun to speak. I started, 'cause he told about Jesus. . . . An' finally I said, "Why they all know him!" I was so happy! an' then they sung this hymn:

Stowe here interjects her own voice, again in contrasting standard English:

(Here Sojourner sang, in a strange, cracked voice, but evidently with all her soul and might, mispronouncing the English, but seeming to derive as much elevation and comfort from bad English as from good):

> There is a holy city,
>   A world of light above,
> Above the stairs and regions,
>   Built by the God of love.
>
> An everlasting temple,
>   And saints arrayed in white
> There serve their great Redeemer
>   And dwell with him in light.
>
> The meanest child of glory
>   Outshines the radiant sun;
> But who can speak the splendor
>   Of Jesus on his throne? . . .

Quoting nine stanzas of Truth's hymn, "There is a holy city," Stowe explains that Truth "sang with the strong barbaric accent of the native African. . . . Sojourner, singing this hymn, seemed to impersonate the fervor of Ethiopia, wild, savage, hunted of all nations, but burning after God in her tropic heart. . . ."

Stowe spins a narrative of Truth and the Dumont-Gedney-Waring family that begins with Peter's sale and recovery, and ends with a character who combines Truth's mistress, Sally Waring Dumont, and her cousin, the mother of the murdered Eliza Waring Fowler.[14] Stowe may well be repeating Truth correctly when she places Truth at her old mistress's deathbed and has Truth caring for her tenderly in her last illness, which occurred in 1846, but her old mistress was not Eliza Fowler's mother.

Stowe quotes Truth as saying, " 'Well, I went in an' tended that poor critter all night. She was out of her mind,—a-cryin', an' callin' for her daughter; an' I held her poor old head on my arm, an' watched for her as ef she'd been my babby. An' I watched by her, an' took care of her all through her sickness after that, an' she died in my arms, poor thing!' "[15] Stowe had used this tableau of the black woman who comforts a white mother whose child is dead in her novel *The Minister's Wooing* (1859), whose slavewoman character, Candace, was probably inspired in part by Truth.[16]

Concluding "The Libyan Sibyl" with a return to the theme of Truth as a work of art, Stowe explains how her vision of Truth came to be portrayed in a statue by Stowe's host in Rome, William Wetmore Story. Stowe says that she told the artist about Sojourner Truth, and the idea of Truth "worked in his mind and led him into the deeper recesses of the African nature." This "African nature" that Story uncovered in his own mind revealed, Stowe maintains, mysterious and "unexplored depths of being and feeling, mighty and dark as the gigantic depths of tropical forests."

When Stowe returned to Rome two years later, she says, Story asked her to repeat her narrative of Sojourner Truth and made a clay model of what would become his *Libyan Sibyl*. Stowe ends her article, not with Sojourner Truth, but with art, and the (vain) hope that Story's two best-known statues—the other was *Cleopatra*—would soon be displayed in the U.S. Capitol building in Washington, D.C.[17]

WILLIAM WETMORE STORY was more securely than Stowe a member of New England's privileged class. His father Joseph had founded and taught in the Harvard Law School, which became the launching pad for an illustrious career in law that ended with a seat on the U.S. Supreme Court. William Story grew up in Salem and Cambridge, trained as a lawyer at Harvard, and wrote well-respected legal textbooks. Like many elite New Englanders in the mid-1840s, he had little patience with abolitionists, whom he saw as troublemakers out to "ruin" Massachusetts.[18] But neither his success nor his indulgence in the prejudices of his class made him a comfortable member of his profession.

Story's twin passions were poetry and sculpture. His emancipation from the law began with his father's death in 1845 and a visit to Italy two years later. On his return to Massachusetts, "dreams of art and Italy" haunted him until 1856, when "I found my heart had gone over from the Law to Art," and he moved his family to Rome for good.[19] Stowe first became acquainted with Story in 1857, when she was writing her first European novel, *Agnes of Sorrento*, published in 1862.[20] Stowe claimed that her word portrait of Truth inspired Story's *Libyan Sibyl;* it in turn provided the title of Stowe's article.

The best-known *Libyan Sibyl* is Michelangelo's, one of the five *Sibyls* of his Sistine Chapel ceiling, a common inspiration for American artists in Rome in Story's time. From the astute *Delphic Sibyl* to the benighted *Libyan Sibyl*, who can gain no understanding from the written word, the Sistine's *Sibyls* represent humanity's loss of knowledge in the pagan world.[21] This *Libyan Sibyl* is a full-bodied figure, partly turned away from the viewer toward a book that she disregards. Her clothing leaves her arms and shoulders bare, but her torso is covered.

Story's *Libyan Sibyl*, in contrast, sits still. A drape covers only her lap and legs. Her arms, breasts, and torso are bare. Once again, a representation of a woman of African descent appears only partially clothed. Story's companion statue, *Cleopatra*, whom he envisioned as Greek, is well covered.

Story himself never connected Truth or Stowe with what he considered his best work. Writing to a friend in Cambridge after the outbreak of the Civil War, Story embraced Africanness in general, but unattached to any particular individual, certainly not any African American. In his new sculpture, the *Libyan Sibyl*, he says, he is "not at all shirking the real African type." But his "real African type" appeared in a form that many Americans found sufficiently attenuated to be attractive. Story's aesthetic lay north of the Sahara; he was an American avoiding a look associated with the enslaved American working classes. His *Libyan Sibyl* was "thoroughly African—Libyan Africa of course, not Congo."

Story explains the figure's pose:

I have taken the pure Coptic head and figure, the great massive sphinx-face, full-lipped, long-eyed, low-browed and lowering, and the largely-developed limbs of the African. She sits on a rock, her legs crossed, leaning forward, her elbow on her knee and her chin pressed down upon her hand. The upper part of the figure is nude, and a rich simple mantle clothes her legs. This gave me a grand opportunity for the contrast of the masses of the nude with drapery, and I studied the nude with great care. It is a very massive figure, big-shouldered, large-bosomed, with nothing of the Venus in it, but, as far as I could make it, luxuriant and heroic.[22]

Ensconced in Rome, distanced by geography and personal politics from antislavery thought, Story could not detect the promise that black abolitionists had immediately recognized in the Civil War. He spoke of slavery as though it were perpetual, not on its

William Wetmore Story's *Libyan Sibyl*, 1860.
Photo courtesy of the Metropolitan Museum of Art,
Gift of the Erving Wolf Foundation, 1979.

way to a swift extinction. Emancipation is nowhere in Story's perspective as he describes his statue's gaze: "She is looking out of her black eyes into futurity and sees the terrible fate of her race. This is the theme of the figure—Slavery on the horizon, and I made her head as melancholy and severe as possible. . . ." Story never mentions Sojourner Truth, and his statue bears no resemblance whatever to her.

Accuracy sometimes eluded Harriet Beecher Stowe, too. "Sojourner Truth, the Libyan Sibyl" is rife with errors, careless and contrived. She writes, for instance, that Truth had come from Africa, though Truth never made such a claim. Even though Truth was very much alive in Battle Creek, at the time and lived until 1883, Stowe calls her dead. Nonetheless, Stowe endowed Truth with visibility and with an identity that lasted well into the twentieth century.[23]

FROM a story in "The Libyan Sibyl" grew a second emblematic phrase: "Frederick, *is God dead?*" The anecdote originated with the aristocratic abolitionist Wendell Phillips, who knew Truth, but not as a close friend. According to Stowe quoting Phillips, Frederick Douglass once spoke emphatically at a meeting in Boston's Faneuil Hall of his lost faith that black Americans would ever gain justice from white Americans. Douglass had concluded that blacks must seize their freedom by force of arms: "It must come to blood; they must fight for themselves, and redeem themselves, or it would never be done."

Truth, sitting in the front row—so Stowe says—rejected Douglass's desperate logic:

> in the hush of deep feeling, after Douglas[s] sat down, she spoke out in her deep, peculiar voice, heard all over the house,—
> "Frederick, *is God dead?*"

Then Stowe adds a paragraph whose imagery would reappear time and again as generation after generation sought to capture Truth's essence in words:

The effect was perfectly electrical, and thrilled through the whole house, changing as by a flash the whole feeling of the audience. Not another word she said or needed to say; it was enough.[24]

"Frederick, *is God dead?*" and "Libyan Sibyl" proved irresistibly attractive to cultivators of Truth's image. During the nineteenth and early twentieth centuries, the phrase, "Libyan Sibyl" appeared in the writing even of people who had known Truth far better than Stowe. After Stowe's article, virtually every mention of Truth until the turn of the century identified her as the "Libyan Sibyl" or some version of that phrase.

"Frederick, *is God dead?*" made Truth an electrifying presence and a symbol of Christian faith and forbearance, a talisman of non-violent faith in God's ability to right the most heinous of wrongs. When Douglass had come to doubt, Stowe's Truth still believed in the power of God and the goodness of white people. To reinforce Truth's attachment to whites, Stowe quotes her revelation when she became a Christian: " 'Dar's de white folks, that have abused you an' beat you an' abused your people.' " Jesus allows Truth to forgive them: " 'Lord, Lord, I can love *even de white folks!* ' "[25]

Thanks to Stowe and the *Atlantic Monthly*, "Frederick, *is God dead?*" became the dominant symbol for Truth. For three-quarters of a century, the image of Stowe's faithful Christian delighted thousands of Americans, while the exasperated, vengeful Truth of the Book of Esther, the blood of Abel, and the taunting question, do you "wish to suck?" remained more obscure. "Sojourner Truth, the Libyan Sibyl" spread the gentleness of spiritualism over Truth's own millennial conviction that there surely would come a day of racial judgment.

AUTHENTICATING the encounter that Stowe said Wendell Phillips had described proves daunting. Stowe provides no dates, and Phillips later denied being present on the occasion. Douglass repeats the anecdote in his 1895 autobiography, but again, without place or date. If Stowe were right about Douglass's desperation, the exchange would most likely have occurred after the 1850 passage of the Fugitive Slave Act. But this is the stuff of allegory, not history, and its importance lies in symbolic meaning rather than verifiable utterance. Every part of Stowe's narrative is open to doubt.

Placing the exchange in Faneuil Hall, Boston, at the hub of her own beloved New England, Stowe honored symbolism over substance. The encounter between Truth and Douglass actually occurred in 1852 in the Salem, Ohio, meetinghouse of the Progressive Friends. Most likely from his own reading of Stowe, Douglass in his 1895 autobiography corroborates the drama of Truth's challenge to his words. "We were all for a moment brought to a stand-still," he recalls, "just as we should have been if someone had thrown a brick through the window."[26] Even so, Truth actually asked a different question: "Is God gone?"[27] Stowe's more trenchant phrase came to stand for the righteousness of God over the rashness of violence—very much a spiritualist message for the times.

"SOJOURNER TRUTH, the Libyan Sibyl" entered American discourse immediately. The renowned Boston Methodist Gilbert Haven, editor of the Methodist newspaper *Zion's Herald*, quickly used Stowe's article to denounce racial discrimination in American churches. Sojourner Truth, Haven said to the New England Conference of the Methodist Episcopal Church in May 1863, "is the rude, ungainly name of a rude, ungainly African of the purest negro blood." Yet Truth, he said, had inspired a statue that had impressed millions at the Great Exhibition in London. It made no sense, Haven implied, for American Methodist churches to segregate people like Truth who were the models for artistry that surpassed the work of Michelangelo.[28] Critical opinion has not supported Haven's comparison of Story and Michelangelo, but his audience understood the lesson—it is folly to judge human worth according to race. Much more such use of Truth as symbol was to come.[29]

Truth herself did not pass over Stowe's mistakes. Evidently in response to an inquiry in June from the abolitionist James Redpath, editor of the Boston *Commonwealth*, Truth corrected Stowe's allegation that she was African: "There is one place where she speaks of me as coming from Africa. My grandmother and my husband's mother came from Africa, but I did not." Truth also charged Stowe with putting words in her mouth: "I never make use of the word honey."[30]

Alert to her image in the historical record and to possibilities of making sales, Truth reminded readers that the facts of her life lay not in Stowe's essay but in her own *Narrative*, six copies of which she sent to Redpath for sale to his readers at 25 cents each. Through her friend Amy Post, Truth also offered objects so new to her that she had not set a price, mementoes that would become more important for her support and her representation of herself in the years to come. These were the first *carte-de-visite* photographs of herself, which in nineteenth-century parlance she called her "shadows."

Flawed as it was as an account of a person and a life, "Sojourner Truth, the Libyan Sibyl" reached an audience of thousands. The power of Harriet Beecher Stowe's prose, the fame of her name, and the prestige of America's leading intellectual journal transformed the persona of Sojourner Truth. From a little-noted evangelist and reformer, she became a celebrity; her presence, of itself, was now news.[31]

18

"Ar'n't I a Woman?"

TRUTH'S feminist comrade Frances Dana Gage was volunteering with the freedpeople in Union-occupied South Carolina in April 1863, when "The Libyan Sibyl" appeared.[1] Stowe's commercialism chagrined Gage, a far less renowned writer still dedicating her talent to reform. Reading Stowe on Parris Island, Gage realized immediately that she possessed the raw materials for a more riveting and true-to-life version of Sojourner Truth. In answer to Stowe's "Frederick, *is God dead?*", Gage reached back to a different setting and invented "and ar'n't I a woman?"

On 23 April 1863, less than a month after the publication of Stowe's "Libyan Sibyl," the New York *Independent* ran Gage's long account of Truth. Its centerpiece was Truth's intervention at the women's rights convention that Gage had chaired twelve years earlier in Akron. This portrait comprises today's essence of Sojourner Truth:

> The story of "Sojourner Truth," by Mrs. H. B. Stowe, in the April number of *The Atlantic* will be read by thousands in the East and West with intense interest; and as those who knew this remarkable woman will lay down this periodical, there will be heard in home-circles throughout Ohio, Michigan, Wisconsin, and Illinois many an anec-

Frances Dana Gage *carte-de-visite*. This *carte* lacks background and was probably taken by an itinerant photographer rather than in a studio, where Truth had her photos taken. Photo courtesy of Dr. Carol Steinhagen and Marietta College.

dote of the weird, wonderful creature, who was at once a marvel and a mystery.

Mrs. Stowe's remarks on Sojourner's opinion of Woman's Rights, bring vividly to my mind a scene in Ohio, never to be forgotten by those who witnessed it. In the spring of 1851, a Woman's Rights Convention was called in Akron, Ohio, by the friends of that then wondrously unpopular cause. I attended that Convention. No one at this day can conceive of the state of feeling of the multitude that came together on that occasion.

The Convention in the spring of 1850, in Salem, Ohio, reported at length in *The New York Tribune* by that staunch friend of Human rights, Oliver Johnson, followed in October of the same year by another convention at Worcester, Mass., well reported and well abused, with divers minor conventions, each amply vilified and caricatured, had set the world all agog, and the people, finding the women *in earnest,* turned out in large numbers to see and hear.

The leaders of the movement, staggering under the weight of disapprobation already laid upon them, and tremblingly alive to every appearance of evil that might spring up in their midst, were many of them almost thrown into panics on the first day of the meeting, by seeing a tall, gaunt black woman in a gray dress and white turban, surmounted by an uncouth sun-bonnet, march deliberately into the church, walk with the air of a queen up the aisle, and take her seat upon the pulpit steps. A buzz of disapprobation was heard all over the house, and such words as these fell upon listening ears:

"An abolition affair!" "Women's Rights and niggers!" "We told you so. Go it, old darkey!"

I chanced upon that occasion to wear my first laurels in public life, as president of the meeting. At my request, order was restored, and the business of the hour went on. The morning session closed; the afternoon session was held; the evening exercises came and went; old Sojourner, quiet and reticent as the "Libyan Statue," sat crouched against the wall on a corner of the pulpit stairs, her sun-bonnet shading her eyes, her elbow on her knee, and her chin resting on her broad, hard palm.

At intermissions she was busy selling the "Life of Sojourner Truth," a narrative of her own strange and adventurous life.

Again and again timorous and trembling ones came to me and said with earnestness, "Don't let her speak, Mrs. G. It will ruin us. Every newspaper in the land will have our cause mixed with abolition and niggers, and we shall be utterly denounced." My only answer was, "We shall see when the time comes."

The second day the work waxed warm. Methodist, Baptist, Episcopal, Presbyterian, and Universalist ministers came in to hear and discuss the resolutions brought forth. One claimed superior rights and privileges for man because of superior intellect; another because of the manhood of Christ. If God had desired the equality of woman, he would have given some token of his will through the birth, life, and death of the Savior. Another gave us a theological view of the awful sin of our first mother. There were few women in those days that dared to "speak in meeting," and the august teachers of the people, with long-winded bombast, were seeming to get the better of us, while the boys in the galleries and sneerers among the pews were enjoying hugely the discomfiture, as they supposed, of the strong-minded. Some of the tender-skinned friends were growing indignant and on the point of losing dignity, and the atmosphere of the convention betokened a storm.

Slowly from her seat in the corner rose Sojourner Truth, who, till now, had hardly lifted her head. "Don't let her speak," gasped a half-dozen in my ear. She moved slowly and solemnly to the front; laid her old bonnet at her feet, and turned her great speaking eyes to me.

There was a hissing sound of disapprobation above and below. I rose and announced "Sojourner Truth," and begged the audience to keep silence for a few moments. The tumult subsided at once, and every eye was fixed on this almost Amazon form, which stood nearly six feet high, head erect, and eye piercing the upper air like one in a dream. At her first word there was a profound hush. She spoke in deep tones, which, though not loud, reached every ear in the house, and away through the throng at the doors and windows.

"Well, chillen, whar dar's so much racket dar must be som'ting out o' kilter. I tink dat, 'twixt the niggers of de South and de women at de Norf, all a-talking 'bout rights, de white men will be in a fix pretty soon. But what's all this here talking 'bout? Dat man over dar say dat woman needs to be helped into carriages, and lifted over ditches, and to have de best place eberywhar. Nobody eber helps me into carriages, or ober mud-puddles, or gives me any best place;" and, raising herself to her full height, and her voice to a pitch like rolling thunder, she asked, "And ar'n't I a woman? Look at me. Look at my arm," and she bared her right arm to the shoulder, showing its tremendous muscular power. "I have plowed and planted and gathered into barns, and no man could head me—and ar'n't I a woman? I could work as much and eat as much as a man, (when I could get it,) and bear de lash as well—and ar'n't I a woman? I have borne thirteen chillen, and seen 'em mos' all sold off into slavery, and when I cried out with a mother's grief, none but Jesus heard—and ar'n't I a woman? When dey talks 'bout dis ting in de head. What dis dey call it?" "Intellect," whispered some one near. "Dat's it, honey. What's dat got to do with woman's rights or niggers' rights? If my cup won't hold but a pint and yourn holds a quart, wouldn't ye be mean not to let me have my little half-measure full?" and she pointed her significant finger and sent a keen glance at the minister who had made the argument. "Den dat little man in black dar, he say woman can't have as much right as man 'cause Christ wa'n't a woman. *Whar did your Christ come from?*"

Rolling thunder could not have stilled that crowd as did those deep wonderful tones, as she stood there with outstretched arms and eye of fire. Raising her voice still louder, she repeated,

"Whar did your Christ come from? From God and a woman. Man had noting to do with him." Oh! what a rebuke she gave the little man. Turning again to another objector, she took up the defense of Mother Eve. I cannot follow her through it all. It was pointed and witty and solemn; eliciting at almost every sentence deafening applause; and she ended by asserting "that if de fust woman God ever made was strong enough to turn de world upside down all her one lone, all dese togeder," and she glanced her eye over us, "ought to be able to turn it back and git it right side up again, and now dey is asking to, de men better let 'em." (Long continuous cheering.) " 'Bleeged to ye for hearin' on me, and now old Sojourner ha'n't got nothin' more to say."

Amid roars of applause she turned to her corner, leaving more than one of us with streaming eyes and hearts beating with gratitude. She had taken us up in her great strong arms and carried us safely over the slough of difficulty, turning the whole tide in our favor.

I have given but a faint sketch of her speech. I have never in my life seen anything like the magical influence that subdued the mobbish spirit of the day, and turned the jibes and sneers of an excited crowd into notes of respect and admiration. Hundreds rushed up to shake hands and congratulate the glorious old mother, and bid her "God-speed" on her mission of "testifying agin concernin' the wickedness of this here people."

Once upon a Sabbath in Michigan an abolition meeting was held. Parker Pillsbury was speaker, and expressed himself freely upon the conduct of the churches regarding slavery. While he spoke, there came up a fearful thunder-storm. A young Methodist rose and, interrupting him, said he felt alarmed; he felt as if God's judgment was about to fall upon him for daring to sit and hear such blasphemy; that it made his hair almost rise with terror. Here a voice sounding above the rain that beat upon the roof, the sweeping surge of the winds, the crashing of the limbs of trees, swaying of branches, and the rolling of thunder, spoke out: "Chile, don't be skeered; you're not goin' to be harmed. I don't speck God's ever heern tell on ye!"

It was all she said, but it was enough. I might multiply anecdotes (and some of the best cannot be told) till your pages would not contain them, and yet the fund not be exhausted. Therefore, I will close, only saying to those who think public opinion does not change, that they have only to look at the progress of ideas from the stand-point of old Sojourner Truth twelve years ago.

The despised and mobbed African, now the heroine of an article in the most popular periodical in the United States. Then Sojourner could say, "If woman wants rights, let her take 'em." Now, women do take them, and public opinion sustains them.

Sojourner Truth is not dead; but, old and feeble, she rests from her labors near Battle Creek, Michigan.

Gage's rendition of Truth far exceeds in drama Marius Robinson's straightforward report from 1851. Through framing and elaboration, she turns Truth's comments into a spectacular performance four times longer than his.

The antiblack setting, though crucial to latter-day users of Sojourner Truth the symbol, is Gage's creation. The call to the conference had specifically invited a wide range of reformers, including antislavery people, the backbone of antebellum feminism. Gage's depiction of a roomful of women unskilled in debate and timorous in their claims applied to only a few in the Akron meeting, to one person in particular: the Pittsburgh journalist Jane Swisshelm, Gage's main rival in the feminist press. Swisshelm plays several invisible roles in Gage's "Sojourner Truth."

Gage introduces Truth in motion: she strides into the church and sits on the pulpit steps. In 1851 someone did stride in to perch on the pulpit steps, but it was Jane Swisshelm, not Sojourner Truth. Swisshelm had sat there because the sanctuary was overcrowded; she had removed her bonnet—normally considered an unladylike gesture—because of the heat.[2] Gage sets Truth in Swisshelm's place, refashions Swisshelm's bonnet into an "uncouth sun-bonnet," and has Truth scandalize by not removing it. Gage informs her 1863 readers that she was presiding at a meeting for the first time in her life, a piece of information that does not contribute to her depiction of Truth but points again to Swisshelm, who had criticized Gage repeatedly for incompetence as chair. Swisshelm had complained that Gage "was a dignified, fine-looking *woman,* but she was *not* a good president. Literary abilities and fine personal appearance are not enough to make a good presiding officer."[3]

To describe Truth during the first day's deliberations, Gage borrows liberally from Stowe with more or less acknowledgment, calling Truth the "Libyan Statue" and copying the pose of Story's sculpture. Her depiction of the events of the second day differs markedly from what appeared in newspaper accounts in 1851. Instead of the confident interchange between Swisshelm, Mary Ann Johnson, Emma Coe, and other outspoken women, Gage hands the initiative to antifeminist ministers seeking to undermine women's claim to equal rights.

In Gage's scenario, Truth addresses male critics and antiblack women, not a meeting full of people who agreed with and supported her. Gage does two things with her set-up: She reiterates a familiar Christian narrative in which a lone preacher—like Sojourner Truth against the rowdies at Northampton—subdues and converts a body of unruly non-believers. And she plays on the irony of white women advocating women's rights while ignoring women who are black. White feminists' hostility is the bedrock of the emblematic Sojourner Truth who emerges from Gage's narrative. Their antagonism proves the power of Truth, the preacher able to convert them.

As Gage builds the scene, Truth rises from a sea of foes. Beginning quietly, in puissant tones, she commands the meeting to hush. Then she establishes an alliance between slaves and the women before her: " 'twixt the niggers of de South and de women at de Norf, all a-talking 'bout rights, de white men will be in a fix pretty soon." In Robinson's 1851 report, this thought had come at the end, not the beginning.

Gage's Truth speaks in an inconsistent dialect that may have been inspired by the South Carolinians around Gage in 1863. As in "The Libyan Sibyl," the dialect serves primarily to measure the distance between Truth and her white audience.

Gage has Truth personify an argument familiar to Gage's work: to anti-women's-righters who declare women too fragile for the rights of men, Gage answers that legions of strong women are already doing men's work without getting men's pay. In 1851, Truth made this argument in a very personal way that Gage repeats in 1863: "I could work as much and eat as much as a man, (when I could get it)." Speaking on woman suffrage platforms in the 1860s, Truth would often reclaim the right of equal pay for equal work, based on her own experience.

"Ar'n't I a woman?" was Gage's invention. Had Truth said it several times in 1851, as in Gage's article, Marius Robinson, who was familiar with Truth's diction, most certainly would have noted it. If he had an unusually tin ear, he might have missed it once, perhaps even twice. But not four times, as in Gage's report. This rhetorical question inserts blackness into feminism and gender into racial identity.

One of only a few black women regulars on the feminist and antislavery circuit, Truth was doing in Gage's report the very same symbolic work of her personal presence in these meetings: she was the pivot that linked two causes—of women (presumed to be white) and of blacks (presumed to be men)—through one black female body. One phrase sums up the meaning of the emblematic Sojourner Truth today: "ar'n't I a woman?"

Gage shines a spotlight on Truth's body: a massive, towering figure straining upward and thundering a riveting refrain, "ar'n't I a woman?" In Gage's "Sojourner Truth," that body is once again undressed and on display. With the force of Truth's use of slave auction imagery in Indiana in 1858, Gage describes Truth's disrobing a part of her body. The naked limb is a mighty right arm, the arm of a worker, the arm of a powerful woman, the body subject to the whip, and again, in counterpoint, "ar'n't I a woman?" The productive labor that Truth describes is men's fieldwork, but Gage inserts the reproductive work of women through an allusion to the tragedy of slave motherhood: the loss of one's children to the slave trade. With the grief of the mother comes one final time, "and ar'n't I a woman?"

Gage's Truth has borne and lost thirteen children. We will never know whether Truth, appropriating her own mother's tragedy, had claimed in 1851 to have lost thirteen children to the slave trade or whether Gage first puts the number thirteen into Truth's mouth in 1863. We know only that Robinson did not have Truth mention thirteen children and that Gage used that number in connection with a slave mother's pain shortly after the Akron convention.

Although she did not write about Truth by name until 1863, Gage had immediately recognized Truth's magnetism and used her as a model in an October 1851 episode of a fictional series she was publishing in Swisshelm's *Saturday Visiter*. She described a fugitive slave whom she called Winna in "Aunt Hanna's Quilt: Or the Record of the West. 'A Tale of the Apple Cellar' ":

> She was black—black as November night itself—tall, straight and muscular. Her wool was sprinkled with grey, that showed her years and sorrows, and her countenance was strikingly interesting. Her features once must have been fine, and even yet beamed with more than ordinary intelligence; her language was a mixture of the African lingo and the manner of the whites among whom she lived.

Winna lamented that all her children had been lost to the slave trade: "I'se had thirteen of 'em. They are all gone—all gone, Miss, I don't know where. . . ."[4]

The Sojourner Truth-like Winna is one of two strong characters in the story. The second is another symbolic type that fascinated Gage and many other American writers, black and white—a type Gage would highlight in her woman suffrage work after the war. Gage was enthralled by the enslavement of near-white women. In "Aunt Hanna's Quilt," the only one of Winna's children said to be of mixed race is subject to sale despite—or because of—her whiteness and beauty.[5]

In "Sojourner Truth," Gage echoes Truth's use of the Bible, but without Truth's skill. Gage recites Truth on original sin, Eve, and woman's ability to set the world right side up again, and she repeats Truth's assertion that God and a woman produced Jesus without any help from man. But Gage is not so agile as Truth in making her way around the Bible. She omits Mary, Martha, and Lazarus, and she stumbles when she has Truth argue for equal rights because "I have plowed and planted and gathered into barns. . . ." This evokes Matthew 6:26, in which the fowls of the air "sow not, neither do they reap, nor gather into barns. . . ." Yet the point in Matthew is that God feeds the birds even without their doing this work, a theme incompatible with what Gage presents as Truth's point: equal work demands equal pay. Truth's biblical allusions always fit her meaning, enabling her Bible-literate public to amplify that meaning, not merely take comfort in the familiarity of her language. Gage closes this section with Truth in the posture of the prophet, silencing the crowd with her "deep wonderful tones," her arms outstretched, her eyes afire.

Gage appropriates from Stowe Truth's single-handed capture and remolding of her audience. As in "The Libyan Sibyl," the white audience is mesmerized. Stowe's Truth electrifies her listeners with a single line, "Frederick, *is God dead?*" Gage's Truth holds them with a spellbinding performance: "I have never in my life seen anything like the magical influence that subdued the mobbish spirit of the day, and turned the jibes and sneers of an excited crowd into notes of respect and admiration." In Stowe's essay, Truth leaves her audience stunned; in Gage's, she moves them from hushed silence to "deafening applause." In both reports, Truth's intervention ruptures business as usual through a logic all her own that cannot be refuted by ordinary (white) people. She puts an end to discussion.

Gage presents Truth as a figure of strength, and that characterization, punctuated with the unforgettable refrain—"ar'n't I a woman?"—has captivated feminists since the late nineteenth century. Not only does Truth exhibit her muscular right arm, she figuratively rescues the timid white women and carries them to safety.[6] Gage overturns Stowe's burlesque of Truth's feminism. Stowe's Truth was impatient with feminists: they should simply take their rights. Gage exhibits Truth as an embodiment of women's power and gives Stowe's throwaway line real meaning. Women can take their rights and make a difference.

Stowe and Gage each append anecdotes to seal Truth's reputation as a natural wit. Gage's Truth demolishes the pretensions of a conventional young Christian with "I don't speck God's ever heern tell on ye!" The stringing together of such stories became a hallmark of Truth narratives, which sometimes were little more than listings of Truth's greatest lines, each abstracted from its context or larger meaning.

WE CANNOT know exactly what Truth said at Akron in 1851, an unusually well reported appearance. We know even less of what she said most other times she spoke. She put her soul and genius into extemporaneous speech, not dictation, and lacking sound recordings or reliable transcripts, seekers after Truth are now at the mercy of what other people said that she said. Accounts of her words in 1851 differ, and today the one that historians judge the more reliable—because it was written close to the time when Truth spoke—is Marius Robinson's.

Unlike professional historians, whose eyes are fixed on accuracy, Truth's modern admirers almost universally prefer the account that Gage presented twelve years after the fact. It fits far better with what we believe Truth to have been like. But this is testimony to the role of symbol in our public life and to our need for this symbol. To Robinson's contemporaneous report in standard English, we prefer the Sojourner Truth in dialect of a skilled feminist writer.

Everything we know of Sojourner Truth comes through other people, mostly educated white women. Does this make Truth unusually remote? Consider the obstacles standing in the way of knowing anyone from the past, whether or not they wrote and preserved testaments to their existence. Every source, every document, comes from a person in a particular relationship to the subject, and every source, every document has a reason for existing. No means of knowing the past is objective, and none is transparent. The layers of interpretation between us and Sojourner Truth are simply different from those that separate us from people who document their own lives and try to supply their own meaning.[7]

After the summer of 1863, Truth began to portray herself in photographs; but photographs, too, have their own rhetoric of representation and are not a transparent window onto history.[8] In every instance, layers of interpretation separate the past from the present. Those who shape their own presentation of self—in words or in pictures—do so for their, not our own ends.

Gage crafted her "Sojourner Truth" carefully, and her sensibility was remarkably modern. Her account is still compelling. But it is by no means the real Sojourner Truth.

PAINTING in 1863 a positive word portrait of a powerful black woman, Gage was as usual in the vanguard. An Ohio abolitionist with roots in Massachusetts, Frances Dana Gage (1808–1884) was known throughout her life as a woman's rights woman. In the early 1860s, her writing appeared now and then alongside Stowe's in the New York *Independent*, the nation's foremost religious newspaper. But whereas Stowe was a featured writer whose Italian travelogues appeared weekly in 1859–60, Gage contributed occasional pieces that most likely were not paid.

Largely self-educated, Gage was a popular public speaker who wrote under the pen name "Aunt Fanny" for a number of feminist and agricultural newspapers in the 1850s and 1860s. She was the first woman suffragist to lecture in Iowa, and in 1856 she toured with Susan B. Anthony.[9] As a western antislavery feminist, Gage was known for being both a sharp critic of the patriarchal family and a folksy wife and mother of eight.

In the mid-1850s, Gage corresponded with Elizabeth Cady Stanton, the leading woman suffragist, to whom she sent this self-deprecating ditty:

> The woman is tallish, but not very slender.
> Her feelings are kind; some think very tender.
> She's some common sense, but is not very witty.
> Her features are coarse and not very pretty.
> Her eyes a clear grey, her hair once was brown,
> Her forehead is narrow and graced with a frown;
> A nose rather flat and lips rather thick,
> A mouth pretty large, a tongue glib and quick,
> A voice middling so-so, a skin without pimples,
> A fairish complexion, a chin without dimples,
> A light merry laugh and a will of her own,
> And a heart as love-craving as ever was known . . .
> She has eight boys and girls (Mrs. Swisshelm said ten) . . .
> She tries with the world to be open and true,
> To do unto others as she's have them, too, do.[10]

As in "Sojourner Truth," Jane Swisshelm plays a role.

Gage's support of woman suffrage stemmed from her temperance convictions. She contended that "*nine-tenths* of all the manufacturers of ardent spirits, of all the drinkers of ardent spirits, and of all the criminals made by ardent spirits, are *men*," while "the greatest sufferers from all this crime, and shame, and wrong, are *women.*"[11] Women needed to vote, hold office, elect representatives, and frame laws that would control the liquor traffic so ruinous to families. At the end of the nineteenth century, this same logic would make Frances Willard, the leader of the Woman's Christian Temperance Union (WCTU), into a woman suffragist, an advocate of what the WCTU called the "home protection ballot."

Gage was radical for her time. Antagonists charged she was for free love because she criticized the institution of marriage as it then existed in the United States; in virtually every state married women lacked the right to control their own wages and property and had no rights in the custody of their children. By rejecting the logic of separate spheres and natural proclivities by sex, and by insisting that women be included as people with full civil, financial, and human rights under state and federal constitutions, Gage placed herself among the extremists in American reform.

Gage contended, for instance, that women would make just as good doctors as men, that they were already doing a good deal of doctoring. Male doctors who cited women's natural unfitness for medicine were hypocrites: "We have always noticed that literary men do not like literary ladies. I suppose from the same reason that the village doctor dislikes his [women] colleagues [who carry] pill-boxes. They don't like competition—are afraid of losing ground by comparison."[12]

When Swisshelm celebrated differences between the sexes, wondering why women would "contend for the right to get upon the housetop and nail shingles," Gage had answers. A widow with children to feed would gladly nail shingles for a dollar a day, for a dollar was more than she could make through knitting or sewing. "[L]et me tell you," Gage harangued Swisshelm, that where there is one lady perched complacently on a stool doing nothing, there are "ten women in this same country of ours that roll logs, mall rails, plough, hoe corn, dig potatoes, burn brush heaps, pitch hay, &c . . . and they do it from necessity."¹³

Throughout her career, Gage focused her women's rights rhetoric on strong, working-class women. Where Swisshelm waxed sentimental about man's strength and woman's weakness, Gage extolled strong women: A woman in rags walked a canal path in Cincinnati with "half a cart load of old fence-rails set into a big sack that was strapped round her neck . . . half bent to the earth with a burden that few men could have carried"; another woman in St. Louis walked two miles "with a child six months old—a large fat boy on her left shoulder, while on her head she is holding some thirty, forty, or fifty pounds of flour. She walks with a firm step, and carries her burden with apparent ease."¹⁴

When antifeminists contended that equal rights would expose women to the rough-and-tumble of economic and political strife, Gage pointed to poor women drowning in an acute struggle for existence, working as hard as men in thoroughly unpleasant circumstances, but handicapped by their lack of civil rights and equal pay.

In 1863, Gage seized on Truth as another working woman who deserved her rights as a worker. Such views were too extreme for readers of prestigious magazines. Unlike the more moderate Harriet Beecher Stowe, Gage never stepped up to the *Atlantic Monthly* or other widely read, fashionable journals. Throughout her life, she remained with the religious and feminist press. Among her eleven books of fiction, those published for temperance organizations predominate.

WITH the publication of the Stowe and Gage profiles during the Civil War, Sojourner Truth became a well-known symbol among liberals, as well as a particular person with her own life history. She began to appear in mainstream newspapers like the Boston *Commonwealth*, the *New York Tribune,* and the Philadelphia *Bulletin,* her access to their columns opened by the wartime influence of the antislavery community. But writers did not invent Truth entirely as they pleased. They nearly always built on Stowe and Gage, whose writing elaborated encounters that Truth initiated. Truth had approached Stowe, and in Akron in 1851 she had turned up on her own and sought permission to speak. Before either woman wrote about her, Truth presented herself to them as a dynamic, attractive person. In light of her tragic youthful experience, this creation represents an extraordinary accomplishment.

When Truth met Stowe and Gage, she had already forged a powerful persona that each writer found compelling—albeit for different reasons. This achievement did not come automatically by dint of Truth's having been enslaved—quite to the contrary, slavery was something she had actively to surmount. As a slave, Truth had been abused, like millions of her counterparts in bondage. Women who have been enslaved and beaten are far more likely to appear depressed than to project intriguing strength of character. They tend to fade from memory rather than make an indelible impression. The legacy of abuse helps explain why Truth's success on the antislavery lecture circuit was unique among women who had actually been enslaved.

Truth in public was extraordinary as an ex-slavewoman, and her vitality needs an explanation. The key lies in Truth's refashioning herself over long years of adult life and through access to uncommon sources of power. Relying on the gifts of the Holy Spirit and a remarkable network of abolitionist, feminist, and spiritualist supporters, she healed the fear and insecurity embedded in her wretched childhood.

A powerfully *re*-made character attracted Stowe and Gage. Truth was no longer a timid victim who might let herself be fondled by Sally Dumont or Ann Folger or beaten by John Dumont or the Prophet Matthias. She was a forceful, indefatigable speaker for political causes that needed the strength and the body she brought to them.

19

Partisan and Aristocrat

A GARRISONIAN abolitionist estranged from the political process, Truth did not embrace politics until the outbreak of the Civil War in April 1861. Once war was declared, she eagerly championed the Union cause, even before it openly challenged slavery, even before black men were allowed to serve. Truth stopped denouncing slavery and started discussing war and Union. For the first time in her life she became the partisan of a secular power—from a vantage point among the elite.

In Steuben County, Indiana, across the state line from her hometown of Battle Creek, Michigan, her embrace of the Union got her into legal trouble as a black woman right away. Truth spoke at meetings large and small, but one of the most memorable was a large pro-Union rally at the Steuben County Courthouse. For this appearance, her good white friends interpreted her dignity flamboyantly and dressed her in an outfit of scandalous provocation. Truth later described her patriotic appearance:

> The ladies thought I should be dressed in uniform as well as the captain of the home guard. ... So they put upon me a red, white, and blue shawl, a sash and apron to match, a cap on my head with a star in front, and a star on each shoulder. When I was dressed I looked in

the glass and was fairly frightened. [I said] "It seems I am going to battle." My friends advised me to take a sword or pistol. I replied, "I carry no weapon; the Lord will reserve [preserve] me without weapons.[1]

Truth drove to the courthouse in a beautiful carriage full of officers and gentlemen, but soon ran afoul of Copperheads—northerners who supported the Confederacy. A small boy on a fence, crying, "Nigger, nigger," forecast the mayhem to come. Truth's party marched into the courthouse between a double file of soldiers to the strains of "The Star-Spangled Banner." "I joined and sang with all my might," Truth recalled, "while amid flashing bayonets and waving banners our party made its way to the platform. . . ."[2]

Truth warned that the Confederacy was arming blacks to fight against the Union and that the federal government should follow suit. A friend reported that she "was armed (stretching out her long bony arm) to fight *for* the North, and if she was ten years younger—(she is now seventy,) she 'would fly to the battle field, and nurse and cook for the Massachusetts troops, *her boys!* and if it came to the pinch, put in a *blow* now and then.' "[3]

At this point, the meeting was mobbed, and Truth was arrested for having contravened Indiana law prohibiting the entry into the state of people of African descent. (The law was rarely enforced, for the tens of thousands of black people living in Indiana in the 1860s belonged to the American culture of mobility. Even so, the climate that permitted the passage of such stipulations in 1851 made Indiana blacks extremely vulnerable.) Embroiled in these charges for ten days, Truth was repeatedly detained, defended by friends, and menaced by mobs. Ultimately she was let go.

Interpretations of this encounter make black and white abolitionist sensibilities interestingly clear. Truth's host, Josephine Griffing, was a white Ohio abolitionist Truth had known since her Salem days in the 1850s. Truth and Griffing would work together again in Washington in the mid-1860s.[4] Griffing saw Truth's difficulties as proof the Union cause was controversial. Without making mention of the 1858 breast-baring episode, Griffing pointed out that Truth had spoken often without incident in Indiana. Truth's retort to the mob, which Griffing quotes, contradicts this interpretation. Where Griffing saw politics, Truth saw race:

Sojourner Truth said, in the Court House, to the mob—"It seems that it takes *my* black face to bring out *your* black hearts; so it's well I came." At another point she said,—"You are afraid of my black face, because it is a looking glass in which you see yourselves."[5]

When it came to the meaning of color, Truth and her assailants seem to agree—blackness was bad, symbolically and literally.

The ambivalence about her color and her race that Truth expressed in Indiana lasted a lifetime, as her later comments about white and black people and her patterns of sociability attest. With the exception of her children, Truth's close associates during her adult life were middle-class white people of education, if not always of standing.

In Steuben County, she associated with the right sort of people. Griffing said Truth was visiting friends, "several of the most wealthy and influential white families."[6] She depicted Truth as she liked to be seen: a gentlewoman in possession of the determining requirement of ladyhood, "unimpeachable moral character." While Truth's fellow feminist and antislavery lecturers (like Lucy Colman of Rochester and Frances Dana Gage) complained of filthy accommodations in the then western states, Truth now stayed with the *crème de la crème*, petted and protected by reform-minded clergymen, lawyers, judges, and their wives.

Rarely did black women keep such company when they were not at work, for these were gentry much like those for whom Truth, as Isabella, had worked in Ulster County and New York City. Now, however, the "Libyan Sibyl" was an honored houseguest who might nonetheless from time to time also help out with the housework. After 1863, middle- and upper-class people saw Truth as an objet d'art or adorable exotic.

Truth had seen enough poverty as slave and household worker to avoid it whenever possible. Given her experience of poor blacks and educated whites in a white-supremacist world, she could scarcely have used blackness as a positive metaphor.

Not even her Washington experiences changed that. Though drawn in the mid-1860s closer to blackness and even poverty—among black troops and then among refugee freedpeople in Washington and northern Virginia—Truth distanced herself from such problems iconographically. All of Truth's photographs project her as the epitome of middle-class decorum.

THE GREAT revolution of the middle of the Civil War was the acceptance of black men, including Sojourner Truth's grandson, into the Union Army. In April 1863, Massachusetts organized its first black regiment, the Massachusetts 54th (memorialized in the 1989 feature film *Glory*). Truth's grandson, James Caldwell, volunteered immediately. So did two of Frederick Douglass's sons. Envisioning military service as the vindication of his masculinity, James wrote: "Now is our time, Grandmother, to prove that we are men."[7] Truth must have been relieved as well as proud, for James, who had accompanied her to Andover to visit Harriet Beecher Stowe in 1853, had a stormy adolescence, much like that of her own son Peter twenty years earlier. Nineteen black men from Battle Creek (not including Caldwell, who joined a Massachusetts regiment) volunteered to serve in the Michigan First Colored Infantry Regiment.[8] By the time the war ended, about 186,000 men, or one-tenth of the Union Army, were black, serving mostly in segregated infantry regiments with white officers.[9]

Truth belonged to the scores of abolitionist women who continued their antislavery work in volunteer service to black troops—and, as a logical extension, to freedpeople. She began in late 1863, going door to door in Battle Creek to collect Thanksgiving food for the First Michigan Regiment of colored soldiers bivouacked at Camp Ward in Detroit.

This effort provides the setting for another often-told anecdote. One neighbor refused to contribute and added gratuitous insults about black people and the Union cause. Caught short by this kind of vituperation in Battle Creek, Truth asked the man his name. To his retort, "I am the only son of my mother," Truth said, "I am glad there are no more," and continued on her way.[10] She delivered the goods she had collected to the soldiers at Camp Ward at Thanksgiving.

Truth stayed in Detroit from Thanksgiving into April 1864 at the home of the Scottish abolitionist Euphemia Cockrane, who, like Amy Post in Rochester, was known for her hospitality.[11] In February, Truth brought more food and clothing from the people of Battle Creek to Camp Ward. On this occasion, at least, she addressed segregated audiences. She spoke to the First Michigan Colored Infantry in a formal ceremony, then chatted with them for over an hour. She sang a song she had composed—full of race pride and revindication—in honor of the First Michigan Colored Regiment to the tune of "John Brown's Body":

We are the valian soldiers who've 'listed for the war;
We are fighting for the Union, we are fighting for the law;
We can shoot a rebel farther than a white man ever saw,
    As we go marching on.
Chorus.—
    Glory, glory, hallelujah! Glory, glory, hallelujah!
    Glory, glory hallelujah! as we go marching on.

Look there above the center, where the flag is waving bright;
We are going out of slavery, we are bound for freedom's light;
We mean to show Jeff Davis how the Africans can fight,
    As we go marching on.—Chorus.

We are done with hoeing cotton, we are done with hoeing corn;
We are colored Yankee soldiers as sure as you are born.
When massa hears us shouting, he will think 'tis Gabriel's horn,
    As we go marching on.—Chorus

They will have to pay us wages, the wages of their sin;
They will have to bow their foreheads to their colored kith and kin;
They will have to give us house-room, or the roof will tumble in,
    As we go marching on.—Chorus.

We hear the proclamation, massa, hush it as you will;
The birds will sing it to us, hopping on the cotton hill;
The possum up the gum tree could n't keep it still,
    As he went climbing on.—Chorus.

Father Abraham has spoken, and the message has been sent;
    The prison doors have opened, and out the prisoners went
    To join the sable army of African descent,
        As we go marching on.—Chorus.[12]

So many whites gathered to hear her that she postponed a second lecture to the soldiers. The white audience took up a collection for her benefit, a custom that may have influenced her decision.[13]

During her time in Detroit, Truth settled on a mission going beyond the needs of black soldiers. By the spring of 1864 she was ready to journey to Washington, where she could serve needy freedpeople within reach of abolitionists while the war was on.

The year 1864 found several of Truth's feminist abolitionist colleagues clustered in and around Washington, working in freedpeople's relief. Josephine Griffing, Truth's host in Indiana in 1861, was with the District of Columbia Freedmen's Relief Association; Lucy Colman, Julia Wilbur, and Harriet Jacobs, all with strong Rochester connections, were attached to the National Freedmen's Aid Association. Jacobs was a fugitive slave from North Carolina, an abolitionist, and author of *Incidents in the Life of a Slave Girl: Written by Herself* (1861). Also a friend of Amy Post, with whom she had stayed while writing her autobiography, Jacobs no doubt encountered Truth in freedpeople's relief. But Truth never mentioned Jacobs, although white women appear as esteemed colleagues in Truth's correspondence. Nor does Jacobs mention Truth; neither may have considered another black woman noteworthy in such obviously historic times. There was a big difference, however, between Jacobs's and Truth's attitudes toward the representation of blackness. Truth thought herself sufficiently important to be photographed repeatedly.

20

Truth in Photographs

SOJOURNER TRUTH found a new means of reaching supporters and raising money in the "cartomania" of the 1860s. As in the 1840s, when the demand for slave narratives enhanced her venture into that profitable line, Truth seized upon new technology for her work of self-representation. In May 1863 in Battle Creek, she joined masses of Americans, high and low, in the rage for photographic *cartes-de-visite*.[1]

This form of portraiture, the invention of André Adolphe Eugène Disdéri of Paris in the mid-1850s, arrived in the United States in the early 1860s. It employed a camera with four, six, eight, or twelve lenses exposing different portions of a single large glass plate. Portrait photography became cheap when Disdéri joined the multi-lens camera with an invention of the early 1850s: collodion wet-plate negative technology, which made it possible to print an indefinite number of prints from a single negative. Simultaneous opening of the lenses produced several small photos of the same pose. If instead the lenses were opened sequentially, the sitter could adjust her pose from one exposure to another.

Once the negative was developed, infinitely many prints could be made, immediately or later on. The prints were then mounted on card stock and cut apart, producing four, eight, or more photographs the size of a visiting card. Having been developed and printed all at once, *cartes-de-visite* were cheap, 25 to 33 cents each. Because they were so small (about 3 1/4″ x 2 1/4″), they did not permit elaborate background or detail, but their cheapness made them the most popular form of portrait in the 1860s. Civil War soldiers by the thousands had themselves photographed in uniform. In their ubiquity, *cartes-de-visite* began to make photographic images as familiar and accepted a means of communication as the printed word.[2]

Truth's fund-raising was only one of a multitude of purposes of *cartes-de-visite* during the Civil War. *Cartes-de-visite* of great men were sold as inspiration to the masses. They became a handy form of publicity for authors (like Harriet Beecher Stowe), politicians (like Abraham Lincoln, whose 1860 *carte* by Mathew Brady was a campaign token), actors, and lecturers (like Frances Dana Gage), who used them as a combination of business card and baseball card, distributing them at personal appearances and through other outlets.

More to the point for Sojourner Truth, *cartes-de-visite* circulated within the Union as anti-Confederate propaganda: images of starved prisoners of war at the notorious Andersonville Confederate prison, the whip-scarred back of the fugitive slave volunteer Gordon, and white-looking children whose lack of color had not protected them from enslavement.[3] These fund-raising *cartes* probably inspired Truth, whose portraits also reminded purchasers that she symbolized the woman who had been a slave.

Had Truth's *cartes-de-visite* served only to wring money from abolitionists, she might have posed in settings or costumes reminiscent of her enslavement. Like Gordon with the mutilated back, she might have featured her right hand, injured during her last year in slavery. Or she might have posed as a worker, as in one of the few non-photographic images made during her lifetime, a drawing from about 1867, purporting to show her in the Northampton Association in the 1840s. In this drawing she does laundry, her bare arms plunged deep into a wash tub.[4]

Truth chose none of these. Her favorite photographs, taken in Detroit in early 1864, are conventional portraits.[5] Most of them are *cartes-de-visite* in the vernacular style, showing no landscape. The props are standard: her own knitting and objects supplied by the photographer (a book and flowers) as simplified tokens of leisure and feminine gentility. As in her other photographs, Truth wears expertly tailored clothing made of handsome, substantial material, here the black or gray and white she favored for public speaking. Sometimes she is dressed in the Quaker-style clothing that feminist and antislavery lecturers wore to distinguish themselves from showily dressed actresses, their less reputable colleagues in female public performance. Her hair is wrapped plainly, but not in the Madras handkerchief that Harriet Beecher Stowe assigned to her after the "manner of her race."[6]

In later photographs, Truth poses in the fashionable clothing she learned to wear in Washington, the only indication that association with middle-class blacks—whom she herself does not mention—might have altered her personal aesthetic. This patterned wardrobe reveals that the Civil War freed Truth, like the fiery lecturer Anna Dickinson, to break away from the simple Quaker dress that had been their style before the war.[7] Whether gray, black and white, or in the style of the time, Truth's clothing was of excellent quality. She presents the image of a respectable, middle-class matron.

Truth's images may appear to be unmediated, the essence of her real self, but in fact they were carefully arranged. In her 1864 studio photographs, she sits with a book, portrait, or knitting in her hands, and a book and flowers on the table. In one favorite photograph, she stands with a cane. This image, now in the Sophia Smith Collection at Smith College, served Susan B. Anthony's purposes shortly after it was made. Anthony was trying to arouse a meeting of the Women's Loyal League. To raise the money she needed, Anthony held up two photographic *cartes-de-visite*, one of Truth standing with her disabled hand resting on her cane, the other of Gordon. Imagine, Anthony urged her audience, that Truth and Gordon were their parents. Would they, in such circumstances, continue to temporize over demands for the irrevocable abolition of slavery? Her resolutions passed immediately and unanimously, and the money was forthcoming.[8] Ordinarily, however, the message in Truth's photos was far more individual than propagandistic.

Sojourner Truth, 1864, *carte-de-visite*, Randall of Detroit probable photographer. This is the image that Susan B. Anthony used to raise money. Photo courtesy of the Burton Historical Collection, Detroit Public Library.

I Sell the Shadow to Support the Substance.

SOJOURNER TRUTH.

One of Truth's favorite *cartes-de-visite*, unidentified photographer, 1864.
Photo courtesy of the National Portrait Gallery, Smithsonian Institution.

I Sell the Shadow to Support the Substance.
SOJOURNER TRUTH.

Sojourner Truth *carte-de-visite*, Detroit, 1864. Reprint of 1864 negative with caption in simpler typeface than original. Photo courtesy of Berenice Lowe Collection, Bentley Historical Library, Michigan Historical Collections, University of Michigan.

I SELL THE SHADOW TO SUPPORT THE
SUBSTANCE.
SOJOURNER TRUTH.

Sojourner Truth *carte-de-visite*, Same sitting, slightly different pose as
previous photo. Photo from the collection of Nell Irvin Painter.

I SELL THE SHADOW TO SUPPORT THE SUBSTANCE.

SOJOURNER TRUTH.

Sojourner Truth *carte-de-visite*, unidentified photographer, 1864. Photo courtesy of the National Portrait Gallery, Smithsonian Institution.

Sojourner Truth, ca. 1860s, format unknown. The photo on Truth's lap
is probably of her grandson, James Caldwell. Photo courtesy of the
Burton Historical Collection, Detroit Public Library.

Drawing, ca. 1867, by Charles C. Burleigh, Jr., of Truth at a washtub in the
Northampton Association. Photo courtesy of Historic Northampton,
Northampton, Massachusetts.

I SELL THE SHADOW TO SUPPORT THE SUBSTANCE.
SOJOURNER TRUTH.

Randall

East Grand Circus Park,
DETROIT.

Sojourner Truth cabinet card, ca. 1870, by Randall of Detroit. The larger cabinet card format (6 1/2″ x 4 1/4″) allows a more elaborate background than the *carte-de-visite*. Photo courtesy of the National Portrait Gallery, Smithsonian Institution.

Truth actually did knit, but in her photographs, she holds her yarn in only one hand, so that it conveys a motherly womanliness central to her self-fashioning. Conforming to conventions of celebrity portraiture, she looks past the camera in weighty seriousness.[9] Her posture is relaxed but upright, communicating an impression of easy composure. For a woman of about sixty-seven, she looks remarkably young, but the relative youthfulness of her appearance takes nothing from the overall gravity of her persona. She is mature and intelligent, not reading, but wearing eyeglasses that might have helped with the knitting and certainly, like the book on the table, lent her an educated air.

In none of these portraits is there anything beyond blackness that would inspire charity—nothing of the piteous slave mother or the weird Matthias Kingdom, no bared arms, no bodice taken down in public, nothing of Stowe's amusing naif. Truth reveals nothing that would make her into an African or into an exotic of any kind at all. The *cartes-de-visite* show a solid bourgeoise who would not speak in dialect. With only her face and hands uncovered, hers is the antithesis of a naked body. Blackness, of course, conveyed its own messages.

Although mid-nineteenth-century African Americans of means had their photographs taken for their own use, bourgeois black portraits were as uncommon as bourgeois blacks.[10] Even well into the mid-twentieth century, long after newspapers had begun to be illustrated, photographs of blacks appeared but rarely in the northern white press, and in the southern white press not at all. Most nineteenth-century photographs of blacks were not taken at the instigation of the subject. Photographs of black men were generally found in the files of metropolitan police, where photography had taken its place as a tool of law enforcement in the 1840s.[11]

One other category of public images took people of color as its subject matter: the anthropological specimen photographs that displayed "types" (usually unclothed) of native peoples to educated metropolitans. In anthropological photographs, captive individuals, stripped and staring directly into the camera, were displayed as examples of otherness, like insects pinned in cases or stuffed mammals in museums. British and French explorers specialized in this genre of natural history photography, but the American biologist Louis Agassiz had several specimen photographs taken of enslaved African Americans in the 1850s.[12] Stowe's verbal portrait of Truth approached this genre in words.

In her letter to the Boston *Commonwealth* rectifying Stowe's misstatements, Truth enclosed six copies of her *Narrative*. Here, she said, her correct history was to be found. She also asked readers to purchase her photograph, in nineteenth-century parlance, her "shadow." Colleagues should buy her *carte-de-visite*, she said, because "I am living on my shadow."[13] In the spring of 1863 she was in her mid-sixties, in ill-health, and restricted to her home in Battle Creek. Henceforth subject to periodic bouts of illness publicized in the antislavery press to encourage donations, Truth increasingly substituted the representation of herself for her presence. Her regular caption became "I sell the shadow to support the substance. SOJOURNER TRUTH."

The caption expressed Truth's lifelong anxieties about money, and lent prominence to the themes of dependence and independence that thread her later years. All along she drew a distinction between selling her artifacts, which was quid pro quo, and charity. Selling books and photographs did not compromise one's independence, for sale was an exchange, transferring value for their price. Similarly, speaking and taking a collection, like working and being paid wages, were not tokens of dependence, for speaking was work for the good.

In 1879 Truth read this theme of independence backwards into the 1840s, recalling her earliest days among abolitionists, before the publication of the *Narrative of Sojourner Truth*. Beginning to make her way at antislavery meetings, she would sell sheets printed with her original song lyrics for 5–10 cents each. She prided herself on an early autonomy: "I was selling songs; for I always had something to pay my way with. Nobody paid me, for I was a free agent, to go and come when I pleased."[14]

A sale of anything, creative work or not, by a person with a black face at an antislavery meeting was invariably accompanied by a frisson of charity. But the better known Truth became, the more she became a celebrity, for whom the sale of the self in American culture carries no hint of charity. The satisfaction Americans take from encounters with celebrity became the currency of Truth's old age.

Truth's photographs gave her an intangible independence, liberating her from the printed words of others. She sat for her first photographic portraits within a month of the publication of Stowe's "Libyan Sibyl." Truth could not write, but she could project herself photographically. Photographs furnished a new means of communication—one more powerful than writing. They allowed Truth to circumvent genteel discourse and the racial stereotype embedded in her nation's language.

As a woman whose person had been the property of others and who remembered being degraded, Truth could cherish her portraits as her own literal embodiment: a refutation of having deserved abuse; a visible rendering of the internal spirit otherwise trapped within. Images like hers were largely missing from American culture, even from the feminist and antislavery subcultures.

Altogether Truth sat for at least fourteen photographic portraits in seven sittings between 1863 and about 1875. Her photographs are in two formats: *cartes-de-visite* (3 1/4″ x 2 1/4″) and cabinet cards (6 1/2″ x 4 1/4″). In the 1860s and 1870s, she stocked copies of these photographs and the *Narrative* to sell through the mail and wherever she made personal appearances. While donations of any size were welcome, Truth seems to have asked about 33 cents for each *carte-de-visite* and 50 cents for the larger cabinet cards, in line with the prices of photographers and publishers: $2.00 to $3.00 per dozen in the early 1860s, less later on.[15]

The substance that Truth supported by selling the shadow went beyond her bodily subsistence, beyond historical memory, to the preservation of her physical image in material artifacts. Had she not reached out to photography, we would lack images of Sojourner Truth fully and respectably clothed. We would see her only at a washtub in the Northampton Association; as William Wetmore Story's *Libyan Sibyl;* or as the field slave at the frontispiece of her *Narrative*. The photographs insist: "I am a woman."

Black woman as lady went against the commonplaces of nineteenth-century American culture. But by circulating her photographs widely, Truth claimed womanhood for a black woman who had been a slave, occupying a space ordinarily off limits to women like her. She refused to define herself by her enslavement.[16]

Seizing on a new technology, Truth established what few nineteenth-century black women were able to prove: that she was present in her times. Her success in distributing her portraits plays no small role in her place in historical memory. Our world, so attuned to images, focuses on the woman whose image is accessible. Given the near absence of black women from nineteenth-century iconography, Truth's *cartes-de-visite* alone would place her at the forefront of black women of her era. Although the composed persona of the photographs conflicts with the thrilling character of the word portraits, the photographs give life to the symbol.

21

Presidents

SOJOURNER TRUTH saw the dawning of a new era in American history in Abraham Lincoln's signing the District of Columbia Emancipation Act in 1862, and the Emancipation Proclamation in 1863. Thrilled, she determined to make her first trip to the nation's capital in 1864. Fifty miles south of Baltimore, Washington was thoroughly southern, but it was now in the land of freedom—the capital of a nation waging war on southern institutions.

Truth announced her intentions in one of her open letters to the *National Anti-Slavery Standard* in February 1864: "I believe the Lord means me to do what I want to do, viz; to go east in the Spring . . . to see the freedmen of my own race." She also intended to see the "first Antislavery President."[1] Truth's fervent and un-stinting commitment to Lincoln led her to embroider her account of their meeting. Setting out, she had no inkling of the retouching that would become necessary in this—and other presidential cases.

Truth's friends had raised enough money to send her and her grandson Samuel Banks on their journey through the East. She and Banks left Battle Creek in the middle of 1864. They stopped often to visit friends and let Truth make campaign speeches for Lincoln's reelection.

In Boston she talked with Harriet Tubman, already well known among abolitionists for escaping from slavery on Maryland's Eastern Shore and returning some nineteen times to rescue her enslaved family, friends, and neighbors.[2] Tubman had earned the appellation "Moses" by bringing more than two hundred people out of bondage.

Truth and Tubman, now so often confounded in the popular mind, did have a lot common—in adventurous pasts, intimate connection with God, singing, and ways of knowing independent of literacy. Both had been hardworking farmers as enslaved girls; doing men's work made them strong and dauntless. The circumstances that made each woman free had also cost each her marriage.[3] As adults, they had made their living like the majority of American women of all races who were not in the field: as household workers. Truth had lived with wealthy people who employed her, often—as in the case of the Latourettes and Elijah Pierson in New York City—as a near equal. Tubman had found employment in hotels where a shifting clientele did not encourage interaction between workers and guests.[4]

The antislavery movement had of course engaged both Truth and Tubman, though in the mid- to late 1850s, Truth was more likely to be found on the platform, and Tubman in the crowd. Both were among the many friends, houseguests, and beneficiaries of a wealthy upstate New York abolitionist, Gerrit Smith (Elizabeth Cady Stanton's cousin). Truth was a generation older than Tubman, who was born in about 1821; we are uncertain about Tubman's birthdate in Maryland, just as we are uncertain of precisely when Truth was born in New York.

Truth was solidly built and nearly six feet tall—reporters called her gaunt, but not slender. Tubman was short, around five feet, and slight. Although Truth could play the naif on the lecture platform, she was also known for her self-confidence as a public speaker and the dignity of her dress and demeanor. Despite her early years in the country, Truth was every inch a northern urbanite. Tubman, whose upper front teeth were missing, was usually dressed in neat but coarse, Quaker-style clothing. Both had worked in barns and parlors, but the mark of southern fields was indelible on Tubman.[5]

Harriet Tubman as a scout for the Union Army. Frontispiece,
Scenes in the Life of Harriet Tubman, by Sarah Bradford
(Auburn, NY, 1869). Photo by Firestone Library,
Princeton University.

Three decades after their encounter, Tubman said that she and
Truth had differed over Lincoln's intentions toward black people.
Truth placed great emphasis on the Emancipation Proclamation,
but Tubman was skeptical. She had been with black Union troops
in South Carolina and knew they were paid less than whites. In

this discrimination she saw Lincoln's hand. Neither woman persuaded the other in August 1864. Immediately afterward, Truth
met Lincoln and published a laudatory open letter in the anti-
slavery press. Her visit, she said, had featured a welcoming and respectful Lincoln. Truth's letter persuaded Tubman that she was
wrong. "Yes," she said many years later, "I'm sorry now I didn't
see Mr. Lincoln and thank him."[6]

THE PRESIDENT Truth visited in 1864 was already known as the
Great Emancipator. He had succeeded where every other American chief executive had failed. Although his measures were dictated by strategy rather than moral conviction and were drawn as
narrowly as possible, Lincoln had set history in motion. Truth was
his ardent adherent, and the journey to Washington was her first
venture onto the campaign trail.

Lincoln was from Illinois, a state divided on both slavery and
the Union cause, with an ample number of negrophobes on both
sides of both issues. His wife came from the slaveholding Todd
family of Lexington, Kentucky. Mary Todd Lincoln's closest companion was her dressmaker and personal attendant, Elizabeth
Keckley, a Virginian and former slave of enormous discretion;
Keckley never sought to attend social gatherings, even public receptions in the White House. Throughout Lincoln's two adminis-
trations, such receptions remained off limits to blacks.

In Washington, Truth discovered that the "Libyan Sibyl" was
not sufficiently prominent to enter the White House. Someone with
influence had to open the way even for her to wait outside Lincoln's office. That someone was Elizabeth Keckley. Not only did
she dress the first lady and chat with the Lincoln family and staff
on a regular basis, she also led a local freedpeople's relief society.
President and motivating spirit of the 1862 Ladies' Contraband Relief Association, Keckley encountered everyone in Washington
working in freedpeople's relief. Unlike Truth, Keckley and other
middle-class black Washingtonians did not work closely with the
various freedpeople's aid associations chartered by white abolitionists. Middle-class black people and middle-class white people
could not work together, even toward the same end. They did, how-

ever, make each other's acquaintance enough for Truth's friend Lucy Colman to secure Keckley's aid in taking Truth to meet the President.

In 1868, Keckley published her narrative, *Behind the Scenes. Or, Thirty Years a Slave, and Four Years in the White House.* It met a hostile reception in the press, which mocked it as "Inside President Lincoln's Kitchen," and unjustly accused Keckley of abusing Mary Todd Lincoln's confidence. A burlesque was entitled *"Behind the Seams" By a Nigger Woman who took in work from Mrs. Lincoln and Mrs. Davis.* The work listed no author, but its preface was signed with an "X" said to be the mark of "Betsey Kickley."[7] Keckley's autobiography said much about the Lincolns but nothing about Sojourner Truth.

Keckley had a keen sense of relative power. She could hardly have imagined that her own stature would rise by having done a good deed for a woman of as little social standing as Truth. Writing in the late 1860s, Keckley could not foresee that as many people would be intrigued later by Sojourner Truth as by Mary Todd Lincoln. Black women, after all, were not viewed as candidates for greatness. No one then saw incongruity in Harriet Tubman's getting down on her hands and knees to scour the filth left in the Colored Orphan Asylum.[8]

At any rate, Keckley was generous toward Truth and used her connections on her behalf. Truth and her white companion, Lucy Colman, secured an appointment to see Lincoln at 8:00 A.M. on Saturday, 29 October 1864. Truth described the visit in her open letter two months later. As they waited, she and Colman watched the people speaking with the President. They also chatted with fellow visitors, one a black woman who needed—and received, thanks to Lucy Colman—the President's help to prevent her eviction. According to Truth's open letter, President Lincoln then welcomed them warmly; he stood up to greet Truth and shook her hand. Both were gestures of civility that whites rarely offered to blacks at the time.

Truth's remarks to Lincoln placed him in the biblical Book of Daniel:

Mr. President, when you first took your seat, I feared you would be torn to pieces: for I likened you unto Daniel, who was thrown into the

Frontispiece to Lucy Colman's *Reminiscences* (Buffalo,
1892). Photo courtesy of the John Shaw Pierson Civil War
Collection, Department of Rare Books and Special
Collections, Princeton University Libraries.

lion's den; for if the lions did not tear you to pieces, I knew it would
be God that had saved you; and I said if He spared me, I would see
you before the four years had expired. And He has done so, and I am
now here to see you for myself.

Lincoln congratulated her on having been spared. She called him
"the best President ever," to which he demurred. Lincoln said that
some of his predecessors, particularly George Washington, were

just as good men, but they lacked the opportunity that secession had presented him. Had the Confederacy not seceded, he would have had no chance to act against slavery.

Truth said she gave him one of her photographs and a song. Lincoln thanked her and showed her a splendid Bible, "beautiful beyond description," which the colored people of Baltimore had presented him.[9] She remarked upon the irony of the colored people's giving a book to the head of the United States. A few years earlier, she said, the laws of this same government had prevented black people from learning to read that very book.

Lincoln signed Truth's autograph book: "For Auntie Sojourner Truth, October 29, 1864. A. Lincoln." She thanked him, grateful for an autograph from the hand that had signed the Emancipation Proclamation.

Truth concluded: "I am proud to say that I never was treated with more kindness and cordiality than I was by the great and good man Abraham Lincoln, by the grace of God President of the United States for four years more."[10] Two giants, Truth and Lincoln, had met, recognizing each other's greatness and treating each other with mutual respect. The version of this letter that appears in the *Narrative of Sojourner Truth* adds an exchange in the middle of Truth's interview that augments these impressions. In this insertion, Truth admitted to Lincoln that she had never heard of him before he became President. "He smilingly replied, 'I had heard of you many times before that.' "[11]

This heart-warming account flourished for more than a century, endlessly embroidered and embellished. Truth becomes a frequent visitor to the White House, her advice solicited by the President.[12] But years after Lincoln's assassination and the dissipation of antislavery politics, Truth's friend Lucy Colman published the story behind the story. This version is closer to prevailing attitudes and scholarly appraisals of Lincoln's racial consciousness.

In Colman's narrative, she and Truth waited three and a half hours as Lincoln joked with male visitors. During that time, a black woman supplicant joined them, and Colman brought her along into Lincoln's office. Lincoln found himself in the presence of three women, two black and one white.

Colman recalled that Lincoln's demeanor changed when he

turned from his white male visitors to Truth, whom Colman introduced as "my friend, Sojourner Truth, a woman widely known, not only in our country, but abroad."[13] Having been relaxed and funny, Lincoln became tense and sour. He called Truth " 'Aunty' . . . as he would his washerwoman," Colman recalled, and he rejected the honor Truth offered him as the first antislavery President.[14] In light of Lincoln's pique, Colman ushered Truth out. The President then called back Colman, not Truth, to help him with the other black woman. Colman sorted out her problem, and they were off. Being loved as the Great Emancipator irritated Lincoln, Colman realized: "He believed in the white race, not in the colored, and did not want them put on an equality."[15]

Other evidence sustains Colman's version. Truth and Frederick Douglass had each been chagrined by initially being turned away from public receptions at the Lincoln White House, though each, upon being called to the President's attention, was allowed in as a special favor.[16] Giles Stebbins, one of Truth's oldest abolitionist friends, drew similar conclusions: Truth "had met Abraham Lincoln, and he, a born Kentuckian, could call her 'anty' in the old familiar way. . . ."[17]

Frederick Douglass came down on both sides. Twelve years after Truth went to see the President, Douglass said that "In his interests, in his associations, in his habits of thought, and in his prejudices, [Abraham Lincoln] was a white man. He was preeminently the white man's President, entirely devoted to the welfare of white men."[18] But Douglass sometimes presented Lincoln as innocent of racial prejudice. Truth and Douglass had their motives for making Lincoln appear as broad-minded as possible. One was a reason of state: Whatever Lincoln's personal limitations, his politics were the best to be had. The other was more personal: When Lincoln patronized them, he violated Truth and Douglass's self-presentation as people commanding respect. The narrowness of Lincoln's spirit threatened to diminish their stature as well.

LINCOLN was Truth's first President, but not her last. She visited with Andrew Johnson and Ulysses S. Grant, who were both cordial, if hurried.[19] Colman again arranged the visit with Johnson, who found Truth easier to deal with than the delegation of black men, headed by Frederick Douglass and George T. Downing (formerly of Isabella's New York City), that sought his support for black suffrage. Johnson would hear nothing of black voting. Instead, he harangued his visitors on his expertise in handling slaves and his knowledge of the Negro. After Douglass's delegation departed, Johnson called them "those d----d sons of b-----s," and complained to his secretary that Douglass was "just like any nigger" and "would sooner cut a white man's throat than not."[20] Among white Washingtonians at the time, Johnson's sentiments were more prevalent than Douglass's.

Truth saw Grant with the assistance of General O. O. Howard of the Freedmen's Bureau, and Giles Stebbins, who accompanied Truth to the White House. Stebbins admitted that the visit began awkwardly: "She expressed her pleasure at meeting him, yet I could see it was not quite easy on either side. . . . Grant was reticent yet kindly." But Stebbins went on to portray a long and warm conversation. Truth thanked Grant for signing the Civil Rights Bill; Grant said it had been a pleasure. Stebbins concluded: "As we were about to leave President Grant rose to his feet and gave her his hand, with a parting word of sincere good will. This mutual respect and sympathy between the president of a great republic and a woman representing an oppressed and despised people was inspiring and admirable."[21]

As in the case of Lincoln, other evidence darkens this rosy picture. In the "Book of Life" section of the *Narrative*, Truth admits that Grant was dreadfully hurried when he gave her his autograph.[22] But partisan politics dictated a version more congenial to abolitionists who had become Republicans. The Civil War brought abolitionists into politics, and politics shaped sunny narratives of human decency.

22

Washington's
Freedpeople

BEFORE the war, Washington was a sleepy, unfinished village of muddy streets full of foraging hogs, animal carcasses, and sewage. But by the time Sojourner Truth and Samuel Banks arrived in the fall of 1864, it was a bustling center of war. Its population had more than doubled in two years, and tens of thousands of former slaves from Maryland and Virginia now took refuge in its unsympathetic embrace.

White southerners had been the main beneficiaries of federal patronage, and their dominance made wartime Washington a nest of "secesh": supporters of the secessionist Confederacy.[1] Republicans saw Washingtonians as "rebels in heart." The poet Walt Whitman, working as a nurse, thought them "secesh of the most venomous kind—they say nothing; but the devil snickers in their faces. . . ."[2]

Washington was a hard place to visit. The antislavery New York editor Horace Greeley disliked this place where "the rents are high, the food is bad, the dust is disgusting, the mud is deep and the morals are deplorable."[3] The city had been planned early in the century, but in the 1860s the roads were paved only intermittently. An English visitor warned that trying to follow Massachusetts Avenue from a map was hazardous: "[Y]ou will find yourself not only out of town, away among the fields, but you will find yourself beyond the fields, in an uncultivated, undrained wilderness."[4] The capital lacked a street railroad until 1860. It began as a Jim Crow institution.

Washington was a slaveholding city until local emancipation by an act of Congress in mid-1862, its black population closely confined by punitive black codes that imposed a curfew and proscribed black businesses. After emancipation and repeal of the black codes, racial discrimination still permeated everyday life. Streetcars were desegregated by federal law in March 1865, but they seldom stopped for blacks, even for a woman in her late sixties in need of public transportation. They caused Sojourner Truth endless aggravation and even personal injury. But not without a struggle: She knew her rights and insisted on having them.

Trying to enter a streetcar behind Josephine Griffing, Truth was dragged several yards because the conductor would not wait for her to mount. She and Griffing took down the conductor's number, contacted the president of the company, a sympathetic northerner, and had the conductor dismissed.

During the battle between Truth and the Washington streetcars, she once signaled a car whose driver and conductor passed her by, pretending not to see her. Another car followed, its driver evidently about to take the same tack. Truth raised her hand and shouted at the top of her lungs: "I want to ride! *I want to ride!!* I WANT TO RIDE!!!" She stopped not only the streetcar but all the other traffic in the vicinity, wedging the streetcar in place. While it was blocked, Truth got on, to the amusement of other passengers, who laughed, "Ha! ha! ha!! She has beaten him." The conductor, not amused, ordered her to "Go forward where the horses are, or I will throw you out." But Truth would not be cowed. No timid Virginian or Marylander, she said she was from the Empire State and knew the laws as well as he did. She stood her ground and rode with the other passengers.[5] A few weeks later, another encounter proved less triumphant.

This time Truth was with a colleague from Michigan, Laura Haviland. Used to being bypassed when alone, Truth expected to be able to ride in the company of a respectable white woman. But an exiting passenger alerted the conductor to her presence by shouting, "[H]ave you got room for niggers here?" The conductor ordered Truth off, and when she stood her ground, he tried to throw her off, wrenching her right arm. Haviland stepped into the fray and pulled the conductor away from Truth. He asked Haviland, "Does she belong to you?" If so, she should take the black woman inside the streetcar and get out of the way.

Haviland answered: "She does not belong to me, but she belongs to Humanity and she would have been out of the way long ago, if you had let her alone." Again, Haviland and Truth noted his number and had the conductor dismissed. Owing to her injury, Truth took the case a step further. She had the conductor arrested and convicted of assault and battery.[6]

Heartbreaking anecdotes became evidence of Truth's pluck, as though uncertainty and physical violence did no lasting damage to her psyche and old frame. But they did. Truth fell ill in the winter of 1866 with pain in her shoulders undoubtedly aggravated by this attack. Such injury was not unusual among black Americans seeking to use public transportation in the nineteenth and twentieth centuries.

Earlier, in 1865, Harriet Tubman had been injured in New Jersey by a conductor and three other men who dragged her out of her seat and threw her into the baggage car.[7] At a time when black civil rights were a lively subject of debate, public transportation throughout the Northeast and in the nation's capital offered daily and nasty lessons in reality. But the war between black people and the railroads began earlier and lasted much longer.

Before the Civil War, Frederick Douglass and David Ruggles had come to blows with conductors trying to deprive them of their seats. In 1858, the most prominent African-American author of the time, Frances Ellen Watkins Harper, had a series of humiliating and bruising altercations on interurban and street railroads in Pennsylvania. George T. Downing reported a railroad altercation during Reconstruction. And after a violent encounter with a train conductor in Tennessee, Ida B. Wells went to court in 1884 for the right to ride first class on a first-class ticket. Examples are legion in the long Jim Crow experience of middle-class blacks.[8]

AFTER meeting President Lincoln, Truth spent three weeks with the feminist journalist Jane Swisshelm, Frances Dana Gage's rival in Akron in 1851. Like Gage and Truth, Swisshelm had been drawn into social work through supporting local Union soldiers. Less well connected than Truth, Swisshelm had not met the President. But she did receive a clerkship in the War Department, where she remained for the duration of the war.[9] Volunteering as a nurse, Swisshelm ran her own newspaper in Washington, the *Reconstructionist*. She did not join the antislavery cohort involved in freedpeople's relief, but she was abolitionist enough to offer a black woman hospitality.

Truth was a celebrity in Washington among the antislavery social workers and their constituents. She held several meetings, including two well-attended benefits for the Colored Soldiers' Aid Society in the Reverend Henry Highland Garnet's Presbyterian church. There she doubtless encountered Washington's black bourgeoisie and philanthropists, such as Elizabeth Keckley and Harriet Jacobs. Truth also spoke at the great celebration of Maryland emancipation in December 1864, where, again, she was with respectable colored Washingtonians.[10]

No record remains of Truth's interactions with Washington's black bourgeoisie. The explanation may lie in the historical process: Truth comes down to us in history mainly through letters in the antislavery press dictated to white friends more interested in slaves and freedpeople than in blacks culturally like themselves. Or perhaps the explanation lies closer to home. By her own lights, Truth may not have valued exchanges with African-American colleagues enough to have them recorded. Only her adoption of fashionable clothing, as revealed in her photographs, hints that she had discovered new associates with more colorful tastes.

TRUTH and Banks's first stop in Washington in 1864 was the refugee camp run by the Reverend D. B. Nichols on Mason's (now Roosevelt) Island. Nichols had first come to Washington as a representative of the Congregationalist-sponsored American Missionary Association, and stayed on as Superintendent of Contrabands for the District of Columbia in May 1862.[11] The Mason's Island camp was one of several the government had set up to house Virginia and Maryland slaves who were fleeing to freedom from the chaos wrought by war. About eleven thousand of the forty thousand black people moving to the Washington area in the mid-1860s were refugees who passed through these camps.[12]

The refugees later came in for much criticism (some from Sojourner Truth) for living in idleness off government largesse, but residents shouldered much of the cost of running the camps. They paid for them and for the Freedmen's Hospital through the withholding of $5 per month from their wages as teamsters and laborers employed by the Quartermaster Corps.[13]

Fugitive slaves in the District (and elsewhere in proximity to theaters of war) were called "contrabands," a term that Union General Benjamin F. Butler had applied to fugitives seeking refuge in Fortress Monroe, at Hampton Roads, Virginia, in May 1861. By considering runaway slaves as contraband of war, Butler found a pretext for not returning fugitives while the Fugitive Slave Act still remained in force. But turning fugitives into contraband also made the federal government the owner of several thousand people.[14] In the non-Confederate city closest to actual hostilities, black refugees quickly became a serious economic problem.

From the end of 1864 through 1868, Truth worked in refugee relief at various camps for the National Freedmen's Relief Association and the Freedmen's Bureau. Headquartered in New York, the National Freedmen's Relief Association was one of many private organizations that helped refugees from slavery to freedom beginning in 1862. The creation of abolitionists, these private freedpeople's relief organizations raised $3–$4 million and supplied volunteers in an effort that inspired the 1865 creation of the federal government's Bureau of Refugees, Freedmen, and Abandoned Lands—popularly known as the Freedmen's Bureau.[15]

The relief effort remained tangled, a mixture of public and private, paid and unpaid support. The National Freedmen's Relief Association provided Truth room and board and sometimes an additional stipend (as, in 1868, $20 for the month of December). In addition, Truth received $390, in 1870, for twenty-six months of work with the Freedmen's Bureau. (She applied the money to the

Freedpeople's shanties, Washington, DC, 1860s. Photo courtesy of the
Mathew Brady Collection, National Archives Still Pictures Branch.

mortgage on her house in Battle Creek.) Lucy Colman occupied a
similarly mixed place as superintendent of the National Freedmen's Relief Association's schools in Washington.[16]

In 1864, Truth's National Freedmen's Relief Association–Freedmen's Bureau post was the Arlington Heights, Virginia, Freedmen's
Village. Her host was the superintendent, a name-dropping
Philadelphian, Captain George B. Carse.[17] Freedmen's Village had
been created out of the Custis-Lee estate of Robert E. Lee and his
wife, the daughter of George Washington's foster son, George W.
Custis. The federal government had seized the property on Arlington Heights early in the Civil War and used it for an army camp
and cemetery, before adding the freedpeople's camp in 1863. In
October 1866, Freedmen's Village consisted of 90 people considered old and infirm at the "Home," plus 250 families renting small
houses and garden plots in the Village.[18]

Like everyone else associated with management of the freedpeople's camps, Carse was delighted with "the great service ren-

dered to the Freedmen and their families by Sojourner." In exchange for visits to the freedpeople and the dispensing of sound
advice on moral living and northern-style sewing, knitting, and
cooking, Truth received use of a house of her own and a meeting
hall. As she had advised black New Yorkers in the 1850s, Truth
exhorted the freedpeople to "[b]e clean, be clean, for cleanliness
is a part of godliness." Seize whatever opportunities they could,
she advised, to acquire education and advance themselves.

Truth's mission was unique, Carse thought, for while white
workers could teach ex-slaves household skills, only another black
person could speak to them frankly. He reported her message to
the refugees in Freedmen's Village:

> she told them they must learn to love the white people, and that they
> had many friends in the North who had been advocating their cause
> for years and were still doing so; that they must learn to be indepen-
> dent—learn industry and economy—and above all strive to show the
> people that they could *be something*.[19]

To Carse's mind, Truth's audience accepted her preaching. Truth
herself had her doubts.

One audience of freedpeople threw Truth out of the building
when she told them they were "in disgrace" for living "off the government."[20] Writing to Amy Post after leaving Freedmen's Village
for similar work at Freedmen's Hospital, Truth acknowledged her
mixed reception. Her service as councillor "for my people" had
been acceptable to "the good" among them, "but not at all times
to those who desire nothing higher than the lowest and the vilest
of habits." Truth flattered herself that differences in status explained differences in her reception. She said she had received only
the "kindest attention" from people in power, including the President.[21]

Freedpeople's relief entailed additional frustrations. Truth
shared other volunteers' conviction that few officers in the Freedmen's Bureau took freedpeople's needs to heart. Josephine Griffing, who joined the Freedmen's Bureau in 1865 after serving as an
agent of the National Freedmen's Relief Association, complained
that the Bureau was replacing abolitionists with pro-slavery army

officers. For her part, Truth grumbled about "the devil" with whom she had to deal. She referred most likely to a Captain Alfred W. Lomas, who succeeded Carse as superintendent of the Freedmen's Village in June 1865 and forced residents to work by reducing their rations.[22]

Truth, Griffing, and Julia Wilbur, the abolitionist from Rochester, accused Freedmen's Bureau officers of neglecting freedpeople and working only for the pay.[23] Meanwhile, conservatives within Congress attacked the Bureau for doing too much, for interfering with natural economic processes. As a consequence of many conflicting pressures, fiscal as well as political, the Bureau soon wound down its operations. It severely curtailed its mission by 1867 and virtually closed its doors in 1868.

WITH the end of the war, Washington's economy soured. The jobs disappeared, and without work there could be no new life. Con-

Barracks at the Freedmen's Village, Arlington Heights, Virginia, where Truth lived and taught in the 1860s. The Village was on the site of what is now Arlington Cemetery. Photo courtesy of the Library of Congress.

gressional support for freedpeople's relief had waned quickly, but the needs of the District's refugees increased.

Inflation aggravated a bad situation, as every necessity of life at least doubled in price. Lewis Douglass, newly appointed to a government clerkship, earned an excellent salary of $100 per month, but the cheapest lodging he could find cost $25 per month. Soaring housing costs (up 344 percent between the outbreak of the war and 1866) defeated ordinary workers. Most working refugees made far less than Douglass: Men made less than $5 and women rarely as much as $4 per month. Ten dollars was excellent pay.[24] For freedpeople entering Washington without money, property, or education, conditions were insufferable.

Josephine Griffing proposed that the Freedmen's Bureau create an office to place unemployed freedpeople in jobs outside Washington. The result, the Freedmen's Intelligence and Employment Agency, placed 5,192 people in jobs in 1865 and 1866 with the energetic support of Griffing and the National Freedmen's

Association.[25] Rather than charging the freedpeople for the services they used, as in early contraband relief, the Bureau shifted the costs to employers, who paid 50 cents for hiring each woman and $1.00 for each man.[26]

The diminution of the Freedmen's Bureau in 1867 took it out of the employment business, but the need for jobs remained staggering.[27] An agent of the Bureau reported being "perfectly horrified at the tales of suffering and want I listened to." Griffing herself described what she found on her rounds:

> Most of these families occupy but one room, in many cases parts of several families are eating, sleeping, propagating and dying in the same room, with but few or no household utensils or facilities to observe the laws of health; or the rules of society.[28]

These crowded conditions spawned a degree of suffering, crime, and disease that appalled Truth and Griffing.

Like many Americans, even friends of the race, Truth cast unemployment in moral terms. She excoriated jobless freedpeople who stayed in Washington as idlers stealing from the government. The race would never get ahead, she feared, if grown men accepted government handouts instead of finding honest work. Sojourner Truth the itinerant preacher proclaimed work as a duty, even when it meant journeying very far from home.

On their own, Truth and Griffing tried to continue the work of the Freedmen's Intelligence and Employment Agency. Throughout the spring and summer of 1867, they placed Washington refugees with employers in other states, notably Michigan and New York. In Battle Creek, Truth's faithful helpers were her friends Frances Titus and Henry Willis. In Rochester, it was the Posts.

Truth later claimed to have placed one hundred refugees. Griffing, working with the Freedmen's Bureau and with Truth, helped between three thousand and five thousand find jobs outside Washington between 1865 and 1868. The federal and private efforts together placed more than eight thousand refugees primarily in Battle Creek, Brockport, Providence, and Rochester. Yet despite such impressive numbers, an odor of failure clung to the entire effort.[29]

The failure to place larger numbers of refugees is not hard to explain, for the demand for labor did not match the supply. Refugees—the labor supply—came to the camps in family groups, with many young children and old people. Employers did not want to hire families; they wanted young men for farm work and women for household help. Few asked for youngsters or elders, let alone the ill and infirm. Faced with the choice between distant employment and their families, most able-bodied refugees stayed in Washington to care for their own.

Soon the blame for the persistence of distressing numbers of unemployed refugees came to rest squarely on the refugees themselves. For Truth as for many others, their reluctance to leave their families for Rochester or other unfamiliar, northern places proved their moral deficiency.

Truth and Griffing's independent employment service did not last long. Two women alone could not compensate for the resources the federal government had withdrawn from the effort. They were bound to meet with frustration. To make matters worse, Truth was hurt by an insinuation amounting to a stab in the back. Julia Wilbur, another volunteer in the Arlington Heights Freedmen's Village, suggested that Truth's collections for job placement appeared to be going into her own pocket.[30] Truth gave up the employment project in the fall of 1867.[31]

Acting on a desire she had voiced the previous year, she returned to Battle Creek, bought a lot with a barn, and asked her abolitionist colleagues for money to help her fix it up. Her withdrawal from the quixotic mission with Griffing did not, however, signal a loss of ambition to resettle freedpeople on land of their own. After Washington, she kept the goal but changed her tactics. She also turned to a reform that preoccupied many other abolitionists during Reconstruction: woman suffrage.

23

Woman Suffrage

In the midst of roaring debates over black and woman suffrage, Sojourner Truth said, "If colored men get their rights, and not colored women theirs, you see the colored men will be masters over the women, and it will be just as bad as it was before." This statement, though less well known than "ar'n't I a woman?" and the 1858 breast-baring incident, belongs to the symbolic Truth and has placed her at odds with other black abolitionists. While Frederick Douglass declares the era of Reconstruction the "Negro's hour," Truth stands beside Elizabeth Cady Stanton and Susan B. Anthony. With Stanton and Anthony, Truth sets votes for women above votes for black men. This picture, woven into the tapestry of Sojourner Truth in Stanton and Anthony's *History of Woman Suffrage*, shrouds Truth's support for black men's civil rights. It obscures the complexity of the woman suffrage movement in the 1860s.

Before the Civil War, Truth, Douglass, Stanton, Anthony, and their friends had worked together against slavery and racial discrimination and for women's rights without seeing these causes as conflicting. Douglass had been Stanton's staunchest supporter in demanding the vote as one of women's rights in 1848; Anthony had been a paid agent of the American Anti-Slavery Society.[1] Truth combined all the issues in her one body.

Most of the men and women who clamored loudest for woman suffrage after the Civil War had been energetic abolitionists. They were black and white, male and female: Stanton, Anthony, Douglass, Lucy Stone and her husband Henry Blackwell, Truth, Parker Pillsbury, Josephine Griffing, Charles Lenox Remond, Frances Dana Gage, Gerrit Smith, Frances Ellen Watkins Harper, William Lloyd Garrison, and Robert Purvis.[2] Douglass, Truth, Remond, Harper, and Purvis were black, but not of one mind as the suffrage issue evolved out of the older demand for women's rights.

Women's rights meant empowering women in a multitude of ways: securing women rights to their wages, their inheritance, and the custody of their children; admitting women to institutions of higher learning and the professions; and permitting women to vote, hold office, and serve on juries. This broad agenda dovetailed with the needs of black people, who also lacked a wide range of civil rights.

During the Civil War, the women's rights–abolitionist community held together seamlessly: In 1863, Stanton and Anthony formed the National Women's Loyal League, the first organization to petition Congress to make emancipation permanent and universal in a Thirteenth Amendment to the U.S. Constitution.[3] But Reconstruction tore abolitionists apart. Southern politics demanded black male suffrage, and black male suffrage galvanized feminists. Feminists glimpsed a victory of their own in the wings.

As long as anyone could remember, black men and (white) women had been powerless together. Now that black men were advancing, why not women? Julia Wilbur of Rochester, Sojourner Truth's co-worker in freedpeople's relief, discovered personal implications in black men's voting. Watching freedmen, whom she considered ignorant and superstitious, voting for the first time in the District of Columbia, Wilbur confessed she felt "a little jealous–the least bit humiliated." In the mid-1860s, words like "humiliation" and "degradation" would become common in one strand of woman suffrage rhetoric.[4]

Suffrage priorities—who should vote first—split reformers. From the breach emerged two competing woman suffrage communities, each seeking the blessing of Sojourner Truth.

ABOLITIONISM was breaking up in 1865. For William Lloyd Garrison, longtime president of the American Anti-Slavery Society, Confederate defeat and the Thirteenth Amendment closed the work of abolition. Suffrage of any sort was separate from emancipation. Many others, including Truth and Wendell Phillips, who then became president of the society, saw black suffrage as necessary to sustain emancipation. Events in Washington and the South reinforced their contention.

After Lincoln's assassination in April 1865, President Andrew Johnson pardoned large numbers of high-ranking former Confederates and welcomed readmission of Confederate states under the leadership of men once hostile to the Union. During the presidential Reconstruction in 1865–66, southern states passed black codes that virtually reproduced slavery. In 1866, a wave of terrorism swept the South. White supremacists murdered and raped black Republicans and their supporters in Memphis and New Orleans. As Phillips became president of the American Anti-Slavery Society, violence in the South was demonstrating that emancipation, of itself, would not transform southern society.

Without some counter to resurgent southern Democrats, the Civil War might just as well not have been fought and won by the Union. In this climate of violent reaction, the American Anti-Slavery Society under Phillips concentrated on the radical Republican goal of enfranchising black men. Blacks were the strongest supporters of the Union and the Republican party in the South, but black women could not be enfranchised without giving the vote to much larger numbers of white women—potential Democrats. Assuring black men the vote required further constitutional amendments, the Fourteenth and Fifteenth, which Congress passed and the states ratified between 1865 and 1870.

In this climate of unaccustomed political progress, universal suffrage supporters formed the Equal Rights Association, an organization important to Sojourner Truth. While she and many other abolitionists agreed with Douglass and Phillips that "This hour belongs to the Negro," she supported woman suffrage in tandem with black male suffrage.[5] Truth championed rights for blacks and for women in the name of black women.

Occupied in Washington with refugee freedpeople, Truth did not attend the founding meeting of the Equal Rights Association in New York in mid-May 1866, or its continuation in Boston at the end of the month.[6] But the poet Frances Ellen Watkins Harper spoke at both meetings, evidently the only black woman to take the floor.

Harper and Truth were a contrasting pair. Harper was born free in Baltimore in 1825 and educated by her abolitionist, schoolmaster uncle, William J. Watkins, also a woman suffragist.[7] After Maryland made it impossible for free blacks to reenter the state, she moved to Philadelphia. There she worked on the underground railroad with well-educated black people like William Still, and published in the African Methodist Episcopal Church's newspa-

Frances Ellen Watkins Harper, from *The Underground Railroad*, by William Still (Philadelphia, 1871). Photo courtesy of the Library Company of Philadelphia.

per, the *Christian Recorder*. In the 1850s, she honed her speaking skills as an agent of the Maine Anti-Slavery Society and published two volumes of poetry. After the death of her husband and the end of the Civil War, she toured the South as an advocate of black civil rights, temperance, education, and high moral standards.[8] Harper was a formidable figure.

Frances Ellen Watkins Harper was ladylike, "slender and graceful," with a speaking voice that was "soft" and "musical" even as it could be assertive.[9] She was too educated, too polished, and too respectable to be taken for an exotic or a foreign work of art. She was not a picturesque character who provoked laughter and affection. Truth was more of an entertainer, whose humor and biblical imagery softened her message. As an uneducated, dark-skinned ex-slave, Truth embodied a black female authenticity that white audiences could not find in Harper.

In the 1866 meetings, Harper sounded vexing themes—themes of race and gender that are with us still. Except on the ideal of women's enfranchisement, she disagreed up and down with Stanton and Anthony. Had formal emancipation in 1865 given black men advantage over white women? Harper said no, Stanton and Anthony said yes. Would the vote, of itself, satisfy the needs of all women? Stanton and Anthony said yes. Harper, pointing to the legacies of class discrimination, slavery, and racism in the lives of poor black women, said no.[10] With Truth and other abolitionists, Harper saw as ongoing the work of emancipation in the South.

An early womanist, Harper refused to separate her sex from her race. Black women were women, she insisted; their concerns were *women's* issues, just as the concerns of white women were women's issues. Most abolitionists were content to pretend that woman suffrage meant the same thing to women of all races. The woman in woman suffrage could be black, white, or red. Harper shredded the pretense. She could hear white women silently appending "white" and "middle-class" to their definition of "woman," and she took them on:

> You white women speak here of rights. I speak of wrongs. I, as a colored woman, have had in this country an education which has made me feel as if I were in the situation of Ishmael, my hand against every

man, and every man's hand against me. Let me go tomorrow morning and take my seat in one of your street cars . . . and the conductor will put up his hand and stop the car rather than let me ride.

Discrimination in transportation was a prime source of grief to black women, including Sojourner Truth. But the experience Harper mentioned at the 1866 meeting was Harriet Tubman's.

We have a woman in our country who has received the name of "Moses," not by lying about it, but by acting it out (applause)—a woman who has gone down into the Egypt of slavery and brought out hundreds of our people into liberty. The last time I saw that woman, her hands were swollen. That woman who had led one of [General] Montgomery's most successful expeditions, who was brave enough and secretive enough to act as a scout for the American army, had her hands all swollen from a conflict with a brutal conductor, who undertook to eject her from her place. That woman, whose courage and bravery won a recognition from our army and from every black man in the land, is excluded from every thoroughfare of travel. (Applause.)

This was black women's reality, Harper said, but white suffragists turned their backs. Until white women acknowledged black women's predicament, she would dismiss woman suffrage as a whites-only affair.

Anger threaded through her taunt to white women. They needed the vote for its educational value: "While there exists this brutal element in society which tramples upon the feeble and treads down the weak, I tell you that if there is any class of people who need to be lifted out of their airy nothings and selfishness, it is the white women of America."[11] This kind of talk was too strong for those soon to be the country's leading woman suffragists. Harper's speeches do not appear in Stanton and Anthony's *History of Woman Suffrage*. A different black woman was needed.

Who better than a celebrity ex-slave to dilute Harper's argument and refute her standing as the representative black woman? In May 1867, Anthony invited Sojourner Truth to a meeting of the Equal Rights Association in New York, and Stanton welcomed Truth as her houseguest. Harper remained in South Carolina, lecturing among the freedpeople. Throughout the convention, Stanton and

Anthony referred to Truth as "Mrs. Stowe's 'Lybian Sybil.' " They habitually misspelled "Libyan Sibyl."[12]

Truth's style was not barbed like Harper's; she disagreed indirectly, without attacking white women straight on. Instead of opposing Stanton and Anthony, she differed from them. Truth came to the podium after Stanton had spoken approvingly of rich southern white women. Acknowledging the cheers that greeted her, Truth warned the audience that had adored Stanton that "I come from another field—the country of the slave."

Stanton and Anthony rejected the Fourteenth Amendment because it introduced the word "male" into the Constitution for the first time. Truth justified it. They saw emancipation as over and done with. Truth stressed its fragility. Slavery had only partially been destroyed, she said, and liberty had not yet been achieved. Truth defended the political rights of black men and vindicated black women. Although she shared with Stanton the long-standing assumption that women owned themselves, Truth made the women in question black. Black women appeared rarely in Stanton's rhetoric. In 1867, Stanton was speaking less of women's self-ownership than of men as the protectors of women's rights.

The middle-class idea of men as protectors figured in Truth's argument only as an absence, one that has characterized black women's thinking for two centuries: "I feel that if I have to answer for the deeds done in my body just as much as a man, I have a right to have just as much as a man." This position was as far as possible from Stanton's argument that women must vote in order to balance the votes of inferior men.[13]

Truth said, "[t]here is a great stir about colored men getting their rights, but not a word about the colored women," and she spoke about women like herself. But when the Stanton-Anthony forces spoke of black women, it was to beat up black men. Paulina Wright Davis, for instance, claimed that freedwomen did not want to marry freedmen out of fear of losing their children and their earnings. Black women were smarter than black men, Davis held, because they had learned from their mistresses. Black men had learned from their masters and wanted only to whip their wives.[14] In the 1860s—as in later times—black women occasionally found white champions, but usually at the expense of black men.

When Truth pointed to the weaknesses of black men as an argument for black women's rights, she focused more on money than personal violence. Money was the context of her famous quote: "if colored men get their rights, and not colored women theirs, you see the colored men will be masters over the women, and it will be just as bad as it was before." Truth said that she wanted to keep agitating for woman suffrage before federal policy hardened.[15] White women needed the vote, but black women needed it even more, having less education and a more limited choice of jobs. "[W]ashing," she said, "is about as high as a colored woman gets."

These legal and economic suffrage arguments sprang from personal experience, for Truth as for Wilbur, Stanton, and Anthony. Recalling the refugees in Washington and perhaps the husbands of her hardworking daughters in Battle Creek, she depicted black men as strutting idlers: "when the women come home, they ask for their money and take it all, and then scold because there is no food." Her view of women's need for legal rights contained another jab at men, but men of a different standing. In Ulster County, Westchester, and Washington, she had been in court three times, she said: "In the courts women have no right, no voice; nobody speaks for them. I wish woman to have her voice there among the pettifoggers."

As a poor working woman, Truth knew life at the bottom of the economic ladder. While Stanton, grounded in her status as a woman of wealth and privilege, might rail at an educated woman's "humiliation" and "degradation" at being treated as the political inferior of poor men, Truth felt needs more economic than political. She returned repeatedly to a theme she had sounded as early as 1851: her right to equal remuneration because she worked like a man. This time she included immigrant women who labored:

> I have done a great deal of work; as much as a man, but did not get so much pay. I used to work in the field and bind grain, keeping up with the cradler; but men doing no more, got twice as much pay; so with the German women. They work in the field and do as much work, but do not get the pay. We do as much, we eat as much, we want as much.

Truth wanted money, and, more fundamentally, the independence that comes of having one's own money. "When we get our rights," she concluded, "we shall not have to come to you for money, for then we shall have money enough in our own pockets; and may be you will ask us for money."[16] A tantalizing prospect for one who so often had to beg money from colleagues for day-to-day survival. Truth's train of thought ranged far from the vote but stayed within the prevailing ideology of woman suffrage, equating women's voting with a recasting of the entire political economy.

After Truth's speech, George T. Downing took the floor. He asked Stanton, point-blank, if she opposed the enfranchisement of black men if women did not get the vote at the same time. Downing's question and Stanton's response went to the heart of the problem of Reconstruction for woman suffragists on all sides.

Speaking from the chair, Stanton first said she would not trust the black man to make laws for her, because "degraded, oppressed himself, he would be more despotic with the governing power than even our Saxon rulers are." If truly universal suffrage were not feasible, she preferred to enfranchise educated people first, for "this incoming tide of ignorance, poverty, and vice" must not be empowered. Without woman suffrage, only the "highest type of manhood" should vote and hold office.

In 1867, at a moment when racial conflict raged in the South, the Fourteenth Amendment waited with the states for ratification, and the meaning of emancipation was still unsettled, Stanton was repudiating the Republican policy of black male suffrage—perhaps not the strongest reed, but abolitionists' best tool for advancing the work of Reconstruction. In doing so, she touched off a firestorm.

Abby Kelley Foster took strenuous exception. Josephine Griffing, the most active woman suffragist in Washington, D.C., was glad that black men were getting the vote. In deep distress, Charles Remond refused to discriminate between a vote for black men or black women. He claimed for his wife and sister all that he claimed for himself.[17] After this heated exchange, a chasm divided the meeting.

Susan B. Anthony brought Truth back to the floor as ex-slave, exaggerating the injury to Truth's right hand and turning it into a drama of slavery: "one of her fingers was chopped off by her cruel master in a moment of anger."[18] Truth was a symbol of slavery rather than of Reconstruction. Everyone in the meeting agreed on slavery; it was Reconstruction that was tearing them apart. Truth lowered the heat and calmed the meeting by playing the part of funny old woman, more entertainer than advocate.

Truth tried to bridge the gulf opening between the political claims of race and of sex: "We are now trying for liberty that requires no blood—that women shall have their rights—not rights from you. Give them what belongs to them; they ask it kindly too. (Laughter). I ask it kindly."[19] She concluded with a funny story about Battle Creek taxes. Her comments, greeted with much laughter, also noted that she was a non-voting woman property owner subject to road taxes.

After the furious Downing-Stanton exchange on competing suffrages, Truth still occupied an intermediate position, along with Charles Remond. Others in the meeting, notably Henry Ward Beecher, the nation's most famous preacher and brother of Harriet Beecher Stowe, also tried not to choose. At this meeting, neither Truth nor Remond acknowledged the increasing distance in 1867 between black male suffrage, now within sight of its goal, and woman suffrage, still chimerical. But both tilted toward black people. Remond closed the meeting with a tribute to black men's service in the Revolutionary and Civil Wars, and Truth welcomed the day when the "colored people might own their soul and body." At this moment—when straddling was still possible in woman suffrage circles—Truth stood for both blacks and women without stating priorities.

TRUTH'S presence in their company served the Stanton and Anthony camp, even though her comments, in this extremely contentious meeting, set her gently on the side of the abolitionists who would soon repudiate Stanton and Anthony's position. The issues were the Fourteenth Amendment, allegiance to the Republican party, and whether black male suffrage should be held hostage to woman suffrage. On every one, Truth disagreed with Stanton and Anthony. In a letter to the *New York World*, Stanton let it be known that Truth was her amusing houseguest. But even the witticisms Stanton reported in her letter set Truth at odds with Stanton.

Stanton supported educational and property qualifications for voting, but Truth did not. She distinguished wisdom from education and worth from wealth. Stanton quoted Truth's denouncing literacy and property qualifications in her own trenchant style:

> You know, children, I don't read such small stuff as letters, I read men and nations. I can see through a millstone, though I can't see through a spelling-book. What a narrow idea a reading qualification is for a voter! I know and do what is right better than many big men who read. And what's that property qualification! just as bad! As if men and women themselves, who made money, were not of more value than the thing they made. If I were a delegate to the [New York] Constitutional Convention I could make suffrage as clear as daylight.[20]

The New York Constitutional Convention that Truth referred to terminated the forty-six-year-old property qualification for black male suffrage without enacting woman suffrage, further antagonizing the Stanton-Anthony faction.

IN 1867 and 1868, Stanton and Anthony set themselves increasingly at odds with their erstwhile comrades in reform who had refused to make woman suffrage their first priority. In Kansas and New York they allied themselves with Democrats willing to back woman suffrage in order to stymie black male enfranchisement. Their principal ally in Kansas, the notorious negrophobe George Francis Train, became their close friend and underwrote their newspaper, *The Revolution*. As they pulled farther away from the ideals of universal suffrage, their language grew increasingly nativist, racist, and classbound.

In the January 1869 meeting of the Equal Rights Association, which Josephine Griffing hosted in Washington, D.C., Stanton set a new note of stridency. She delivered a fiery keynote that disparaged the "dregs of China, Germany, England, Ireland, and Africa" who were polluting the American polity. Stanton thought it disgraceful that "Patrick and Sambo and Hans and Yung Tung" should make laws for women like herself. How could American politicians fall so low as to "make their wives and mothers the political inferiors of unlettered and unwashed ditch-diggers, bootblacks, butchers, and barbers, fresh from the slave plantations of the South, and the effete civilizations of the Old world . . ."? Poor men, black and white, endangered women's rights more than had southern slaveholders. She called universal manhood suffrage an "appalling question."[21]

Truth missed this meeting, but Harper, Douglass, and Stephen S. Foster, a veteran abolitionist and the husband of Abby Kelley Foster, did not. The men denounced Stanton for bigotry and disregard for the Reconstruction amendments so crucial in the South. For Douglass, this was a tragic moment. His beloved abolitionist community lay a pile of smoking ashes. He could only deplore Stanton's politics, but he had to pause to acknowledge the past generosity of his old friend and comrade in arms. Recalling her hospitality in the days when respectable white people turned away blacks, he praised her for personal freedom from racial prejudice.[22]

Harper, too, rushed to defend the morals and rights of freedmen. As black women so often have done when black men come under attack, Harper fell silent on the rights of black women. Concluding that she must now choose between her identity as a woman and her identity as a Negro, she abandoned black women and rallied to the side of black men: "[w]hen it was a question of race, she let the lesser question of sex go."[23] In the conflict between black men and white women, black women disappeared.

Torn apart in 1869, the Equal Rights Association gave way to two new organizations dedicated to woman suffrage. Stanton, Anthony, some old abolitionists (Josephine Griffing, for example), and many women new to the cause founded the all-female National Woman Suffrage Association (NWSA). The NWSA turned its back on black male suffrage and the issues of Reconstruction that as early as 1868 Anthony had declared the "dead questions of the past."[24]

Unable to stomach Stanton's rhetoric and Anthony's Democrats, supporters of black male suffrage and the Republican party in turn founded the American Woman Suffrage Association (AWSA). Its leaders, Lucy Stone and Henry Blackwell, had waged the Kansas campaign with Anthony but had no use for George Francis Train. Harper, also a founder, addressed AWSA meetings in 1873 and 1875.[25]

Truth still sought a middle road, avoiding NWSA/AWSA politics while speaking for women's political rights in generalities. In western New York from August to October 1868, she convened meetings nearly every day, speaking sometimes more than once a day. Over seventy at the time, she kept a strenuous schedule and addressed crowds that numbered in the thousands. Reports of this tour omit the content of her speeches, noting only that she spoke for more than an hour at a time "in her usually impressive and sarcastic manner, much to the satisfaction of the majority present."[26]

But a choice was unavoidable. Like Frances Dana Gage, who had also tried to straddle, Truth came finally to rest with the AWSA. She attended their meetings in New York in May 1870 and in Boston in January 1871.[27] Truth spoke briefly at the Boston meeting, saying that women ought to have their rights not only for themselves, as others had contended, but "for the benefit of the whole creation, not only the women, but all the men on the face of the earth, for they were the mothers of them." Woman deserved her "God-given right, and be the equal of men, for she was the resurrection of them."[28]

Even after finding her place in the AWSA, Truth sought to heal divisions in her community. In Battle Creek in 1872 she took a heroic step in concert with Susan B. Anthony and other friends in Rochester, including Amy Post. Truth voted—or at least tried to— in the presidential contest that reelected Ulysses S. Grant, for whom she had campaigned.[29] Anthony's arrest in Rochester made the 1872 vote a milestone in the history of woman suffrage. Truth's vote embedded her deeper in the Stanton-Anthony version of that history.

The passions that rent woman suffrage in 1869 kept its two branches at loggerheads for the next twenty years. Stanton and Anthony's strategies did little to advance the cause of woman suffrage, but their upper-class radicalism drew in a new generation of wealthy, young adherents. The less militant AWSA limped along under the inattentive leadership of Henry Ward Beecher. When the two groups reunited in 1890, the new National American Woman Suffrage Association carried Stanton and Anthony's stamp.

THE POLITICS of woman suffrage produced a new symbolic Truth—the Stanton-Anthony suffragist—and eventually gave new resonance to another—Gage's 1863 "ar'n't I a woman?" Truth. The Stanton-Anthony Truth tends first and last toward women. For her, the Fourteenth Amendment portends worry, not triumph, if "colored men get their rights" before women are enfranchised. This Truth blots out the womanism of Frances Ellen Watkins Harper, who would not separate the woman in her identity from the black. Only one strong black woman emerges from the white sea of the *History of Woman Suffrage:* Stanton and Anthony's Truth.

Even while creating its own Sojourner Truth, Stanton-Anthony suffragism amplified the need for Gage's Truth through its racial exclusivity. Coming of age after abolitionism and women's rights were one, the new generation turned its back on race and made "woman" white, middle- and upper-class. By the turn of the century, these new suffragists were reenacting Gage's drama of white women feminists afraid of blacks.

24

Kansas

DIVINE command drove Sojourner Truth to her last great mission, a "crowning work," the culmination of her whole life's experience.[1] Truth wanted the government to allot western land for resettlement of refugee freedpeople still unemployed in Washington, D.C. Her model was the Indian reservation. In the late 1860s and early 1870s, when she was agitating for her plan, Indian wars, and hence Indian policy, were much in the news. The abolitionist press featured Indian news alongside reports of atrocities in the Reconstruction South.[2]

Truth's work in Washington had impressed upon her the wages of destitution: depression, crime, perverted childhoods, and blighted adult lives. The refugee freedpeople "had a dreamy look, taking no note of time; it seemed as if a pause had come in their lives—an abyss, over whose brink they dared not look."[3] Her colonization plan was urgently necessary, "the only way to prevent a large amount of misery, degradation and crime in the present and future generations."[4] Such senseless human waste would make black independence impossible, and independence was now her desideratum in life. In the black "humbug idlers" of Washington, she detected a people becoming "trash."[5]

Unemployed, needy freedpeople still congregated in Washington in 1870. Scandalized that they should still be living off the government, Truth concluded that charity was making them lazy and thieving. "When I saw able men and women taking dry bread from the government to keep from starving," she said, she decided to devote herself "to the cause of getting land for these people, where they can work and earn their own living in the West. . . ."[6]

Truth, like Julia Wilbur, Frances Dana Gage, the freeborn, well-educated black Philadelphian Charlotte Forten, and other abolitionists who served in freedpeople's relief, recognized that freedpeople were "sinned against as well as sinning." Enslavement had rendered them dependent and deprived them of morals.[7] In 1870, slavery was a thing of the past, yet the freedpeople stagnated.[8] Something dramatic must occur lest the next generation inherit the debilities of slaves.

Envisioning massive resettlement, Truth was more ambitious than she and Griffing had been in 1867. In both initiatives—transporting freedpeople to jobs in the North and now colonization in the West—Truth was grappling with a problem as large and as old as civilization: How to get rid of poor people without redistributing wealth.

In a sense, early American history tells the story of attempts to solve this problem as posed in eighteenth-century England, Scotland, and Wales, and nineteenth-century Ireland. The African slave trade represented a variation on the theme. Entirely involuntary, it had conveyed captives to places where other people needed them as workers. Migration within America, largely a voluntary movement, inspired Truth as she worried about blacks in the nation's capital.

In the 1860s and 1870s, as in earlier times, black migration was no simple matter of going from here to there. As in so many aspects of American life, blacks encountered unique impediments when they acted on the same impulses as whites. Before the Civil War, states such as Indiana and Illinois crafted laws to discourage their entry, and Kansas was not open to settlement until the contentious mid-1850s. Black migration, even for the eager and able, remained severely constrained.

Truth's plan drew on what she saw of Gilded Age politics and ideas circulating among abolitionists and blacks. Could not the

West replicate the Freedmen's Village of Arlington Heights, Virginia, where she had worked in the mid-1860s, with "suitable buildings erected, and schools established where the now dependent thousands of colored people may go, and not only attain an independence for themselves, but become educated and respectable citizens"?[9] The federal government, she knew, had allotted millions of acres to Indian tribes and railroad companies. Why not put some of this land at the disposition of needy freedpeople, where they could "work and earn their own living"?[10]

As Truth and Griffing's experience had already demonstrated, relocating large groups of people required more than jobs. Freedpeople feared strange places would prove hostile. To be sure, a new employer might be tolerant, but somewhere trouble lay in wait. Accustomed to itinerancy and traveling alone, Truth usually disregarded their fears. When she did confront freedpeople's hesitancy, she blamed them for weakness. Government handouts made them "apathetic and indifferent," and the men were becoming shiftless. She mocked—in dialect—the response of able-bodied men who questioned the need to leave Washington: " 'What fo' I go way? gubernment feed me, gib me close, I's doin' well enuff,' and so say they all, or at least a great part of them."[11]

She gave little thought to persuading the people she would move. As in 1867, Truth the saviour knew what was best; with the help of northern supporters, she would deliver freedpeople to a better place. She and her friends would *get* them out of Washington and *put* them in the West.[12] Freedpeople's initiative had no part in it.

The same logic prevailed among her friends. In antislavery meetings and black labor conventions, the demand surfaced repeatedly: Land for the southern freedpeople appeared as the only means of ensuring their independence. Most of these discussions focused on land in the South, where the people were already located, not in the West, as in Truth's plan. Wendell Phillips, president of the American Anti-Slavery Society, and Aaron Powell, editor of the *National Anti-Slavery Standard*, spoke out most prominently among abolitionists. Powell urged the point to a Washington meeting of the National Colored Labor Convention in December 1869, and a delegation from the convention subsequently visited President Grant to present in person a request for land.[13]

In Washington, Battle Creek, Boston, and New York, reform leaders worked from the top down. Their way was to formulate a solution to the problems of the freedpeople and petition the federal government. Unbeknownst to them, there was also ferment at the grass roots.

In Louisiana and Tennessee, freedpeople themselves conceived of migration. In Louisiana, the most articulate advocate was Henry Adams of Shreveport. A slave in Georgia and Louisiana for twenty antebellum years, the newly emancipated Adams was so sickened by the wholesale slaughter of his fellows that he joined the occupying Union Army in 1865 to help restore order and, coincidentally, learn to read and write. After his discharge in 1868, Adams, like many veterans, turned toward politics. As a Republican organizer, he rallied his voters against a backdrop of Democratic terrorism.[14]

The Reconstruction South was providing fertile ground for the newly formed Ku Klux Klan and similar armed, white-supremacist organizations using violence to forestall change. Adams and his associates, horrified by the loss of black life and property following every exercise of political rights, founded "the Council" to investigate racist political outrages in northern Louisiana and the adjoining sections of Mississippi and Texas. Their reports to the U.S. Justice Department only temporarily alleviated the terror. By the mid-1870s, Adams and other Council members were reaching a dour conclusion: The preservation of life and freedom might require leaving the South.

Near Nashville, Tennessee, Benjamin "Pap" Singleton was drawing similar conclusions. Too old to have served in the Union Army and absorbed its lessons in citizenship, he was less politically minded than Adams. Singleton belonged to Truth's generation and listened to the voice of God. God told him that black people should leave Tennessee, where they were just so much fodder for terrorists. In the mid-1870s, Singleton and his associates formed the Edgefield Real Estate Association to transport blacks from Edgefield County to rural Kansas, settle them, and help them into a safe prosperity. With black Tennesseeans already trickling into Kansas, Singleton sought to augment and rationalize a movement already under way.

Singleton and Adams were in close touch with potential migrants, but Truth was not. She addressed not migrants but Congress, through the submission of a petition bearing masses of signatures. Her petition spoke the language of charity:

Petition

To the Senate and House of Representatives, in Congress assembled:

Whereas, through the faithful and earnest representations of Sojourner Truth (who has personally investigated the matter), we believe that the freed colored people in and about Washington, dependent upon Government for support, would be greatly benefitted and might become useful citizens by being placed in a position to support themselves.

We, the undersigned, therefore earnestly request your Honorable Body to set apart for them a portion of the public land in the West, and erect buildings thereon for the aged and infirm, and otherwise so to legislate as to secure the desired results.[15]

Reflecting Truth's hazy goals, her wording was vague. As a preacher, her forte was principles, not details; she relegated particulars to others who could read and write. And as a woman, she lacked access to the structure and idiom of government. Now that she was trying to influence federal policy, she felt the handicap of her disfranchisement keenly. Throughout this crusade, she advocated votes for women alongside land for freedpeople.[16]

Truth had fifty copies of the petition printed at her own expense and urged her supporters to make and circulate more. The Reverend Gilbert Haven, her friend in Boston, soon to be bishop of the Methodist Episcopal Church, was supposed to forward the signed petitions to Congress. The strongest endorsement that Haven could muster said: "She ought to win this battle. Any one who wishes to aid in such a work, can circulate petitions like the following, and send them to this office."[17]

Between August 1870 and March 1871, Truth and her grandson Samuel Banks toured New England and the Mid-Atlantic states collecting signatures. She financed their expedition by selling her photographs, accepting donations, and staying with friends like the Havens and Garrisons.[18]

The schedule was hectic, as it had been for most of her life as a lecturer. She kicked off her resettlement campaign in Providence, Rhode Island, in February 1870.[19] In March, she was back in Washington for a Fifteenth Amendment celebration, and she stayed on for some weeks. There she met President Grant and several prominent radical Republican senators, including Charles Sumner, Henry Wilson, George W. Julian, and "H. R. Revels, Senator, Miss., Colored."[20] In the balance of 1870 she was up and down the East Coast in pursuit of her mission.[21]

On New Year's Day, 1871, Truth was in Boston for a massive meeting at Tremont Temple celebrating the eighth anniversary of American emancipation. The National Association for the Spread of Temperance and Night Schools Among the Freed People of the South sponsored this meeting, chaired by its president, the fugitive slave narrator and historian William Wells Brown. The audience consisted of supporters, but the newspaper report was written in a style typical of these prejudiced times. Truth's speech appeared in dialect now itself a curiosity:

> I been to Washin'ton, an' I fine out dis, dat de colud pepul dat is in Washin'tun libin on de government dat de United Staas ort to gi' 'em lan' an' move 'em on it. Dey are libin on de gov'ment, an' dere is pepul takin' care of 'em costin' you so much, an' it don't benefit him 'tall. It degrades him wuss an' wuss. Therefo' I say dat these people, take an' put 'em in de West where you ken enrich 'em. . . . Dey say, Let 'em take keer of derselves. Why, you've taken dat all away from 'em. Ain't got nufin lef'.[22]

Massachusetts newspapers repeated the customary exaggerations about Truth, whose person roused more interest than her message. She was said to be older than eighty (not her actual seventy-three or seventy-four), to have been enslaved for forty years (not her actual thirty). According to a Springfield report, she had outlived most of her thirteen children. In fact, three of her five children were living near or with her in Battle Creek.[23]

Newspaper reporters often presented Truth as a character from the pen of Harriet Beecher Stowe. She was likened to Dinah, in *Uncle Tom's Cabin,* but most often she became the Libyan Sibyl: "the colored American Sibyl," "the Libyan *Sibyl,*" the "Africain Sybil," a "real Sibyl," and, twisting the motif completely beyond recognition, "a Christian sibyl."[24] By transforming her into something more familiar—a fictional character—reporters gave her a recognizable identity and conveyed her entertainment value. Truth did not protest such recasting, though she followed her press coverage closely. She understood the dynamics of publicity.[25]

Truth's last great speaking campaign produced mixed results. At times she drew full and enthusiastic crowds, at times crowds sparse and lethargic. Sometimes her voice was strong and her message focused, sometimes her remarks were scattered.[26] The mistress appeared to be faltering. The fascination with her age rather than her message annoyed her: "I have been hoping that some body would print a little of what I am doing, but the papers seem to be content simply in saying how old I am."[27] She jokingly charged $5 of a man (who turned out to be the radical Republican mayor of Washington) for having asked her age.[28]

During her petitioning, Truth spoke to woman suffragists, Methodists, temperance people, and spiritualists. Her far-flung network of former abolitionist colleagues now opened to her every corner of postwar reform. To all these people she preached woman suffrage, temperance and prohibition, and the corruption of Gilded Age politics, but she kept her leading motif. Whatever the venue, whoever her audience, she called for resettling freedpeople in the West.

Truth had long consorted with spiritualists in the persons of Progressive Friends. Now their beliefs became increasingly her own. Over seventy, she accepted their tranquil notion of life after death. Pentecostal judgment at the end of time fell out of her expectation.[29]

AS 1870 was ending, after nearly a year of talk, Truth had enlisted no powerful allies and was no closer to a concrete proposal. She still knew nothing of the West where she would move her freedpeople. All her exhortation to audiences large and small had brought her no closer to achieving her goal. Growing increasingly frustrated, she complained that "Everybody says this is a good work, but nobody helps."[30] Then, suddenly, in December 1870, came an answer to her prayers: a letter from Kansas. Kansas possessed enormous symbolic value for blacks and abolitionists. The quintessential free state—home of the martyred John Brown and firmly Republican—Kansas stood for the best of the West.

Posing as a longtime admirer of Truth and, presumably, an abolitionist, Byron M. Smith invited Truth to visit Topeka as his guest for as long as she wished. He neglected to identify himself as a land agent.[31] Smith offered to pay all her expenses, including train fare. In September 1871, Truth left Battle Creek for Kansas with her helpful twenty-year-old grandson, Samuel Banks. Between their arrival and their departure in February 1872, Truth spoke regularly throughout Kansas and Missouri.[32] They stayed with well-placed people as she continued her advocacy of resettlement, temperance, and woman suffrage. Political corruption was a popular theme. Until women could vote, she contended, misgovernment and corruption would continue unabated.[33]

Westerners held Truth at arm's length. A Kansas newspaper found that she presented her colonization mission "not very intelligently." A Missouri newspaper called her a man lecturing under the name of Sojourner Truth.[34] Even her supporters found fault. A Congregationalist minister in Emporia, Kansas, saw an occasional "gleam of wit or a sparkle of wisdom" and heard the odd "burst of powerful, but strange, eloquence." But at bottom he found "[h]er speaking is disjointed, and her 'lectures,' as she calls them, quite variable . . . she just drifts along."[35]

The journey to Kansas made no difference. Truth and Smith forged no more concrete basis for her mission, perhaps for lack of adequate funding and prospective buyers of land. When Truth and Banks went to Iowa, Wisconsin, and Missouri after Kansas in the winter of 1872, her scheme remained as vague as in 1870.

Vagueness may not have dismayed her, for she was after signatures. Staying with old friends like Joseph Dugdale, a spiritualist Progressive Friend from Pennsylvania who now lived in Iowa, Truth collected many more signatures in 1872. She returned to Battle Creek, in the words of her friend Frances Titus, "with scrolls of signatures and trophies of success, over which she felt as jubilant as 'great Caesar bringing captives home to Rome.' "³⁶

THE FIRST phase of Truth's mission to colonize freedpeople in the West ended in the spring of 1874, when she and Banks traveled to Washington to present her petition. As usual, they stopped with friends in the East, including a son of William Lloyd and Helen Benson Garrison: Wendell Phillips Garrison. Young Garrison wrote his father about Truth's visit, to which William Lloyd Garrison replied: "[Truth] is indeed a remarkable woman, and always deserving of considerate and kind treatment; but, at her extreme age, (she is older than 83, probably close on to 90) it is a pity that she cannot remain quiet at her home in Battle Creek, in stead of perambulating around the country, compelling hospitality whether or no."³⁷

I doubt Truth presented her petition to Congress. She explained later that "there was a new bill [possibly one of several unsuccessful land policy bills] introduced and her petition was ignored."³⁸ No report of submission survives. Then Samuel Banks fell ill, necessitating an early return to Battle Creek, where he died in February 1875.³⁹

Banks's death at twenty-four deprived Truth of a beloved companion, the family member who shared her years in Washington and the signature-collecting tours of the early 1870s. Financial drain compounded her grief. Truth had no money to speak of, but she refused to put Banks in a pauper's grave. She mortgaged her little house and went $300 to $400 into debt to cover the costs of his medical care and burial.⁴⁰

In January 1876, the Centennial celebration in Philadelphia presented Truth a fine opportunity to see old comrades and sell her new, augmented 1875 edition of the *Narrative of Sojourner Truth*, compiled by Frances Titus, her neighbor, friend, and informal manager in Battle Creek. Through sales at the Centennial, Truth hoped to repay the $350 Titus had borrowed to cover the cost of printing 5,000 copies.⁴¹ But illness prevented Truth's making the trip.

Grounded in Battle Creek during the mid-1870s, Truth was suf-

Frances Titus, Truth's friend and informal
manager, editor of the 1870s and 1880s edi-
tions of the *Narrative of Sojourner Truth*.
Photo courtesy of the Berenice Lowe
Collection, Bentley Historical Library, Michigan
Historical Collections, University of Michigan.

ficiently restored by the end of the decade to travel as far as
Rochester, where she saw her old friend and co-worker in feminist abolition, Lucretia Mott. Truth and Mott compared their age-
ing. Mott asked, "Why, Sojourner, how is it that I am so wrinkled,
and your face is just as smooth as can be?" Truth remarked later
that "She is not as old as I am, but she is all broke down." In fact,
Truth was about four years younger than Mott, but age did not figure in her explanation: "I have two skins; I have a white skin
under, and a black one to cover it."[42]

THE EXODUS to Kansas of 1879 revived Truth's "crowning work."
This spontaneous, millenarian movement took tens of thousands
of poor, rural blacks out of Mississippi, Louisiana, Texas, and Tennessee to Truth's Kansas. The Exodusters fled out of fear of a
return to slavery following the Democrats' recapture of state gov-

PART SECOND.

"BOOK OF LIFE."

THE preceding narrative has given us a partial history of Sojourner Truth. This biography was published not many years after her freedom had been secured to her. Having but recently emerged from the
gloomy night of slavery, ignorant and untaught in all
that gives value to human existence, she was still suffering from the burden of acquired and transmitted
habits incidental to her past condition of servitude.
Yet she was one whose life forces and moral perceptions were so powerful and clear cut that she not only
came out from this moral gutter herself, but largely
assisted in elevating others of her race from a similar
state of degradation. It was the "oil of divine origin" which quickened her soul and fed the vital spark,
that her own indomitable courage fanned to an undying flame. She was one of the first to enlist in the
war against slavery, and fought the battles·for freedom by the side of its noble leaders.

A true sentinel, she slumbered not at her post. To
hasten the enfranchisement of her own people was
the great work to which she consecrated her life; yet,

A   (129)

The opening page of Frances Titus's "Book of Life," 1875.

ernments.[43] Benjamin Singleton and Henry Adams have been
identified with the Exodus, for they gave the most riveting testimony at Senate hearings investigating the movement. But neither
man led the Exodus, which had no leader at all. Adams remained
in New Orleans, barred from returning to Shreveport after his
Senate testimony; Singleton stayed in Tennessee.

The Exodus to Kansas of 1879 upstaged Truth's plan, but she
supported it enthusiastically. As in 1864, she traveled to the side
of needy freedpeople and gave them her help. Although they depended on charity in St. Louis and Topeka, the Exodusters were
doing what Truth had wanted for Washington's unemployed freedpeople: They were leaving the South for a state where they might
become independent farmers. They needed aid in the short term,
which Truth was pleased to offer.

Truth was certain the Exodus would regenerate the freedpeople, make them into what she called "a people." She doubted that

"God has had them robbed and scourged all the days of their life for nothing." She had prayed "so long that my people would go to Kansas" because they could never amount to anything as long as whites were in control in the South. In Kansas they would "get the Northern spirit in them," grow prosperous, and even return south to instruct the poor white people how to get ahead.[44]

In her delight at the Exodus, Truth parted company with Frederick Douglass, alone among eminent blacks in deploring it. George T. Downing, so prominent in the recent suffrage controversies, eloquently defended the Exodus.[45]

The atrocities that had driven the Exodusters from home shocked Truth into anger. Mississippi had "abused and heathenized" the freedpeople, who had every reason in the world to flee.[46] She railed against white southerners' Christian hypocrisy: "That such things should take place in an intelligent community, filled with Christian churches [,] without any public expression of dissent or abhorrence, is a disgrace to the civilization of the present century."[47]

Exodusters' relief called out abolitionist women as in the mid-1860s. Two longtime social workers, Laura Haviland and Elizabeth Comstock, joined Truth and Titus among the volunteers. Truth's health was still fragile, but she managed to offer encouragement and instruction as she had done at the Freedmen's Village in Arlington Heights, Virginia, and the Freedmen's Hospital in Washington. Exodusters were needy as Washington's freedpeople had been needy, but the difference between the 1860s and the 1870s gratified Truth: Nearly all the youngsters she encountered could read and write.

Truth spoke in churches, black and white, soliciting support for the Exodusters and upholding the idea of emigration out of the South. In a black church in Topeka, she declared the Republican governor of Kansas, a supporter of the Kansas Freedmen's Relief Association, an instrument in the furtherance of God's creation. The Exodus to Kansas she saw as the working out of God's plan for African Americans: "God still lives and means to see the black people in full possession of all their rights, even if the entire white population of the South has to be annihilated in the accomplishment of His purpose."[48]

In these words of the late 1870s, Truth returned to her theme of the desperate 1850s: vengeance. The 1870s, too, were cruel, a prelude to even harsher decades to come. After the Panic of 1873 and the depression that spawned a wave of labor unrest, most Americans cooled to the Civil War issues of race and Reconstruction.[49] With labor and money topping the national agenda, supporters of black rights in and out of Congress found advocacy hard going. In 1875, as a last act of radical Reconstruction policy, Senator Charles Sumner managed to shepherd through Congress a watered-down Civil Rights Act, which the Supreme Court would find unconstitutional in 1883. In a climate increasingly hostile to the needs of the black poor, frustration moved Truth to show her anger straightforwardly.

The Exodus to Kansas tapered off after the spring of 1879 and was over by 1880. In synchrony with it, Truth's strength gave out when she returned to Battle Creek in January 1880. She had been one of many yearning for black migration after the Civil War, but the actual movement—an expression of independent black action—had caught her completely by surprise.

25

The End of a Life

SOJOURNER TRUTH'S life had myriad endings—many more beginning than end. The end of her enslavement in 1827 began a life of freedom. It marked, she said, the beginning of her living, for she did not know when she was born.[1] Isabella's life ended with the beginning of "Sojourner Truth" in 1843. Later proclaimed endings from the 1850s onward also brought renewal. Truth seemed old and dying practically forever, and people were always ushering her out in documents conceived as memorials.

The 1850 *Narrative of Sojourner Truth* concludes with Truth old and infirm, a mother whose children could not or would not support her old age. Please buy this book, Olive Gilbert entreated, to take poor old Sojourner through to her death. That was in 1850, before the words and deeds that now define her meaning.

"The Libyan Sibyl" announces that "Sojourner Truth has passed away from among us as a wave of the sea. ..."[2] In 1863, Harriet Beecher Stowe thought Truth already dead, a misrepresentation Frances Dana Gage was delighted to correct. Gage resurrects Truth, but not by much. Truth was, Gage says, "not dead; but, old and feeble, she rests from her labors near Battle Creek, Michigan."[3] There was something to Gage's description, for Truth passed through her first great public illness in 1863. The antislavery

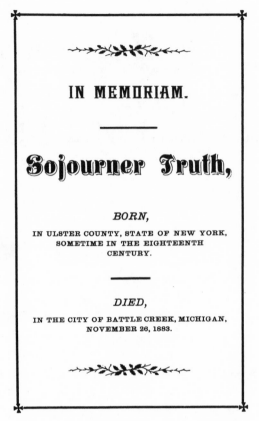

First page of "In Memoriam" chapter by
Frances Titus, 1884 edition of the *Narrative of
Sojourner Truth*. This is also the text of
Truth's gravestone.

press solicited donations that carried her through recuperation.

The Civil War gave Truth renewed strength. She quit smoking in late 1868 for reasons of health. Reported in the antislavery press, this accomplishment gratified her temperance friends enormously.[4] But more endings soon followed. Truth's Battle Creek helper Frances Titus rounded out Truth's life again in late 1874 in an edition of the *Narrative of Sojourner Truth* that included her scrapbooks. In the mid-1870s, another serious illness paralyzed her entire right side and left her legs with gangrenous ulcers that never healed completely.

Truth credited a woman doctor, Sallie Rogers, and a veterinarian with enabling her to walk again after two months in bed. This ordeal took her so close to death that in 1876 word spread among abolitionists that she had indeed died. In Philadelphia, where Truth had hoped to attend the Centennial, reporters called upon William Still, an old ally and one of her few black friends. Still retold Stowe's "Frederick, *is God dead?*" anecdote, but fumbled for words of his own to describe Truth. She was not easily described, Still conceded, but he summed her up as a "strangely-made creature," who would "dauntlessly face the most intelligent and cultivated audiences" to advance the interests of the slave. The American Woman Suffrage Association memorialized her as a figure of native genius: "one of the most remarkable women of the age. . . . She has rare natural gifts; a clear intellect; a fine moral intuition and spirited insight, with much common sense."[5]

Despite illness and obituaries, Sojourner Truth did not die. There followed a lecture tour in 1878, the Exodus to Kansas of 1879, and more speeches in the Midwest. Truth did much as an old woman. With so many endings to choose from, when began her end?

After her return from Kansas, Truth was ready to go on the road again in 1880. She traveled little outside southern Michigan, but her words reached thousands of readers. The Philadelphia *Christian Recorder*, organ of the African Methodist Episcopal Church, the church of her daughters, and the Philadelphia *Woman's Tribune*, associated with the AWSA branch of woman suffrage, both reprinted her 1880 New Year's greeting to the Chicago *Inter-Ocean*, a writing full of spiritualism. She echoed her old views, but no longer in apocalyptic tones: "We talk of a beginning, but there is no beginning but the beginning of a wrong. All else is from God, and is from everlasting to everlasting." Once a pentecostal associating with spiritualists, Truth now preached spiritualist themes. In 1880, her God was not a judge but

a great ocean of love; and we live and move in him as the fishes in the sea, filled with his love and spirit, and his throne is in the hearts of his people. . . .

These ideas have come to me since I was a hundred years old. . . . This has become a new world.[6]

Engraving of Truth in old age, from a photograph no longer in existence. This illustration
comes from the 1884 "In Memoriam" chapter
of the *Narrative of Sojourner Truth.*

Though immobilized, Truth reached the public as a local tourist
attraction, one of the few famous people in Battle Creek. (The others were Mother Ellen White and Dr. John Harvey Kellogg, both
of the Seventh-Day Adventist Church, headquartered there.) Now
Truth's public came to her. In the words of one caller: "She is always ready for visitors, who come and go freely. . . ."[7] She was the
"celebrated colored woman" of Battle Creek, whom sightseers
called upon to "listen to her quaint wisdom and bright sayings."[8]
The considerate left something material in exchange for her time,
a help toward her living expenses now she could no longer travel.

During her last years, as in all her time in Harmonia and Battle Creek, Truth lived with her daughters. The youngest, Sophia
Schuyler, occupied Truth's Harmonia house with her husband,
Thomas Schuyler; three sons, Sojourner, Edward, and Wesley;
and their daughter Frances's son, Charles. Sophia was in her fifties
in the early 1880s.[9] Truth lived eight miles away on Cottage Street

in Battle Creek, in "a little dove cote of a house with a background of sunflowers and beds of quaint blossoms leading to the door."[10]

Living with and caring for Truth were her two older daughters, Diana and Elizabeth.[11] Diana was now about sixty-five. She and her husband Jacob Corbin had one son, Frank, but neither son nor husband lived in the Cottage Street house. Jacob and Diana had separated in 1869, and Jacob lived near the Kalamazoo River Dam in Battle Creek. Their son Frank, a cook, seems never to have married or had children. Elizabeth had married twice, first to the father of Samuel Banks and then, in about 1861, to William Boyd. Boyd had deserted Elizabeth in 1872, after several years of difficulties.[12] Their son, William, died in 1887.

Diana, Elizabeth, and Sophia are the only living children we know Truth had in those years. Peter had disappeared at sea in the 1840s. She had told of having five children in her *Narrative*, but we know nothing about the fifth. It is possible that the fifth child was grandson James Caldwell's mother.[13]

An 1880 visitor to Truth departed from custom and commented on her family: "Her two daughters live with her, and one [Diana] especially resembles her in her stately bearing and intellectual face.

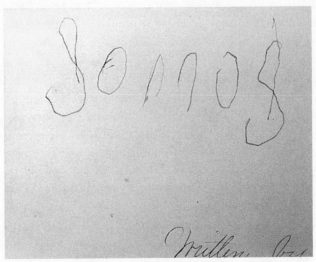

Sojourner Truth's only known signature. Photo courtesy of the Archives of the Historical Society of Battle Creek, Michigan.

Her grandchildren are all promising young people, but it is doubtful if there will ever be another Sojourner Truth."[14] Ordinarily, friends and reporters passed in silence over the presence and character of her accompanying daughters and grandsons, as though they were not of significance, or, indeed, did not exist.

In the prose of other people, Truth seemed usually to abide by herself, an isolated black presence among a mass of genteel, reformist whites. A notable rhetorical exception is Harriet Beecher Stowe's description of James Caldwell, who was about nine years old at the time of their encounter in Andover. Stowe called Caldwell, whom she did not name, "the fattest, jolliest woolly-headed little specimen of Africa that one can imagine. He was grinning and showing his glistening white teeth in a state of perpetual merriment. . . ."[15]

The silence around Truth's family stems in part from the discomfort her white comrades felt in dealing with African Americans who could not be made into singular and entertaining characters. Admittedly the effacement of family occurred elsewhere in the nineteenth century; the families of prominent people of any race or sex receded from view into homebound obscurity. But this was especially true for black families. We know, for instance, little of Anna Murray Douglass, the wife of Frederick Douglass from the first days of their escape from Maryland until her death in 1882. Only one photograph of Anna Douglass exists, the single image that preserves her from complete invisibility.

Like Sojourner Truth and her daughters, Anna Douglass did not read or write. Cultured people may have felt ill at ease with illiterate (though well-dressed) black women. But this formulation contains its own silence. Even during most of the twentieth century, the educated families of middle-class blacks were not welcome in the family resorts of their white peers. Intellectuals like W. E. B. Du Bois and the biologist E. E. Just traveled alone.[16] Black families of any level of sophistication were too awkward for the admirers of well-known blacks to deal with on a footing of equality, and so family members disappear.

With the exception of James Caldwell and Samuel Banks, Sojourner Truth's family never posed the problem that colleagues of Just or Du Bois faced. Truth's daughters and sons-in-law never

Diana Corbin, Sojourner Truth's oldest daughter, cabinet card, ca. 1880,
Perry studio, reissued ca. 1900 by Canfield. Photo courtesy of Local
History Collection, Willard Library, Battle Creek, Michigan.

presumed to enter her elevated circles. All three daughters worked
as domestic servants and died poor: Elizabeth Boyd died at home
on College Street of "nervous prostration" in June 1893; Sophia
Schuyler died in the county poorhouse of "old age" in March
1901; and Diana Corbin died of chronic ill health in the county
poorhouse after being an object of private charity for ten years.[17]

All of Truth's descendants who survived well into the twentieth century descend from Sophia's daughter Frances.[18] But this is to get ahead of the story, for Sojourner Truth, nursed by her daughters, is dying, but not yet dead.

TRUTH lay mortally ill for about two months in the late fall of 1883. Doctors, including the famed John Harvey Kellogg of the Seventh-Day Adventist's Battle Creek Sanitarium, made heroic efforts to cure the ulcers on her legs. Decades later, Kellogg told a questionable story (given what we know about tissue rejection) of having grafted his own skin onto Truth's leg, producing "a ring of white skin around the colored woman's limb."[19] Whether or not this treatment occurred as described, it did not heal Truth's legs. By late November 1883 she was wasted and weak, too emaciated to wear her false teeth.

A reporter from Grand Rapids paid Truth her last public visit. Although toothlessness rendered her words indistinct and shortness of breath curtailed her expression, her eyes were bright and her mind keen. Truth husbanded her strength and conducted the visit with as much vigor as possible while dying. She exhorted the reporter on the need to continue her resettlement project. And she sang one of her favorite songs:

> It was early in the morning,
> It was early in the morning,
> Just at the break of day,
> When He rose, when He rose, when He rose,
> And went to Heaven on a cloud.

Her last words were: "Be a follower of the Lord Jesus."[20]

She died before dawn on 26 November 1883. Everyone, herself included, thought she was at least one hundred and five years old.[21] She was actually about eighty-six.

Truth's funeral, one of the biggest in Battle Creek, was held not in a Methodist church or in the Spiritualist Friends' Meeting House she had attended, but in the tony Congregational and Presbyterian Church. The Reverend Reed Stuart preached, and her old friend Giles Stebbins, now of Detroit, spoke to a congregation of a thousand people. She lay in her open coffin dressed in black and white, a spray of white flowers in her (crippled) right hand, arranged perhaps as evocation of her enslavement. A long procession of carriages accompanied her remains to Oak Hill Cemetery, where she and her family are buried together. Frances Titus concluded that Truth had risen "from the mud and slime of basest enslavement, sought and found her level among the purest and the best."[22]

TRUTH'S first obituaries came from the great men of abolitionism. The day after her death, Frederick Douglass eulogized her from Washington, D.C., Wendell Phillips from Boston. With the caution of all his forty years' acquaintance with Truth, Douglass restrained his admiration: "Venerable for age, distinguished for insight into human nature, remarkable for independence and courageous self-assertion, devoted to the welfare of her race, she has been for the last forty years an object of respect and admiration to social reformers everywhere." Phillips, too, was careful. He praised Truth's "natural wit and happiness in retort," and recalled the "rich, quaint, poetic, and often profound speech of a most remarkable person, who used to say to us, 'You read books; God himself talks to me.' "[23]

Educated blacks celebrated Truth as a hero of her race and sex. The *Christian Recorder* ran a brief obituary, calling her "one of the most remarkable characters of the day. . . . A real Sibyl," with access to the most important men in the land.[24] The *New York Globe*, also a black newspaper, appreciated her remarkable intelligence despite her utter lack of education, and her service to the great men of abolitionism.[25] The National Colored Convention, meeting in Nashville in March 1884, passed two resolutions recognizing Truth's labors as an abolitionist who left her people a "rich legacy of [N]egro enthusiasm, virtue, and noble womanhood."[26]

Both branches of woman suffrage saluted her memory. Volume 3 of Elizabeth Cady Stanton and Susan B. Anthony's *History of Woman Suffrage*, appearing not long after Truth's death, noted her passing at one hundred and ten. Quoting the Chicago *Inter-Ocean*, Stanton and Anthony called Truth "the most wonderful woman the colored race has ever produced."[27] Warmer admiration came from Truth's preferred branch of woman suffrage, the American Woman Suffrage Association. For the second time in seven years, Lucy Stone composed Truth's obituary in the AWSA's Boston *Woman's Journal.* This time Stone said Truth had been born in Africa, died at one hundred and ten, and "bore the marks of the lash till her dying day. She was a tall, muscular woman with a face as black as night." Stone had heard Truth speak, and like Douglass and Phillips captured her genius: a "wonderful power of expression and the logic which toppled down the defences built on lies, and a good deal more."[28]

In a society in which geographical inheritance—one's Africanness or Europeanness—threatened to dictate one's abilities, this African theme haunted Americans, black and white. Many believed intelligence to be racial, not individual. They thought races gained or lost points in a competition for numbers of prominent people— "men and women of genius." Part of Truth's fascination for Americans was her apparent lack of white ancestry, which would have offered a facile explanation for her intelligence. As a woman of pure African descent, her intelligence did not have to be subdivided: it all increased the African total.

Pondering the significance of Truth's racial background, one obituary compared hers to Douglass's obviously mixed heritage. "The fact that Sojourner was wholly of African extraction is a feature which lent no small degree of interest to her character and was with herself oftentimes a matter of pleasant boast," said the Battle Creek *Daily Journal* immediately after her death. "Her intellect, her energy and her quick wit in which she far surpassed most people of her time, are all to be credited to the race from which she sprang."[29] Truth's blackness, as opposed to the brownness or yellowness of most other prominent Negroes of her time, burnished her luster as a symbol of her race.

T. Thomas Fortune, a young journalist writing in the *New York Globe,* hoped Truth would be permanently memorialized as an important figure of the past and the most visible black woman in the abolitionist movement. But he foresaw difficulties in explaining her to the postwar generation. Foreshadowing a conundrum of the twentieth century, Fortune recognized that "[a]lthough the name of Sojourner Truth is familiar to many people, not more than one colored person out of ten knows who she is."[30] He traced this confusion to geography: Truth had operated in the North rather than the South so thoroughly identified with the African race. There was much more to the confusion, of course, but the unorthodoxy of her life would not make her less durable as a symbol. Whatever did not fit the tight mold of *the* black woman—such as Truth's pentecostalism or the gentility of her appearance in her photographs—fell out of the making of a symbol.

26

The Life of a Symbol

A GREAT woman, a heroic life, yes. But wherein lay the greatness
and heroism? Some said talking with presidents made the proof.
For others, breast-baring and muscle-flexing conveyed greatness.
"Sojourner Truth" has enjoyed a fine but kaleidoscopic reputation.
The symbol was not made by a relative or admirer toiling over unfinished manuscripts, painstakingly collecting journals and letters,
and burning those compromising the reputation. No harmonious,
flattering biography emerged. Because neither Truth nor her
memorialists cemented her brilliant fragments into a whole, suc-
cessive purveyors of her memory have each magnified their favorite piece.

Did Truth's descendants try to preserve their ancestor's reputation? If so, their efforts were lost. Poor and illiterate domestic
servants, Diana Corbin, Elizabeth Boyd, and Sophia Schuyler inspired a degree of compassion in their employers, but nothing
enabling them to memorialize their famous mother. Nor has any
subsequent familial attempt to lay claim to Truth's cultural legacy
come to light. Perhaps the issue was as much a matter of custody
as of means.

Even in the 1880s, Truth as a public figure belonged more to
her middle- and upper-class admirers than to her family. Accord-

ing to Frances Titus, the Battle Creek widow who was Truth's closest companion after the 1860s, "Some of the more prominent citizens of Battle Creek acted as pall-bearers" at her funeral, in which none of Truth's family members took noticeable part.[1] Titus, rather than Corbin, Boyd, Schuyler, or their children, became the keeper of Truth's flame.

The only person in the Truth memorial business in the 1880s and 1890s, Frances Titus laid the cornerstone of Truth's memory in one great labor of love: the 1870s and 1880s editions of the *Narrative of Sojourner Truth*. In 1875, Titus republished Olive Gilbert's 1850 *Narrative* together with Truth's "Book of Life"—her scrapbooks. After Truth's death, Titus added the 1884 "Memorial Chapter."[2] As the 1850s editions of the *Narrative* are extremely rare, libraries and reprint houses have depended on Titus's more numerous 1870s editions. The 1875 edition most closely approximates an authorized biography. Often reprinted, it provides the foundation for every subsequent description of Truth.

For all her earnestness and affection, Titus presented Truth in lumps that later investigators have strained to digest.[3] To the persistent and well-informed reader, the 1870s and 1880s editions yield much information, but they baffle the newcomer to Sojourner Truth's milieux.

It did not have to be this way: In the spring of 1872, Theodore Tilton, the antislavery, feminist editor of the New York *Independent*, one of the great weekly newspapers of the era, wanted to write Truth's life. She said no, "she expected to live a long time yet, and was going to accomplish 'lots' before she died, and did n't want to be 'written up' at present."[4]

By late 1874 Truth had changed her mind, but the offer from Tilton no longer held. Her aspiration for sales at the 1876 American Centennial in Philadelphia probably motivated the new edition of the *Narrative*, which Titus completed in late 1874.[5] This edition was to finance Truth's old age.

An uncommonly dedicated friend, Titus traveled with Truth after Samuel Banks's death. Their shared spiritualism and Titus's family ties to Amy Post had probably brought Truth and Titus together in Battle Creek in the 1850s.[6] After Truth's death, Titus collected $44 for the first of three successive grave markers, erected in 1890 or 1891 and engraved with the words: "Frederick, is God dead?"[7] Titus memorialized Truth in words, stone, and image before she herself died of Bright's disease in 1894.[8]

Titus gave us the most famous image of Truth after the *cartes-de-visite*. She engaged Frank C. Courter, a professor of art at Albion College, to paint Truth's legendary meeting with Abraham Lincoln. Courter had never seen Truth or Lincoln, but he specialized in Lincolniana and over his lifetime painted scores of Lincoln portraits. He completed the painting in 1893. Featured in the Michigan pavilion of that year's Chicago World's Fair, the painting later returned for permanent display in the Seventh-Day Adventists' Battle Creek Sanitarium. The sanitarium burned down in 1902, destroying the painting, but a local professional photographer, Frank E. Perry, had photographed the portrait before the fire.[9]

Courter's painting depicts Truth seated and Lincoln standing—a highly unlikely arrangement, given their relative status. Lincoln is showing Truth the Bible given him by the colored people of Baltimore. He looks down, she gazes into the distance, as in her *cartes-de-visite*, from which Courter may have worked. Despite its eccentricity, this painting is often reproduced as though it were painted from life in 1864.[10]

In her editions of the *Narrative*, Titus presented Truth to posterity as a woman noteworthy for living long, traveling widely, elevating her race, and hobnobbing with famous people. She sought to efface the shortcomings of the figure of Truth in the first edition, which, Titus wrote, was published "not many years after her freedom had been secured to her." (Those "not many years" equaled nearly a quarter century.) In those long-ago days of the 1840s, Titus held, Truth was still handicapped by the legacy of her enslavement: "Having but recently emerged from the gloomy night of slavery, ignorant and untaught in all that gives value to human existence, she was still suffering from the burden of acquired and transmitted habits incidental to her past condition of servitude."[11] Titus most likely referred to the affectionate paean to her master with which Truth closed her 1850 account, and the pages that precede the "Last Interview with her Master," which present an impoverished, pathetic figure, a bad mother whose religion is fervent but whose outlook is paranoid. Titus wanted to replace this persona with an antislavery lecturer and woman of the world. Her choices are with us still.

When Truth enters the scene in the "Book of Life," she is in the chamber of the U.S. Senate during the Civil War, surrounded by senators rushing toward her with compliments and handshakes.[12] There follow Frances Dana Gage's 1863 rendition (undated in the "Book of Life") of Truth in Akron in 1851; several anecdotes of Truth's brilliant repartee as an abolitionist; Harriet Beecher Stowe's "Sojourner Truth, the Libyan Sibyl"; page after page of press clippings; and greetings from important people. These chunks form Titus's Truth in words.

While Titus's compilation is crucial to Truth biography, it creates problems of its own. With neither single author, coherent viewpoint, nor chronological order, Titus's editions of the *Narrative* present a fractured portrait. The result is the perpetuation of the puzzle that T. Thomas Fortune identified in his 1883 obituary in the *New York Globe:* Many people know Truth's name without understanding why. Even admirers often admit their ignorance of whatever she might have done.

Truth's own means of communication blur her memory. She was preeminently a speaker, and we remember her for spontaneous commentary, not deeds. But the spoken word is notoriously unstable. Truth depended upon disparate amanuenses for the preservation of her identity. They represented her according to their own lights, often in dialect of their own invention. Depending on the reporter, Truth can appear as a northerner or a southerner, an insightful commentator or an ignoramus.

The symbolic Truth lacks religion. Having in 1843 left the company of pentecostals, she was lost to the very people most suited to understand her religion. Her memory fell into the hands of successors to abolitionists and woman suffragists, politically minded reformers whose religions or lack thereof were far from the beliefs she held most of her life. Linked inextricably to feminists and insurgent blacks, her persona lost the religion of her free woman's life.

No context, few comparisons, little sense of tradition have guided the placement of Truth in her times. As a result, she often floats

Frank Courter's 1893 painting of Sojourner Truth visiting President Abraham Lincoln. Photo courtesy of the Berenice Lowe Collection, Bentley Historical Library, Michigan Historical Collections, University of Michigan.

outside history, a symbol without a life, an isolated black woman among a mass of educated whites. Unmoored by possessive descendants, the idea of Sojourner Truth has been available for several purposes and been put to a multiplicity of uses.

APPEARING together in the "Book of Life," Stowe's and Gage's accounts contributed equally to Truth's legend until well into the middle of the twentieth century. African Americans leaned slightly toward the Libyan Sibyl, while white feminists tended somewhat toward Gage's "ar'n't I a woman?" Truth, with a great deal of overlap.

Stanton-Anthony woman suffragists claimed Truth first by reprinting Gage's "Sojourner Truth" in Volume 1 (1881) of the *History of Woman Suffrage*, where activists quickly picked it up.[13] In Memphis, for example, Lide Parker Meriwether set Gage's Truth to routing antisuffragists, in this instance, the Reverend Thomas Dixon, the fiercely negrophobic author of *The Clansman* (1905), which inspired the movie *Birth of a Nation*. Quoting Gage liberally, Meriwether added that Truth had recently died at the age of one hundred and ten, and, "[l]ike many of our old negro mammy [sic], Sojourner was a character."[14]

Gage's Truth took two more giant steps into American popular culture at the turn of the century in magazines reaching large, middle-class audiences. In 1887, she appeared in *The Chautauquan*, organ of the Chautauqua Literary and Scientific Circle, the acme of American self-cultivation. In *The Chautauquan*, Truth speaks dialect, but is "a figure of remarkable muscular development, straight, gaunt, and nearly six feet in height." A woman of great common sense, she indelibly impresses herself on history.[15]

A popular muckraking journalist, Ida Tarbell, brought Gage's Truth to the sizable readership of *The American Magazine* in 1910 in a series on "The American Woman." Like virtually everyone who wrote about Truth in the twentieth century, Tarbell failed to integrate her into her historical contexts. Truth sticks out among Tarbell's formal, photographic portraits of well-dressed white feminists. There appears not Truth's photograph, but the *Narrative*'s woodcut of her as a slave. In the company of ladies, Truth is a working woman.[16] Tarbell's Truth irritated W. E. B. Du Bois, the most prominent black intellectual of the time. Teaching at Atlanta University and about to become editor of the *Crisis* magazine, organ of the newly formed National Association for the Advancement of Colored People, Du Bois gave Tarbell mock praise for finally ceasing to write as though no blacks existed in the United States. He criticized her Truth as "only a caricature," speaking "a hideous and ridiculous dialect such as no human being ever spoke."[17]

In the early twentieth century, Truth's memory changed hands. For several decades, she became more black, less feminist. As woman suffragists' consciousness became more and more white, Truth disappeared from their iconography. Black intellectuals and academics began forging a usable Sojourner Truth of their own.

Black Sojourner Truth appeared in collected biographies of great Negroes compiled as inspiration to the young. One of the earliest and best was John W. Cromwell's *The Negro in American History*, published in 1914 in Washington, D.C., by the American Negro Academy, in which Cromwell was a motivating spirit. Cromwell uses Titus and Stowe as well as Gage. He repeats Stowe's scenario of Truth's electrifying her audience and altering its mood. Confronting a despairing Frederick Douglass, "Sojourner Truth rose in the audience and stretching forth her arms in a shrill voice exclaimed, 'Frederick, is God dead?' The effect was electrical. By a flash the sentiment of the house was changed to one of hope and assurance."[18]

Cromwell borrows the breast-baring episode from Titus's "Book of Life" and quotes Gage's Truth in Akron as saying ("in 1857"): "Well, chillen, when dar is so much racket dar must be something out of kilter . . . and *ain't I a woman? . . .*" His illustration shows a full-page "Libyan Sibyl" with a tiny portrait of Truth in the upper-right corner. The caption: "Art Masterpiece inspired by Sojourner Truth." Cromwell's text happily juxtaposes the latinate *"Sibylla Libyca"* of a great American sculptor and Sojourner Truth.[19] Cromwell may well have been influenced by his neighbor, Freeman Henry Morris Murray, author of a study of the theme of emancipation in American sculpture. Murray opens his book with Story's *Libyan Sibyl* and mentions Truth in this context.[20]

Truth appears again in 1926 in Hallie Q. Brown's *Homespun Heroines and Other Women of Distinction*, a collective biography of black women. Thanks to Brown's prominence as temperance advocate, teacher, and president of the National Association of Colored Women, her Truth influenced later renditions.[21] Brown exaggerates Truth's uniqueness by calling her—with Frederick Douglass—one of only two noted ex-slave abolitionists. Drawing heavily on Stowe, Brown repeats "Frederick, is God dead?" complete with electrical effect. Brown's quaint Truth visits the White House repeatedly and persuades Abraham Lincoln to issue the Emancipation Proclamation. After the Civil War, this Truth often speaks in state legislatures, and "Presidents, Senators, Judges, Authors, Lecturers—all were proud to grasp her hand and bid her God Speed on her noble mission."[22]

Brown avoids "ar'n't I a woman?" She makes her Truth "the Libyan Sibyl of Harriet Beecher Stowe and the ideal *Sibilla Libica* [sic] which the chisel of the eminent sculptor, Mr. Story, has given to the world." To show the young they could grow up to forge policy for presidents, Brown illustrates her piece with Courter's "Sojourner Truth and Abraham Lincoln." Contributing a lasting note of pure theatricality, Brown tells of a visit she made to Truth, complete with corny ending: "As we left that heroic character she said, 'I isn't goin' to die, honey, Ise goin' home like a shootin' star.' "[23]

In the 1930s, the Sojourner Truth legend benefitted from the initiative of a Howard University professor, Benjamin Brawley, who included Truth in his *Negro Builders and Heroes* (1937). Brawley's Truth still asks whether God is dead and changes the "sentiment of the gathering" in a flash. Again, "the effect was electrical," but Stowe makes no appearance by name. Brawley mentions Gage and cleans her up a bit: " 'Nobody ever helped me into carriages, or ober mud puddles, or gibs me any best place,' and raising herself to her full height, with a voice pitched like rolling thunder, she asked, 'And a'n't I a woman?' " Truth returns to her "corner" "amid roars of applause." Although Brawley's Truth brings business as usual to a halt, she does not bare her breast or inspire sculptors. She wisely urges her people toward practical education before exiting with Hallie Q. Brown's shooting star.[24] *Negro Builders and Heroes* inspired a series of Negro biographies by the University of North Carolina Press for use in schools. Two actually appeared: Brawley's own biography of the poet Paul Laurence Dunbar; and the first full-length biography of Truth, by Arthur Huff Fauset.[25]

Fauset was the principal of Joseph Singerly High School in Philadelphia. His *Sojourner Truth: God's Faithful Pilgrim*, a lively piece of writing, was first published in 1938 and reissued in 1971. For historical context, Fauset leaned mainly on the complete 1884 version of the *Narrative* and on secondary sources. He dedicates half the book to Truth's pre-1843 life, covered in detail in the *Narrative*. Fauset canonized the four incidents now constituting the symbolic Sojourner Truth: "Frederick, is God dead?"; "ar'n't I a woman?" at Akron; breast-baring in Indiana; and the warm welcome from President Lincoln. The "Libyan Sibyl" recedes into brief mention as a metaphor for Truth and a piece of artwork she inspired. Fauset portrays Truth as a Christian radical—"God's Shadow" and "a restless shadow." But he shows none of the photographs she called her shadows.[26]

By the early 1940s, Truth was well enough known as a Negro to have the black section of a new housing project in Detroit named for her. As that section was to open for black occupants in February 1942, white tenants rioted. The melee led to hundreds of arrests and tens of injuries. Only months later and under the protection of state troopers could blacks move in.[27]

Walter White, executive secretary of the National Association for the Advancement of Colored People in the 1930s and 1940s, published the most influential midcentury "Sojourner Truth" in a series on "American Movers and Shakers" in the *New Republic* in 1948. White begins with Frederick Douglass's being interrupted by "a gaunt, shabbily dressed black woman," who almost dwarfs Douglass with her height. Her comment silences him, and "an avalanche of applause swept away the despair which had enveloped the hall. Sojourner Truth had saved the day." White quotes four paragraphs of Gage and "ain't I a woman?" but with less emphasis on the phrase than on its repercussion: "The disruptive clergymen were silenced." White's Truth is every inch a militant, baring her breasts and once again electrifying audiences.

White's Truth comes out of the movies, a far more dramatic

character than even Arthur Huff Fauset's. A figure of "ragged, un-prepossessing appearance," she has "flashing eyes" and a "reso-nant voice that rumbled incongruously out of a woman's body." She strides into churches, where "her amazingly imaginative and poetic speech ha[s] an electric effect." In Indiana, the charge that she was a man "angered" her, and she "ripped open her dress, shouting above the tumult: 'My breasts have suckled many a white baby when they should have been sucklin' my own. . . .' "

White's Truth makes a mistake: She tries to take black people out of the mainstream with her western colonization plan, which, because wrong-headed, is bound to fail. A rolling stone after her emancipation, this Truth ends up in Battle Creek in Hallie Q. Brown's prose, heightened by White's own staging: "The aged woman smiled as she shook her head. Then after a pause, the old spark blazed again as she looked at death: 'I ain't goin' to die, honey, I'm going' home like a shootin' star!' "[28]

Walter White was Sojourner Truth's twentieth-century Harriet Beecher Stowe: He made Truth visible to a vast reading public. He wrote in the context of a wide impulse among black club women to memorialize the great figures in Negro history. The Na-tional Council of Negro Women (NCNW) was especially active in this effort and organized materials for use in black schools during Negro History Week. In 1946 the NCNW produced a radio pro-gram featuring Truth, along with Harriet Tubman and the eighteenth-century poet Phillis Wheatley. The NCNW and White's article together probably inspired the change in name of the black chapters of the Woman's Christian Temperance Union. Originally named after Lucy Thurman, the organizer of separate black chap-ters at the turn of the century, these chapters changed their name to "Sojourner Truth" in the late 1940s.[29]

After White's *New Republic* piece and the work of the NCNW, Truth could not easily be overlooked when the topic of abolition-ism came up. This happened with increasing frequency in the 1950s and 1960s. The civil rights movement trained the sights of professional historians and the reading public on abolitionism's great crusade for racial justice. The 1960s and 1970s brought ap-pearances by Sojourner Truth in several new scholarly and pop-ular books on civil rights pioneers.

Truth always appears in histories of the antislavery movement, but she scarcely fits into the narrative. Louis Filler in 1960, James M. McPherson in 1964, Carleton Mabee in 1970, and Benjamin Quarles in 1972 all mention Truth, but virtually in passing. Their academic histories came out of documents, and Truth did not write her part in the primary sources.[30]

The civil rights revolution also created a market for books aimed at general readers. Two full-length biographies of Truth appeared in the 1960s, both by left-leaning women of European birth. The first, Austrian actress and playwright Hertha Pauli, had sought refuge in the United States after the Nazi occupation.[31] One day in the library she encountered this remarkable exchange:

> "Mr. Lincoln," [Truth] said, "I never heard tell of you before they put you up for president."
> "But I heard of you," the President said, smiling."[32]

Frances Titus's made-up dialogue, together with the early 1960s drama of the second reconstruction—sit-ins, freedom rides, and marches—inspired Pauli's Truth biography.

Pauli portrays Truth as a courageous public figure, not quite as theatrical as Hallie Q. Brown, Arthur Huff Fauset, or Walter White's Truth, but definitely of legendary stature. Hers is a full-blown Truth of unwavering greatness along the lines of Gage's production. Carefully researched but lacking notes and peppered with swashbuckling fiction, Pauli's biography cannot be relied upon without corroboration.[33]

Five years later, in 1967, Jacqueline Bernard, born in France but educated in the United States, published *Journey Toward Freedom: The Story of Sojourner Truth*. Bernard, like Pauli, was a New Yorker, and *Journey Toward Freedom*, like Pauli's *Her Name Was Sojourner Truth*, is strongest on Truth's years in New York State. Bernard's great innovation is generous illustration; hers is the first Truth biography with visual documentation of Truth's surroundings. Although Gage is discernible, Bernard tones down the fervor Gage inspired elsewhere and refuses her dialect. The drama remains. Bernard's breast-baring episode, for instance, substitutes quiet passion for the intensity in Pauli, Fauset, and White. This Truth acts deliberately, her anger simmering:

> Quietly, her fingers steady, Sojourner began to untie the white kerchief across her breast. Slowly her hands moved to undo the buttons at the top of her dress.
>
> "I will show my breast," she announced as the last button came undone, "but to the entire congregation." And as she opened her blouse, she added with slow emphasis, "It is not my shame but yours that I do this."[34]

Bernard's biography became a best-seller (25,000 copies sold) and appeared in an inexpensive paperback edition in 1969, but by the early 1970s and second-wave feminism, it was out of print.

The feminist biography of the 1970s was by a young scholar, the first full-length study of Truth by a woman of color. Born in Mexico, Victoria Ortiz grew up in Europe and North America. She published *Sojourner Truth: A Self-Made Woman* in 1974 as a New York University graduate student in comparative literature.[35] In its frank turn toward scholarship, Ortiz's book marks a watershed in Truth biography. Ortiz avoids histrionics and stays closer to the sources than any previous biographer. Where the biographies of Fauset, Pauli, and Bernard read like novels, Ortiz's looks like scholarship.

For all their individuality, these four biographies agree in one aspect with older journalism: They all present Frances Dana Gage's Truth in Akron as fact. With each succeeding biography, Truth and "ar'n't I a woman?" intertwine ever more tightly. Quaintness falls out of view. Keeping pace with the twentieth century, Truth becomes a modern ancestor.

In the 1970s and 1980s, Sojourner Truth received new forms of recognition. The first black woman in Congress, Shirley Chisholm, inaugurated her presidential campaign at Truth's gravesite in 1972.[36] Later in the 1970s, the portion of Michigan state highway M-66 running through Calhoun County, in which Battle Creek lies, was named the "Sojourner Truth Memorial Highway."[37] Alongside the birth control advocate Margaret Sanger, Truth was inducted into the National Women's Hall of Fame in 1981. As if to illustrate her family's permanent disinheritance, a former secretary of the Sojourner Truth Memorial Association in Battle Creek accepted the award in Truth's name. In the twentieth century, the keepers of Truth's memory in Battle Creek have been local people like Frances Valentine and Forest H. Sweet, and those who carried on Truth research: a retired schoolteacher, Berenice Bryant Lowe, whose collection of Truth material is deposited in the Bentley Historical Library at the University of Michigan at Ann Arbor; and Dorothy and Michael Martich, who work with the Battle Creek Historical Society and have compiled a clipping file on Sojourner Truth in the Willard Public Library in Battle Creek.

PARADOXICALLY, the rise of women's history in the 1970s and 1980s narrowed Truth's range and aggravated the disappearance of the historical figure. In the work of secular-minded feminists resenting orthodox religion's power to oppress women, Truth's religion, always a puzzle for biographers, disappeared entirely. Truth's identity became little more than Gage's report. Her Truth appeared in the anthologies that circulated most widely in academia, notably Bert James Loewenberg and Ruth Bogin's *Black Women in Nineteenth-Century American Life* and Linda K. Kerber and Jane Sherron De Hart's *Women's America: Refocusing the Past.*

Loewenberg and Bogin introduce Truth as a woman with "a flair for dramatic communication," who "electrified her listeners on numerous occasions." They took Gage's Truth from the *History of Woman Suffrage,* but, as they explain in a footnote, "the dialect Mrs. Gage attempted to record has been dropped." These historians operated as though altering nineteenth-century texts could reveal a reality lying beneath the record of Truth's comments. Rewriting Gage's already invented report, Loewenberg and Bogin seek to present a better Truth, a truer Truth—a Truth, nevertheless, who is still a concoction.[38]

Thoroughly professional historians, Kerber and De Hart do not edit within quotes. Yet the first edition of their *Women's America* claims to present "our only account of impassioned oratory by this black abolitionist." This Truth comes by the familiar route: the

Sojourner Truth's grave marker, erected in 1946 at Oak Hill Cemetery, Battle Creek, Michigan. Photo courtesy of the Burton Historical Collection, Detroit Public Library.

History of Woman Suffrage. Now entitled "A'n't I a Woman?" the speech bears the date "May 29, 1851," as though Gage wrote contemporaneously with Truth's speaking.[39]

Certified by scholars like Loewenberg, Bogin, Kerber, and De Hart, Gage's Truth quickly made her way into the broad stream of feminist scholarship. Though the dialect sometimes had to be cleaned up for print, Gage's scenario of white hostility and fear was tailor-made for the feminist struggles of the 1970s and beyond. Black and white feminists were searching for a poor black woman to insert into a women's movement projecting an all-too white and middle-class image.[40]

While Gage's Truth was making her way into academic discourse, the memory of Truth was also finding a place in popular culture, where black power had its own use for her. Earlier in the twentieth century, Truth had appeared as a patient Christian, a rolling stone, an itinerant preacher, a quaint speaker. Now she needed to be angry.

Black oral culture of the late twentieth century produced a composite Sojourner Truth comprised of one single, speech act dated 1851–or, often, 1852. This Truth faces down a hostile audience, defies doubters as to her sex, rips open her bodice to bare her breast, and shouts, sneeringly, "and ain't I a woman?!!" "Ar'n't" became "ain't" in the interests of authenticity. As presented on stage in one-woman plays, Truth is a nineteenth-century female Black Panther, an Elaine Brown and Kathleen Cleaver rolled up into one and projected back in time.

Malcolm X's and Black Power's repudiation of middle-class and educated blacks delegitimized existing black scholarship, which emphasized contributions to American history. Black history had to be invented in place of Negro history. In the transition from Negro to black history, only two nineteenth-century black women survived: Sojourner Truth and Harriet Tubman. Tubman acted; Truth talked. Tubman stayed rooted in the historical contingencies of slavery, but the talking figure of Truth was portable. Truth endured as a necessary commentator on American racism and sexism.

The vessel of Sojourner Truth contained timeless black womanhood. As the strong black woman, or, simply, *the* black woman in history, she had to deliver every black woman's message, even Frances Ellen Watkins Harper's. Although a temperate Truth had replaced a confrontational Harper in 1867, the symbol of Sojourner Truth now stood for Harper's scathing commentary on white women's need for education as much as for her own issues—equal pay for equal work, the heterogeneity of womanhood. Truth now filled Harper's space as well as her own.

The trailblazing black feminist essayist bell hooks reached for the one phrase synonymous with black women and entitled her first collection of essays in black women's studies *"Ain't I a Woman."*[41] Only Gage's original phrase, by now considered a weaker version, remained for Deborah Gray White's classic 1985 study of southern plantation slave women, *"Ar'n't I a Woman?"* Three years later, Elizabeth Fox-Genovese went beyond White to employ Truth as a spokeswoman for southern slavewomen. Never mind that Truth was a northerner, that her bondage ended before the antebellum era began, and that she never set foot on a plantation. Even professional historians like White and Fox-Genovese used Truth to stand for black women in slavery in the South.[42]

Thanks to her success in distributing her *cartes-de-visite* widely, the figure and image of Sojourner Truth proliferated in the late twentieth century: T-shirts, postcards, lapel buttons, a 1986 postage stamp, one-woman shows, and black women's organizations named "Ain't I a Woman?" made her visually and verbally omnipresent as the embodiment of black womanhood. In the 1990s, she became Americans as a whole. The Sojourner Truth Congregation, "an intentionally diverse religious community," meets in Washington, D.C., under the leadership of the Reverend Alma Faith Crawford. Truth went into space in 1995 as "Sojourner"—a twenty-five-pound, six-wheeled American robot on its way to Mars.[43]

Sojourner Truth has become American material culture's female equivalent of Malcolm X. Her image demonstrates the wearer or owner's political correctness. For all their appeal to authenticity, however, these items refashion Truth. The posters and postcards available from several outlets invariably replace Truth's caption: "I sell the shadow to support the substance. SOJOURNER TRUTH," most often by a quotation from Gage's version of the Akron speech—in the very dialect Du Bois found "hideous and ridiculous."

At the same time that Truth was becoming a fashion statement, black women's studies embedded her more deeply into academia. The maturation of black women's studies in the late 1980s spurred scholarly production and nurtured black women scholars' reclamation of Truth. As white feminist critics continued to use Truth metonymically as *the* black woman, abstracted from history and theory, black feminist critics were now fighting back. One of the more lively debates over Sojourner Truth engages Deborah McDowell, Donna Haraway, and Denise Riley in struggle over definitions of "women" and whether black women can symbolize theory as well as spontaneous action.[44]

Historians, curious about the person behind the popular symbol of Sojourner Truth, have also been seriously at work since the

I sell the Shadow to Support the Substance
Sojourner Truth
Historical Society of Battle Creek, Michigan

This postcard of Truth (date, photographer, and format unknown)
reproduces Truth's familiar caption, but to raise funds for the
Battle Creek Historical Society. Photo courtesy of Creeko Creations,
Johnson Creek, Wisconsin.

Sojourner Truth

Sojourner Truth

ABOVE. Two similar Sojourner Truth lapel buttons of the sort commonly available through mail-order outlets. The button on the right is from Ferne Sales & Manufacturing Company, West Orange, New Jersey.

BELOW. T-shirt with a plaid-clad, puzzled Truth, by Ethnique Heritage Collection.

On this magnet, a glamorous, light-brown-skinned,
close-mouthed Sojourner Truth preaches from behind a
lectern, minister-style. Both her cap and shawl appear
more elaborately than in her own *cartes-de-visite*. Magnet
by Chelsea House from a painting by Alan Nahigian,
used with the artist's permission.

mid-1980s. In 1993, Carleton Mabee, an emeritus professor of history at the State University of New York at New Paltz, in Truth's
own Ulster County, published (with his daughter, Susan Mabee
Newhouse) *Sojourner Truth: Slave, Prophet, Legend,* a thoroughly
researched account of Truth's life and immediate surroundings. A
year later, Erlene Stetson, a professor of English, Afro-American

A brown-clothed, open-necked, smiling Sojourner Truth figurine with lace shawl holds her Bible tight. Hand-painted by Cheryl, used with permission of Anna's Rainbow of Colors.

Studies, and Women's Studies at Indiana University, and her collaborator, Linda David, an independent scholar in Bloomington, Indiana, published *Glorying in Tribulation*, a biographical analysis from a black women's studies perspective of Truth's lifework of "talking aloud."[45] The present study rounds out the full-length Sojourner Truth biographies of the mid-1990s.

TRUTH iconography—the T-shirts, lapel buttons, and postcards—pulls in one direction, toward flattening out, simplifying, and widely distributing the symbolic Sojourner Truth. These objects publicize her as emblem and inspiration, a heroic Truth who never tires, never doubts, achieves in the most discouraging of circumstances. She was, after all, a slave.

Serious scholarship pulls in another, contrary direction, toward a detailed elaboration of Sojourner Truth's long life's experience, toward too nuanced a mixture of frustration and triumph to work as inspiration. Historians, of course, respect the juggernaut of popular culture and recognize that a simplified Sojourner Truth out-

Twixt the Negroes of the South and the women at the North, all talking about rights, the white man will be in a fix pretty soon.
Sojourner Truth, 1851

Postcard from Helaine Victoria Press, Inc., from a photograph from the Sophia Smith Collection. Truth's caption has been replaced by a version of Gage's 1863 rendition of Truth's 1851 speech, as though it were a quote from Truth in 1851. Photo courtesy of the Sophia Smith Collection, Smith College

side history will continue to flourish; yet we aim our investigations toward a reading public willing to transcend the simplicity of slogans.

Biographies of the mid-1990s allow students, colleagues, and readers to see Sojourner Truth not simply as an electrifying symbol and outsized force of nature, but as a figure in historical context. At least among scholars, the symbol makes room for the

Plastic pin with a young Truth in an old Truth's clothing, with a version of Gage's 1863 rendition of Truth's 1851 speech as "ain't I a woman?" By the Pyramid Complex.

nineteenth-century woman who developed as she aged, learned from her associates, and moved in identifiable human networks. Among thoughtful people, a life as well as a symbol of Sojourner Truth emerges. Although knowledge may not triumph over myth, it becomes at least a rival. Or does it? After several eye-opening encounters over the past few years, I am no longer certain.

Coda: The Triumph
of a Symbol

THOUGH our biographies differ, Mabee, Stetson and David, and I have one tactic in common: We all treat Frances Dana Gage's version of Truth critically. We separate Gage's article from whatever Truth might actually have said, which, we agree, can never be known.[1] In short, we query the symbolic Sojourner Truth so dependent on Gage's text. During the six or so years I worked on this biography, the creation and perpetuation of the symbolic Sojourner Truth became a central theme. But I found Truth's fans less fascinated than I by the process of making a symbol. Gage's Truth overshadows my research and produces unexpected responses to my work.

I should have realized something was awry when my undergraduate students and I kept misunderstanding each other. In my black women's studies course at Princeton one year, I assigned an article, "Representing Truth," that I had published in 1994.[2] Intended for professional historians, this essay may be too dense for undergraduates. But even as I worked through its points in class orally, I still encountered resistance. Faced with Marius Robinson's 1851 report of Sojourner Truth's comments, on the one hand, and with Frances Dana Gage's stirring essay written twelve years later, on the other, some of my students insisted that Gage's Truth, the

Truth of "ar'n't I a woman?" was more "true." Black, white, and Latina students insisted Robinson's uneventful reportage could not be the "real" Sojourner Truth.

I would go over the material methodically and explain, in good historian's fashion, why Robinson's report is more reliable than Gage's. "Historians have criteria for deciding which documents to trust," I would say. We examine the proximity of the report to the event and prefer the more immediate; we ask how well the reporter knew the speaker, and we go for the more familiar. We investigate motives. I would ask them to look at the particulars. Robinson knew Sojourner Truth better than Gage, because Truth made her northern Ohio base the offices of the Salem *Anti-Slavery Bugle,* which Robinson edited. She had spent days with her hosts, Marius and his wife Emily. Frances Dana Gage, however, had not met Truth before the meeting.

While Gage was busy chairing—and this was her first time as a chair—Marius Robinson was the designated recording secretary. His report of Gage's keynote address captures spoken English and demonstrates his ability to take down what people said as they were talking. Above all, Robinson published his report within weeks of Truth's speech, while Gage waited twelve years. We also know that in verifiable details, her account contradicts the historical record. Finally, Gage was in competition with Harriet Beecher Stowe, whereas Robinson did not write against anyone else. This competition supplied her a motive for heightening rhetorical effect. Applying all these criteria for weighing evidence, I would say, Robinson's report wins hands down.

This explanation convinced—or at least silenced—most of my students, but the dogged ones persisted. Gage provided the drama that they knew belonged to "Sojourner Truth," and her use of dialect reinforced the semblance of authenticity. At first I was vexed, thinking my students refused engagement with professional historians' demanding intellectual processes. I should have known that something more was at stake, for Princeton undergraduates are not simply recalcitrant. But at this point I did not understand. It took four more personal experiences, reinforced by news of other people's conversations, to awaken me to the balance of power between my historical understanding and the symbol of Sojourner Truth.

One morning I was walking with a friend along the Delaware and Raritan Canal running beside the Millstone River in Princeton. My friend, an experienced writer familiar with African-American history, knew Gage's "Sojourner Truth." I had also sent her a draft of my chapter 14 of this book, describing the Akron meeting as it emerges from the 1851 historical sources. We discussed that chapter as we walked. "Fascinating research," she told me. "Great stuff." I accepted the compliments gratefully as she reviewed the scenario I had described. Then she stopped me short with a preference for Gage's more lively Truth. She found Robinson's Truth too flat "really" to be Sojourner Truth. Now I began to recognize a bigger problem than undergraduate stubbornness.

Somewhat later, a historian spending a year at Stanford told me of her experience in a faculty seminar at the Stanford Institute for Research on Women and Gender. Some years earlier, when I had been at the Center for Advanced Study in the Behavioral Sciences, I had attended that seminar, too. I knew its members as thoughtful, conscientious readers. The historian told me they had read my "Representing Truth," but after a long discussion, she added, several women announced they still believed Gage's version. Gage's Truth, they concluded, was "the real Sojourner Truth." This came from scholars. But, then again, many of them were in literature, not history. Perhaps the explanation for miscommunication lay in their unfamiliarity with historical method. Perhaps.

But maybe not. I was totally unprepared for a comment from one of my most constant supporters, a scholar of American religion and African-American history who is also a former minister, New York Public Library administrator, and longtime collector of books. At his desk at the W. E. B. Du Bois Institute for Afro-American Research at Harvard, my friend was reading the manuscript of this book as I drafted it. He has heard me talk through the issues, including the reliability of the two versions of Truth's 1851 speech. After he read chapter 18, we speculated on the reading public's reception of my message that Gage, not Truth, invented "ar'n't I a woman?" At the close of our conversation, he joked: "I

think she said it. It sounds like her." With earlier frustrations ringing in my ears, I could only sigh, "That's not funny."

My experience at the 1995 meeting of the Organization of American Historians, an association of professional historians of the
United States, really was not funny. Every year in late March,
American historians gather to share their research and hear their
colleagues' critiques. The whole point of the meeting is hearing
other historians criticize one's work, for criticism is the lifeblood
of scholarship.

I was attending a session with two excellent papers on former
slavewomen's concept of self. As usual, I sat listening and knitting,
taking in fresh scholarship. I was astonished when one presenter
ended her paper by quoting Frances Dana Gage as Sojourner
Truth. The historian spoke as though Carleton Mabee's 1993 biography and my 1994 "Representing Truth" had not been published. I was floored. And I said so.

The effect of my critique was—to quote Stowe and many a Truth
biographer—"electric." The young historian fell to pieces, stutter-
ing that she admired my work and had, in fact, cited it in the
footnotes of her paper. Her incapacity momentarily brought the
session to a halt, for she needed several moments to collect herself. You can imagine my chagrin at hearing a historian deeply engaged with the scholarship of nineteenth-century black women
seem to miss one of the main points of my article. At first it seemed
a terrible disregard of my work.

As I later related this incident to friends, all these episodes with
students, friends, and colleagues began to fall into place, and others besides. One example: At the 1993 meeting of the Berkshire
Conference on Women's History, Carleton Mabee read a paper
charging that Gage had fabricated a Sojourner Truth personage
that feminists had connived to advance throughout the nineteenth
and twentieth centuries. When women in the audience received
him combatively, I thought his debunking tone had aggravated
them. I understand now that his tone was only part of what was
going on.

After all this instruction, I finally realize Americans of goodwill
deeply need the colossal Sojourner Truth, the black woman who
faces down a hostile white audience and, with a few choice words,

gives direction to muddled proceedings. We need an heroic "Sojourner Truth" in our public life to function as the authentic black woman, as a symbol who compensates for the imperfections of individual black women—especially educated, and thereby inauthentic, black women like me.[3] As useful in scholarly discourse as in popular culture, this eloquent genius of Sojourner Truth appears sometimes at the beginning, but usually at the end of scholarly writing. She cuts off discussion with one sharp comment, or as Harriet Beecher Stowe concluded in the "Libyan Sibyl" in 1863, "it was enough."

Another example: A few years ago, a historian unaware of my biography of Truth used her to close a comment addressed to me. We were exchanging views in a forum on the languages of race and money in the *American Historical Review,* bandying about Michel Foucault, Jacques Lacan, and Marshall Sahlins. At the end of his rejoinder, the historian said:

> I think immediately of Sojourner Truth's bared arm and her famous question—"a'n't I a woman? I have ploughed, and planted, and gathered into barns, and no man could head me! And a'n't I a woman?"[4]

As this was written before I published "Representing Truth," the historian had little reason to doubt the quote. He was free to use Truth in the way Americans have loved to use her: as an electrical presence who terminates debate. For professional historians as for lay people, the symbolic Sojourner Truth is extremely valuable.

Sojourner Truth belongs to a company of "invented greats." Jesus and Joan of Arc are only two of the most glorious among many figures known purely through the agency of others, who have constructed and maintained their legends. American culture has invented greats of its own. As one of them, Truth is consumed as a signifier and beloved for what we need her to have said. It is no accident that in each case, other people writing well after the fact made up what we see as most meaningful.

Mason "Parson" Weems invented the story of young George Washington's chopping down a cherry tree about which he was unable to tell a lie, a story that played a major role in Weems's biography of Washington.[5] Perhaps less well known is the fiction behind the legend of Betsy Ross, the woman celebrated for sewing the first American flag. Elizabeth Griscom Ross Ashburn Claypoole was, in fact, a seamstress living in Philadelphia when the Declaration of Independence was being drafted. But her tale is the invention of her grandson, William Canby, who concocted it all in 1870. The house the city of Philadelphia has designated a historical place, where the Betsy Ross doll is for sale for $19.95, was actually a bar. The bones in her grave are unidentified. Canby's Betsy Ross fills the need for a Founding Mother among the parade of men personifying the birth of the United States of America.[6]

A more recent invention is the legend of *Brother Eagle, Sister Sky*, a best-selling tract said to be an 1854 speech by wise old Chief Seattle, a Native American environmental prophet. Even though the Earth Day U.S.A. Committee distributes the book as a fundraiser, it is actually the creation of a screenwriter from Texas named Ted Perry, who wrote the text in 1971 and is horrified that it has been attributed to Chief Seattle rather than to him.[7] As with Sojourner Truth's "ar'n't I a woman?" and Betsy Ross's American flag, what makes Chief Seattle work as Chief Seattle in American culture has more to do with our need for myth than with his history.

Americans who buy Sojourner Truth's image invest in the idea of strong women, black or not. As in the nineteenth century, Americans consume Sojourner Truth as the embodiment of a construct necessary for their own cultural formations, even though its meaning has changed radically since Harriet Beecher Stowe first polished its contours.

Having opened my eyes to this enterprise, I see how my colleagues have used Sojourner Truth to silence other scholars. I see also how I myself have functioned as a sort of Sojourner Truth. Returning to that session at the 1995 meeting of the Organization of American Historians, we see that the process of "doing" Sojourner Truth did not end with the historian's paper and my critique. When the proceedings came to a standstill after my comment, I was functioning as a Sojourner Truth. My words were reenacting "Frederick, is God dead?" and "ar'n't I a woman?" Certainly not what I had intended.

Even among scholars, even almost a century and a half after

Harriet Beecher Stowe and Frances Dana Gage described Sojourner Truth's electrified audiences, the assertive words of a black woman can halt the world they pierce. Black women are not ordinarily speakers and consequently are difficult to integrate into ongoing business. The scenario of rupture has more to say about the dynamics of American public life than about the power of particular black women.

Whatever the fundamental meaning of these encounters, they have taught me two new lessons: The symbol of Sojourner Truth is stronger and more essential in our culture than the complicated historic person; and the process that makes a black woman speaking firmly into a show-stopper has not come to an end. I can explain to you the making of the symbol of Sojourner Truth, the electrifying black presence in a white crowd. But I cannot talk you out of the convictions you need to get through life. The symbol we require in our public life still triumphs over scholarship.

A Note on the Sources

THIS enterprise provokes puzzlement from general readers and historians alike: What are your sources? Sometimes the emphasis falls on Truth's illiteracy, meaning her inability to generate the primary documents—letters, journals—biographers ordinarily use. But sometimes the question carries broader implications: What sources can generate a history of the kind of person Truth was—black, female, poor, nineteenth-century? Do people like Truth *have* a history?

People like Truth do have a history, of course. But a Truth biographer, like the biographer of any poor person, any person of color, or a woman of any stratum, cannot stick to convention, for conventional sources mostly are lacking. This history demands more or less uncommon research methods, starting with the richest potential resource: newspaper articles published by friends, colleagues, and competitors, principally, in Truth's case, the antislavery press and articles reprinted in the *History of Woman Suffrage*. Newspapers, pamphlets, and other ephemera useful in Truth research illuminate unexpected corners of American life, but only rare repositories collect them for the early nineteenth century. Luckily the American Antiquarian Society in Worcester, Massachusetts, is full of such sources. I recommend it to others researching the histories of non-elite Americans in the eighteenth and early nineteenth centuries. Local historical societies—in this case the Battle Creek Historical Society and the Willard Library in Battle Creek, Michigan, and the Westchester County Archives in New York—can also be extremely useful.

Ordinarily we think of rare book collections and private libraries as places to study the elite, but they hold a variety of treasures. One of the first places I found Sojourner Truth was the Library Company of Philadelphia, which owns a copy of Gilbert Vale's invaluable investigation of the Kingdom of Matthias, based largely on interviews with then Isabella Van Wagenen.

Between my own Princeton University library and Speer Library at the Princeton Theological Seminary, I found most, but not all, of what I needed to read. Interlibrary loan gained me access to rare books, unpublished dissertations, and master's theses examining esoteric topics so crucial to understanding Truth's human and historical contexts. I count myself fortunate that I had access to Firestone Library at Princeton, whose interlibrary loan services work so efficiently.

For Truth, specifically, the challenges exceeded the usual lack of sources about a figure who was not white, male, or educated. Not only did she not write, she also belonged to religious communities that did not prize mere horizontal communication—communication between people. While abolitionists and feminists wrote to one another and published newspapers almost compulsively, Truth's perfectionists communicated vertically with the Holy Spirit. New York perfectionists generated virtually nothing in print. Happily, one New Haven perfectionist, John Humphrey Noyes, departed from habit. In the columns of his newspapers, Noyes excoriated James Latourette, a pivotal figure in Isabella's religious formation. Without Noyes's published enmity, the evolution and career of Isabella as a perfectionist would remain yet more shadowy.

Sojourner Truth seldom appears in the correspondence and memoirs of her abolitionist colleagues. A black woman, an uneducated person, and a pentecostal preacher, she remained outside the human worlds they captured easily in words—in private correspondence, at least. Although Truth appears from time to time in the correspondence of William Lloyd Garrison and Isaac and Amy Post, her fullest descriptions were composed for publication in the antislavery press—e.g., by the séance-attending Rochester abolitionist Elizabeth Lukins—or in books by Frederick Douglass, Gilbert Vale, and Lucy Colman. Another rich resource, Berenice Bryant Lowe's "Sojourner Truth" Collection in the Bentley Historical Library at the University of Michigan, Ann Arbor, contains unexpected gems. A retired schoolteacher in Battle Creek, Lowe painstakingly collected every bit of information she could find on Truth, shared it with Hertha Pauli, and gave it to the Bentley Historical Library in 1964. Dorothy Martich has continued that work in a series of notebooks in the Willard Library in Battle Creek. The people of Truth's town have not neglected her memory.

As my notes attest, the secondary sources—material generated by scholars—are wide-ranging and abundant. Trained conventionally as an American historian, I knew practically nothing of popular religion, which I now see as absolutely necessary for an understanding of American culture. Fortunately for me, the history of popular religion has been flourishing, producing studies of unorthodox religions like spiritualism and perfectionism as well as the less-known manifestations of Methodism.

Writing the biography of someone who did not write demanded my emancipation from purely verbal sources. I needed to learn to read the sources that Truth generated herself: her photographs. Her *cartes-de-visite*, I discovered, conveyed their own messages, needing as much to be heard as what she said in words. Portraits often do not exist for poor subjects, but when available, they require as careful analysis as written documents. Deciphering photographs sends the historian to libraries of art history, a trip well worth making for the study of images generally, not simply photographs.

Scholarly readers will find full citations in my notes. I hope their variety invites other historians into the literatures of fields besides our own.

Notes

PART I

PART I
CHAPTER 1 Isabella,
Sojourner Truth,
and American Slavery

1. Berenice Bryant Lowe, "How Tall Was Sojourner Truth?" 1975, Berenice Bryant Lowe Collection, Folder 13, Michigan Historical Collections, Bentley Historical Library, University of Michigan, Ann Arbor. Howard Gardner posits the existence of "several relatively autonomous human intellectual competences" that would help explain Truth's inability to learn reading and writing coextensive with a ready intelligence and sharp wit. See his *Frames of Mind: The Theory of Multiple Intelligences* (New York: Basic Books, 1985), pp. 8–9. See also pp. 39–40, 60–61, 73–98, 242–243.

2. The classic text in this regard is Gloria T. Hull, Patricia Bell Scott, and Barbara Smith, eds., *But Some of Us Are Brave: Black Women's Studies* (Old Westbury, NY: Feminist Press, 1982).

3. See Roland Barthes, *Mythologies*, ed. and trans. Annette Lavers (1957; reprint New York: Farrar, Straus & Giroux, 1972), pp. 58, 123, 127, 143.

4. "Pentecostal" is a twentieth-century word that appears here at the forbearance of the reader. Although Truth's beliefs were what we now call pentecostal, in her own time, people like her were called "perfectionists." As "perfectionist" now pertains to secular people who are impatient with human weakness, I am importing "pentecostal," on the ground that while it is anachro-

nistic, it is more likely to convey my meaning than the nineteenth-century word.

5. Truth called herself a self-made woman. See [Olive Gilbert and Frances Titus], *Narrative of Sojourner Truth; A Bondswoman of Olden Time, Emancipated by the New York Legislature in the Early Part of the Present Century; with a History of her Labors and Correspondence Drawn from her "Book of Life"* (1878; reprint Salem, NH: Ayer Company, 1990), p. v.

6. Cf. A. J. Williams-Myers, *Long Hammering: Essays on the Forging of an African American Presence in the Hudson River Valley to the Early Twentieth Century* (Trenton, NJ: Africa World Press, 1994), pp. 34, 43, 60.

7. T. F. Gordon, *Gazetteer of the State of New York.* Vol. 2 (Philadelphia: Printed for the author, 1836), pp. 736–738. Alphonso T. Clearwater, ed., *The History of Ulster County, New York* (Kingston, NY: W. J. Van Deusen, 1907), p. 263. Augustus H. Van Buren, *A History of Ulster County Under the Dominion of the Dutch* (Kingston, NY: [n.p.], 1923), pp. 13–14.

8. In the eighteenth century, the local Indians, then called Esopus, were divided into white Esopus and black Esopus, giving Ulster County four rather than three races. Williams-Myers, *Long Hammering*, p. 6.

9. Alice P. Kenney, *Stubborn for Liberty: The Dutch in New York* (Syracuse, NY: Syracuse University Press, 1975), p. 95. According to a Swedish botanist visiting the Hudson Valley in 1749, the wheat flour from around Albany was considered to be the best milled in all the Americas, with the exception of that from Esopus (the old name for Kingston) in Ulster County.

10. Isaac Weld, Jr., *Travels Through the States of North America, and the Provinces of Upper and Lower Canada, During the Years 1795, 1796, and 1797.* Vol. 2 (London: John Stockdale, 1800), p. 372.

11. The breakdown was 26,334 whites and 3,220 blacks, of whom 157 were free. Edgar J. McManus, *A History of Negro Slavery in New York* (Syracuse, NY: Syracuse University Press, 1966), pp. 25, 30, 42–43, 176, 200. Shane White, *Somewhat More Independent: The End of Slavery in New York City, 1770–1810* (Athens, GA: University of Georgia Press, 1991), p. 82.

12. White, *Somewhat More Independent*, pp. 17, 189–190. See also J. L. Dillard, *A History of American English* (London: Longman, 1992), pp. 24–29.

13. Ibid., p. 190.

14. H. Hendricks, "Sojourner Truth," *National Magazine* XVI (1892): 671.

15. An undated and mostly illegible clipping [1879], Berenice Bryant Lowe, Sojourner Truth, Section IX.

16. For detailed discussion of *Uncle Tom's Cabin*, see Eric J. Sundquist, ed., *New Essays on Uncle Tom's Cabin* (Cambridge, ENG: Cambridge University Press, 1986), especially Richard Yarborough, "Strategies of Black Characterization in *Uncle Tom's Cabin* and the Early Afro-American Novel," pp. 45–84.

17. United States Department of Commerce, Bureau of the Census, *Negro Population, 1790–1915* (1918; reprint New York: Arno Press and the New York Times, 1968), pp. 45, 51, 57.

CHAPTER 2 Isabella, A Slave

1. The place of Isabella's birth is located on Dorothy Dumond's map of the town of Esopus (Kingston), Ulster County, March 1991.

2. This information and all that follows about Isabella's childhood comes from [Olive Gilbert and Frances Titus], *Narrative of Sojourner Truth; A Bondswoman of Olden Time, Emancipated by the New York Legislature in the Early Part of the Present Century; with a History of her Labors and Correspondence Drawn from her "Book of Life"* (1878; reprint Salem, NH: Ayer Company, 1990).

3. Nathaniel Bartlett Sylvester, *History of Ulster County, New York, With Illustrations and Biographical Sketches of Its Prominent Men and Pioneers.* Part 2 (Philadelphia: Everts & Pack, 1880), pp. 147–148, 154, 169.

4. Gary B. Nash and Jean R. Soderlund, *Freedom by Degrees: Emancipation in Pennsylvania and Its Aftermath* (New York: Oxford University Press, 1991), pp. 188–192.

5. *Narrative of Sojourner Truth*, pp. 15–16.

6. "Chronology, Notes, and Sources on the Life of Sojourner Truth," p. 1, lists the exact place names where Isabella worked as a slave in Ulster County. Berenice Bryant Lowe Collection, Michigan Historical Collections, Bentley Historical Library, University of Michigan, Ann Arbor.

7. *Narrative of Sojourner Truth*, p. 26.

8. Brant F. Steele calls attachment disorders—in Isabella's case, bad attachments—one of the most troubling long-term effects of child abuse. "Notes on the Lasting Effects of Early Child Abuse Throughout the Life Cycle," *Child Abuse and Neglect* 10 (1986): 289.

9. *Narrative of Sojourner Truth*, pp. 30–32.

10. Steele, "Notes on the Lasting Effects of Early Child Abuse . . . ," pp. 285–286. Just as the abuse that Isabella suffered damaged her psychic development, her fearful punishment of her hungry children would have made them vulnerable to low self-esteem as well.

11. See, e.g., Saunders Redding, *Lonesome Road: The Story of the Negro's Part in America* (New York: Doubleday, 1958), and Hertha Pauli, *Her Name Was Sojourner Truth* (New York: Appleton-Century-Crofts, 1962).

12. *Narrative of Sojourner Truth*, pp. 37, 81.

13. Diana E. H. Russell, *Sexual Exploitation: Rape, Child Sexual Abuse, and Workplace Harassment* (Newbury Park, CA: Sage Publications, 1984), pp. 219,

224, 231. Russell points out that even though genital penetration is more salient in the imagery of child sexual abuse, most perpetrators fondle children's genitals or persuade the child to manipulate theirs (p. 229).

14. *Narrative of Sojourner Truth*, p. 82.

15. See Arthur M. Kelly, *Vital Records of Low Dutch Church of Klyn Esopus, Ulster Park, New York, 1791–1889* (Rhinebeck, NY: Arthur M. Kelly, 1980), pp. 8, 14, 119, 129. On the wider, familial ramifications of child sexual abuse, see David Finkelhor, *A Sourcebook on Child Sexual Abuse* (Newbury Park, CA: Sage Publications, 1986), p. 72.

16. *Narrative of Sojourner Truth*, pp. 33–34.

17. Dorothy Martich, "Sojourner Truth Chronology," Willard Public Library, Battle Creek, Michigan.

18. *Narrative of Sojourner Truth*, pp. 83–84.

19. Ibid., p. 66.

20. Ibid., pp. 36–37, says that a slave preacher, i.e., not an ordained minister, married Isabella and Thomas. Gertrude Dumont recalled Isabella and Thomas as living together without having been married. Their five children would make this a common law marriage, quite common among poor and rural people. H. Hendricks, "Sojourner Truth," *National Magazine* XVI (1892): 668–669. On slave marriages, see Edgar J. McManus, *A History of Negro Slavery in New York* (Syracuse, NY: Syracuse University Press, 1966), p. 178.

21. "Sojourner Truth: Data collected and edited by Berenice Lowe," Lowe Collection.

22. "Sojourner Truth—As Seen by Diana Corbin. Her Interesting Daughter Knows Many Anecdotes of Days Gone By," Battle Creek *Sunday Record*, 4 February 1900, Lowe Collection, Section VII.

23. Battle Creek, [no paper name], 25 October 1904, "Sojourner Truth," Lowe Collection, Section VII.

24. A fugitive, unsigned document, dated 29 January 1884 and found in an Ulster County home near where Isabella lived, says that John Dumont's son (probably Solomon) said her marriage to Thomas was not happy. This letter is in the possession of Carl Van Wagenen of Ulster County, New York.

CHAPTER 3 Journey Toward Freedom

1. If psychologists studied the traumas of earlier times, they would probably classify emancipation as a thoroughly disorienting life event, even though slaves saw it as a positive change. Fraught with uncertainty, freedom would have entailed a major reorientation of one's usual activities. See John W. Reich and Alex J. Zautra, "Direct and Stress-Moderating Effects of Positive Life Experiences," in Lawrence H. Cohen, ed., *Life Events and Psychological Functioning: Theo-*

retical and Methodological Issues (Newbury Park, CA: Sage Publications, 1988), pp. 152–156.

2. H. Hendricks, "Sojourner Truth," *National Magazine* XVI (1892): 669. Binding is tying together stocks of cut wheat after the cradler has cut it with a scythe. Truth was later to speak proudly of having been able to keep up with the cradler.

3. Carl Nordstrom, "The New York Slave Code," *Afro-Americans in New York Life and History* 4, no. 1 (January 1980): 19–20.

4. J. Saunders Redding's treatment of Isabella as a mother is unfairly harsh. He criticizes her for not keeping her children with her after she left Dumont and for taking only Peter with her to New York in 1828. Yet none of her children but Peter (whose illegal sale released him from indenture) was able to leave Dumont at that time. Saunders Redding, *Lonesome Road: The Story of the Negro's Part in America* (New York: Doubleday, 1958), pp. 66, 67.

5. In every northern state, as the date set for general emancipation approached, slaves and owners entered into intricate, personal negotiations in which slaves sought more or less successfully to reduce their remaining time in bondage. In Connecticut, the state legislature decreed in 1788 that everyone born after 1792 would be free, but that the enslaved born before that date must serve until they turned twenty-five. James Mars, born in Canaan in 1790, was to have served his master until 1815, but Mars negotiated an early emancipation and the same freedom bounty that indentured white men received. Many others, especially young men, simply ran away. James Mars, *Life of James Mars, A Slave Born and Sold in Connecticut. Written By Himself* (8th ed., 1869; reprint Miami: Mnemosyne Publishing, 1969), pp. 29–31.

6. Jan Todd to Nell Irvin Painter, Bethel, Maine, 5 September 1992.

7. [Olive Gilbert and Frances Titus], *Narrative of Sojourner Truth; A Bondswoman of Olden Time, Emancipated by the New York Legislature in the Early Part of the Present Century; with a History of her Labors and Correspondence Drawn from her "Book of Life"* (1878; reprint Salem, NH: Ayer Company, 1990), p. 60; Albert J. Raboteau, *Slave Religion: The "Invisible Institution" in the Antebellum South* (New York: Oxford University Press, 1978), pp. 212–215; Milton C. Sernett, *Black Religion and American Evangelicalism: White Protestants, Plantation Missions, and the Flowering of Negro Christianity, 1787–1865* (Metuchen, NJ: Scarecrow Press, 1975), pp. 101–103.

8. *Narrative of Sojourner Truth*, pp. 59–61. See also Harold A. Carter, *The Prayer Tradition of Black People* (Valley Forge, PA: Judson Press, 1976), p. 33.

9. See also Benjamin E. Mays, *The Negro's God As Reflected in His Literature* (Boston: Chapman & Grimes, 1938), p. 14.

10. Memoir and genealogy from Carl Van Wagenen, 8 March 1991, based on a letter found in the home of Beatrice Jordan of St. Remy, New York, written on 29 January 1884.

Wagondale (Wahkendall in Truth's *Narrative*) is now called Bloomington and is in the town of Hurley.

11. G.[ilbert] Vale, *Fanaticism; Its Source and Influence, Illustrated by the Simple Narrative of Isabella in the Case of Matthias, Mr. and Mrs. B. Folger, Mr. Pierson, Mr. Mills, Catherine, Isabella, &c. &c. A Reply to W. L. Stone, with Descriptive Portraits of All the Parties, While at Sing-Sing and at Third Street.– Containing the Whole Truth–and Nothing But the Truth.* Part I (New York: G. Vale, 1835), pp. 17–18.

CHAPTER 4   Sanctification

1. Russell E. Richey, *Early American Methodism* (Bloomington, IN: Indiana University Press, 1991), p. 82. For the journal of a late eighteenth-century New Jersey itinerant Methodist preacher who gloried in "tearing up old Calvin," see John Ffirth, *The Experience and Gospel Labours of the Rev. Benjamin Abbott: to which is Annexed a Narrative of his Life and Death* (Philadelphia: Ezekiel Cooper, 1801).

2. H. Hendricks, "Sojourner Truth," *National Magazine* XVI (1892): 669.

3. Antebellum holiness people used a variety of phrases that evoked the Pentecost: "Pentecostal outpourings of the Holy Spirit," "outpouring of the Spirit," "effusions of the Holy Spirit," "a return of apostolic days," and "Pentecostal revival." See Richard Wheatley, *The Life and Letters of Mrs. Phoebe Palmer* (New York: W. C. Palmer, 1881), pp. 302, 264, 341–342.

4. In the Netherlands, Pinkster is still recognized as an official national holiday.

5. A. J. Williams-Myers, "Pinkster Carnival: Africanisms in the Hudson River Valley," *Afro-Americans in New York Life and History* (January 1985): 9–14; Shane White, *Somewhat More Independent: The End of Slavery in New York City, 1770–1810* (Athens, GA: University of Georgia Press, 1991), pp. 95–106.

6. In the 1880s, Gertrude Dumont presented a very different version of Isabella's flight. According to Dumont, Isabella "returned to us soon afterward and wanted father to keep her child, but he said it was too young to be left without its mother, although we did take the child afterward. Isabel begged father to take her back also, but he refused. He said he has always treated her well; and now since she had run away he would have nothing more to do with her." Hendricks, "Sojourner Truth," p. 668.

It is not possible to find out what actually happened. Truth gave her version twenty years after the event; Dumont spoke more than fifty years afterward. But even had they recorded their views in 1827, they would probably have been discrepant. Each woman had a larger narrative, based on her position within Ulster County society and her individual experience, into which this incident had to fit. Isabella's story, which I present here, is the pivot of her religious formation, without which her sanctification cannot occur.

The discussion of the sometimes competing claims of experience and language (or "discourse") is current in feminist theory. See, for example, Kathleen Canning, "Feminist History after the Linguistic Turn: Historicizing Discourse and Experience," *SIGNS* 19, no. 2 (Winter 1994): 368–404.

7. [Olive Gilbert and Frances Titus], *Narrative of Sojourner Truth; A Bondswoman of Olden Time, Emancipated by the New York Legislature in the Early Part of the Present Century; with a History of her Labors and Correspondence Drawn from her "Book of Life"* (1878; reprint Salem, NH: Ayer Company, 1990), p. 65.

8. See Christian R. Davis, "The Rhetoric of Nineteenth-Century American Evangelical Autobiography," unpublished Ph.D. dissertation, Pennsylvania State University, 1985, p. 25.

9. *Narrative of Sojourner Truth,* pp. 66–68; James H. Cone, *God of the Oppressed* (San Francisco: Harper San Francisco, 1975), pp. 31–32, 35, 105, 139.

10. Arthur A. Stone et al., "Coping with Stressful Events: Coping Dimensions and Issues," in Lawrence H. Cohen, ed., *Life Events and Psychological Functioning: Theoretical and Methodological Issues* (Newbury Park, CA: Sage Publications, 1988), p. 187.

11. Jacquelyn Grant, *White Women's Christ and Black Women's Jesus: Feminist Christology and Womanist Response* (Atlanta: Scholars Press, 1989), pp. 104, 144, 211–212, 215.

12. Cheryl Townsend Gilkes, " 'Together and in Harness': Women's Traditions in the Sanctified Church," *SIGNS* 10, no. 4 (1985): 678–699.

13. Stone et al., "Coping with Stressful Events," p. 188. See also Gayraud S. Wilmore, *Black Religion and Black Radicalism: An Interpretation of the Religious History of Afro-American People* (2nd ed. Maryknoll, NY: Orbis Books, 1983), pp. 12–14, 57–60.

CHAPTER 5 Plaintiff and Witch

1. Memoir and genealogy from Carl Van Wagenen, 8 March 1991, based on a letter found in the home of Beatrice Jordan of St. Remy, New York, written on 29 January 1884.

2. For one example, see Solomon Northup, *Twelve Years a Slave*, Sue Eakin and Joseph Logsdon, eds., (1853; reprint Baton Rouge: Louisiana State University Press, 1968).

3. [Olive Gilbert and Frances Titus], *Narrative of Sojourner Truth; A Bondswoman of Olden Time, Emancipated by the New York Legislature in the Early Part of the Present Century; with a History of her Labors and Correspondence Drawn from her "Book of Life"* (1878; reprint Salem, NH: Ayer Company, 1990), pp. 44–45.

4. Ibid., p. 70.

5. G.[ilbert] Vale, *Fanaticism; Its Source and Influence, Illustrated by the Simple Narrative of Isabella in the case of Matthias, Mr. and Mrs. B. Folger, Mr. Pierson, Mr. Mills, Catherine, Isabella, &c. &c. A Reply to W. L. Stone, with Descriptive Portraits of All the Parties, While at Sing-Sing and at Third Street.– Containing the Whole Truth–and Nothing But the Truth.* Part I (New York: G. Vale, 1835), p. 11. The New York Manumission Society, which flourished at the turn of the century, helped recover New York slaves illegally sold to the South, but it had been most active in New York City.

6. See John Bowlby, *Attachment and Loss.* Vol. II. *Separation: Anxiety and Anger* (New York: Basic Books, 1973), pp. xii, 19, 21.

7. *Narrative of Sojourner Truth*, pp. 52–54. See also Timothy McMillan, "Black Magic: Witchcraft, Race, and Resistance in Colonial New England," *Journal of Black Studies* 25, no. 1 (September 1994): 103–106.

8. Jon Butler, *Religion and Witchcraft in Early American Society* (St. Charles, MO: Forum Press, 1974), p. 2; Keith Thomas, *Religion and the Decline of Magic: Studies in Popular Beliefs in Sixteenth and Seventeenth Century England* (London: Weidenfeld and Nicolson, 1971), pp. 264–267, 502–507. See also Henry H. Mitchell, *Black Belief: Folk Beliefs of Blacks in America and West Africa* (New York: Harper & Row, 1975), p. 112; Eugen Weber, *Peasants into Frenchmen: The Modernization of Rural France, 1870–1914* (Stanford, CA: Stanford University Press, 1976), p. 26.

9. *Narrative of Sojourner Truth*, pp. 55–58.

10. "Chronology, Notes, and Sources on the Life of Sojourner Truth," Sojourner Truth data collected and edited by Berenice Lowe, Michigan Historical Collections, Bentley Historical Library, University of Michigan, Ann Arbor.

CHAPTER 6 New York Perfectionism

1. G.[ilbert] Vale, *Fanaticism; Its Source and Influence, Illustrated by the Simple Narrative of Isabella in the case of Matthias, Mr. and Mrs. B. Folger, Mr. Pierson, Mr. Mills, Catherine, Isabella, &c. &c. A Reply to W. L. Stone, with Descriptive Portraits of All the Parties, While at Sing-Sing and at Third Street.– Containing the Whole Truth–and Nothing But the Truth.* Part I (New York: G. Vale, 1835), p. 18; [Olive Gilbert and Frances Titus], *Narrative of Sojourner Truth; A Bondswoman of Olden Time, Emancipated by the New York Legislature in the Early Part of the Present Century; with a History of her Labors and Correspondence Drawn from her "Book of Life"* (1878; reprint Salem, NH: Ayer Company, 1990), p. 86; Whitney R. Cross, *The Burned-Over District: The Social and Intellectual History of Enthusiastic Religion in Western New York, 1800–1850* (Ithaca, NY: Cornell University Press, 1950), p. 240.

2. See E. P. Thompson, *The Making of the English Working Class* (rev. ed. Harmondsworth, ENG: Penguin Books, 1968), p. 417.

3. *Narrative of Sojourner Truth*, pp. 80–81.

4. Ibid., p. 78; Lyman Ezra Latourette, *Latourette Annals in America* (Portland, OR[?]: Lyman Latourette, 1954), pp. 1, 50. Latourette died in 1841. On Hutchinson, see Philip F. Gura, *A Glimpse of Sion's Glory: Puritan Radicalism in New England, 1620–1660* (Middletown, CT: Wesleyan University Press, 1984), pp. 49–61.

5. Richard P. Heitzenrater, *Wesley and the People Called Methodists* (1992) unpublished ms., pp. 34, 46, 89–90, used with the permission of the author; Ithaca, *The Witness*, vol. I, no. 10 (25 September 1839): 74; vol. I, no. 3 (23 September 1837): 19. See also, for example, the lay Methodist preacher Diana Morris, a poor millworker of "sincere unpremeditated eloquence," in George Eliot's *Adam Bede* (1859).

6. William L. Stone, *Matthias and His Impostures: Or, the Progress of Fanaticism. Illustrated in the Extraordinary Case of Robert Matthews, and Some of His Forerunners and Disciples* (3rd ed. New York: Harper & Brothers, 1835), pp. 316–317.

7. Ibid., pp. 314–316. Ithaca, *Witness*, vol. I, no. 10 (25 September 1839); John Humphrey Noyes, *Confessions of John H. Noyes. Part I. Confession of Religious Experience: Including a History of Modern Perfectionism* (Oneida Reserve, NY: Leonard & Company, 1849), pp. 85–86. See also John Leland Peters, *Christian Perfection and American Methodism* (New York: Abingdon Press, 1966); Whitney R. Cross, *The Burned-Over District*.

8. See Elizabeth Blackmar, *Manhattan for Rent: 1785–1850* (Ithaca, NY: Cornell University Press, 1989), pp. 75–76, 107, 117; Sean Wilentz, *Chants Democratic: New York City and the Rise of the American Working Class, 1788–1850* (New York: Oxford University Press, 1984), pp. 109–117. Vale, *Fanaticism.* Part I, pp. 24–25; Stone, *Matthias and His Impostures*, pp. 46–50, 59.

Holiness ideals attracted people as disparate as the fiery New York evangelical preacher Charles Grandison Finney; Phoebe Palmer, who held holiness meetings in her respectable New York City home to which came the upper-class New England college professor Thomas Upham; the migratory New England author Harriet Beecher Stowe; an anonymous black preacher in Florida; and New Yorkers of various classes, races, and religious backgrounds. See Charles Edwin Jones, *Perfectionist Persuasion: The Holiness Movement and American Methodism, 1867–1936* (Metuchen, NJ: Scarecrow Press, 1974), pp. 1–8. The Florida preacher is cited in Ulrich B. Phillips, *American Negro Slavery: A Survey of the Supply, Employment and Control of Negro Labor as Determined by the Plantation Regime* (New York: Appleton-Century, 1940), pp. 294–295.

In the midst of the roaring 1820s, when prosperous merchants regarded their wives and homes as showplaces of success, the women around Frances Folger refused this role. In 1829, Folger, followed by some of her adherents, moved to Bowery Hill, a woodsy suburban neighborhood. Folger and her co-religionists had reached out first to other members of the bourgeoisie, but in the early 1830s they welcomed poor black women like Isabella into their ranks, another practice encouraged by the eighteenth-century example of John Wesley.

9. New York *Journal of Commerce*, 1 June 1831.

10. Blackmar, *Manhattan for Rent*, p. 164.

11. In the late 1820s, some of Latourette's followers spoke in tongues, though there is no direct evidence that Isabella did. At least into the mid-1840s she did share the expectation of an imminent apocalypse. See Melvin E. Dieter, *The Holiness Revival of the Nineteenth Century* (Metuchen, NJ: Scarecrow Press, 1980), pp. 4–25; Vinson Synan, *The Holiness-Pentecostal Movement in the United States* (Grand Rapids, MI: Eerdmans, 1971), pp. 13–30; Charles Edwin Jones, *The Perfectionist Persuasion*, pp. xvii–6. Timothy L. Smith, "The Doctrine of the Sanctifying Spirit: Charles G. Finney's Synthesis of Wesleyan and Covenant Theology," *Wesleyan Theological Journal* 13 (Spring 1978): 92–113; Charles Edwin Jones, *Black Holiness: A Guide to the Study of Black Participation in Wesleyan Perfectionist and Glossolalic Pentecostal Movements* (Metuchen, NJ: Scarecrow Press, 1987), pp. xix, 1, 37, 83–84; Mark A. Noll, *A History of Christianity in the United States and Canada* (Grand Rapids, MI: Eerdmans, 1992), pp. 386–388; Timothy L. Smith, "The Theology and Practices of Methodism, Part 3," in *The History of American Methodism*. Vol. II, Emory Stevens Bucke, ed. (New York: Abingdon Press, 1964), pp. 606–611; Lycurgus M. Starkey, Jr., *The Work of the Holy Spirit: A Study in Wesleyan Theology* (New York: Abingdon Press, 1962), pp. 9, 22–26, 63–78; and Paul Boyer, *When Time Shall Be No More: Prophecy Belief in Modern American Culture* (Cambridge, MA: Harvard University Press, 1992), pp. 4, 11, 93, 178.

12. Jean McMahon Humez, ed., *Gifts of Power: The Writings of Rebecca Jackson, Black Visionary, Shaker Eldress* (Amherst, MA: University of Massachusetts Press, 1981), pp. 92–93. In the early 1830s Jackson and another black woman, Jarena Lee, were preaching sensations around Philadelphia. Humez, p. 21. See also Timothy Merritt, *The Convert's Guide and Preacher's Assistant* (9th ed., New York: Carlton & Porter, 1857), p. 152.

13. H. Hendricks, "Sojourner Truth," *National Magazine* XVI (1892): 669.

14. Richard Cordley, "Sojourner Truth," Boston *Congregationalist*, 3 March 1880.

15. Cordley, "Sojourner Truth." See also Christine Stansell, *City of Women: Sex and Class in New York, 1789–1860* (New York: Alfred A. Knopf, 1986), pp. 93, 163–165.

16. Debra Clyde, " 'A People Called Methodists': The Van Coortlandts and Methodism in Early America, Historic Hudson Valley, Tarrytown, NY," in *Westchester Historian* 66, no. 3 (Summer 1990): 51–56; C. W. Christman, Jr.,

The Onward Way: The Story of the New York Annual Conference of the Methodist Church Commemorating the 150th Session of the Conference, June 16, 1800–May 12, 1949 (Saugerties, NY: Catskill Mountains Publishing Corp., 1949), p. 12. The Croton camp meeting lasted from 1805 to 1831, when it was superseded by the Mount Pleasant camp meeting.

17. Latourette quoted in Vale, *Fanaticism*, Part I, p. 21; Part II, p. 126.

18. Moses Elsemore, *An Impartial Account of the Life of the Rev. John N. Maffitt, With a Narrative of the Difficulties Attending His First Marriage* (New York: John F. Feeks, 1848), p. 11.

19. Vale, *Fanaticism*, Part I, p. 21; Roswell Rice, *An Oration with Monumental Inscriptions, on the Rev. John N. Maffitt* (Troy, NY: Whig Publishing, 1874), pp. 3, 13; James Mudge, *History of the New England Conference of the Methodist Episcopal Church, 1796–1910* (Boston: Published by the Conference, 1910), p. 92.

20. Catherine A. Brekus, " 'Let Your Women Keep Silence in the Churches': Female Preaching and Evangelical Religion in America, 1740–1845," unpublished Ph.D. dissertation, Yale University, 1993, pp. 1–2, 91, 160–161, 244, 283–286; Noyes, *Confessions*, Part I, p. 42.

21. *Narrative of Sojourner Truth*, pp. 87–88.

22. Ibid., pp. 96–97.

23. *The Magdalen Report. First Annual Report of the Executive Committee of the New-York Magdalen Society. Instituted, January 1, 1830* (New York: New-York Historical Society, 1831). See also Bertram Wyatt-Brown, *Lewis Tappan and the Evangelical War Against Slavery* (Cleveland: Press of Case Western Reserve University, 1969), pp. 51–55, 60–70.

24. *History of the First Presbyterian Church, Morristown, NJ*, Part II. *The Combined Registers, From 1742–1885*, p. 183; Paul E. Johnson and Sean Wilentz, *The Kingdom of Matthias* (New York: Oxford University Press, 1994), pp. 14–19, 25–26; Vale, *Fanaticism*, Part II, p. 19; *Memoirs of Matthias the Prophet, with a Full Exposure of His Atrocious Impositions, and of the Degrading Delusions of His Followers* (New York: New York Sun, 1835), p. 8.

25. *Memoirs of Matthias the Prophet*, p. 8; Malachi 4:5.

26. *Narrative of Sojourner Truth*, pp. 88–89. Katy was a slave in Virginia, and in order for her to be able to return to Virginia to visit her children, Pierson bought her freedom for $400. Stone, *Matthias and His Impostures*, pp. 80–82.

CHAPTER 7 In the Kingdom of Matthias

1. *Memoirs of Matthias the Prophet, with a Full Exposure of His Atrocious Impositions, and of the Degrading Delusions of his Followers* (New York: New York Sun, 1835), pp. 4–9. On chromo likeness: [Anonymous], *An Authentic History*

of Remarkable Persons, Who Have Attracted Public Attention in Various Parts of the World: Including a Full Exposure of the Iniquities of the Pretended Prophet Joe Smith, and of the Seven Degrees of the Mormon Temple; also an Account of the Frauds Practised by Matthias the Prophet, and Other Religious Impostors (New York: Wilson & Company, Brother Jonathan Press, 1849), p. 35.

In Matthew 16:13–19, Jesus asks the disciples: "Whom do men say that I the Son of man am?" The disciples report the thoughts of the people to Jesus, who asks them who *they* say he is. Peter replies, "Thou art the Christ, the Son of the living God." Jesus blesses Peter and promises that Peter will build his church and hold the keys of the kingdom of heaven.

2. [Olive Gilbert and Frances Titus], *Narrative of Sojourner Truth; A Bondswoman of Olden Time, Emancipated by the New York Legislature in the Early Part of the Present Century; with a History of her Labors and Correspondence Drawn from her "Book of Life"* (1878; reprint Salem, NH: Ayer Company, 1990), p. 93.

3. Matthias's predecessors in New York included Johnny Edwards, a Welsh immigrant scale-maker, and a preacher named Dorothy Ripley who joined him in 1810. They tried to start a revival in Wall Street, where using a three-foot-long tin trumpet Edwards warned the moneylenders to repent before the world ended on 10 June 1810. In Potters Field on the Fourth of July 1826, a gardener named David Whitehead preached that God would destroy the rich, self-indulgent "pretty set" of the city. Sean Wilentz, *Chants Democratic: New York City and the Rise of the American Working Class, 1788–1850* (New York: Oxford University Press, 1984), pp. 81–82.

4. William L. Stone, *Matthias and His Impostures: Or, the Progress of Fanaticism. Illustrated in the Extraordinary Case of Robert Matthews, and Some of his Forerunners and Disciples* (3rd ed. New York: Harper & Brothers, 1835), pp. 18–30, 120–122, 128; *Memoirs of Matthias*, pp. 4–5, and *Authentic History of Remarkable Persons*, p. 36. See also Donald W. Dayton, "The Doctrine of the Baptism of the Holy Spirit: Its Emergence and Significance," *Wesleyan Theological Journal* 13 (Spring 1978): 114–126.

5. The Bible (Acts 1:23, 26) contains little information about the original Matthias beyond his identity as the disciple chosen to take Judas' place. The biblical Matthias' importance for this New York story lies more in his function, which was to fill a vacancy and allow the Apostles to receive the gift of the Spirit at Pentecost. *The Anchor Bible Dictionary*, David Noel Freedman et al., eds. Vol. IV (New York: Doubleday, 1992), p. 644.

As Matthias of New York explained himself, he was "a traveller," who possessed the Spirit of Truth and the Spirit of God, which he used interchangeably. This Spirit, he said, had originally been imparted to Adam and then become spread abroad over the earth as mankind multiplied. With so wide a dispersal, the Spirit lost its power and was in need of reconcentration in one individual, who would have "knowledge of all the iniquities of mankind, which always led to the destruction of man." Matthias said he had the power to exercise the wrath of God. *New York Courier and Enquirer*, 17 April 1835; *New York Commercial Advertiser*, 2 October 1834; *New York Sun*, 17 April 1835.

6. *Memoirs of Matthias*, p. 7; Stone, *Matthias and His Impostures*, pp. 120–122, 132.

7. Stone, *Matthias and His Impostures*, pp. 142–143, 219, 318.

8. Vale, *Fanaticism*, Part I, p. 61.

9. Stone, *Matthias and His Impostures*, pp. 45–46; Vale, *Fanaticism*, Part I, p. 61; Part II, p. 20.

10. See Charles Rosenberg, *The Cholera Years: The United States in 1832, 1849, and 1866* (Chicago: University of Chicago Press, 1962), pp. 42–54.

11. These inventories are in the Westchester County Records and Archives in Elmsford, New York, in a folder of legal materials pertaining to Matthias.

12. Stone, *Matthias and His Impostures*, p. 220.

13. One of Matthias's sons was six or seven years old, the other eleven.

14. Stone, *Matthias and His Impostures*, p. 179; *New York Courier and Enquirer*, 20 April 1835.

15. *New York Courier and Enquirer*, 17 April 1835; 20 April 1835.

16. *New York Courier and Enquirer*, 17 April 1835; 20 April 1835.

17. Matthias believed that people possessed both male and female spirits, and that the male did not resist his teaching, though the female "had never been subdued." Men or women who resisted him were actuated by a female spirit that needed to be tamed. In his city of the New Jerusalem, men would reclaim their power, and women would relinquish to their husbands any hold on the governing spirit. Husbands and fathers should rule everyone in their households exclusive of any influence from outside, so their spirits would fill their wives and children, for women, like children, were inferior beings. In Matthias's vision of complete male control, children should not attend school, in order that the spirits of their parents rather than the spirits of their teachers would rule them. *Memoirs of Matthias*, p. 10; Stone, *Matthias and His Impostures*, pp. 154–159, 261.

18. Stone, *Matthias and His Impostures*, pp. 154–159, 276; Vale, *Fanaticism*, Part II, pp. 126–127.

19. Vale, *Fanaticism*, Part II, p. 94.

20. Ibid., Part II, pp. 90–91.

21. Matthias's sons John and James were under eleven; Pierson's daughter Elizabeth was older than five but younger than twelve; Catherine Galloway seems to have had a young child; and there seem to have been two other children, aged about seven and ten. Matthias Trial Record and Elijah Pierson Papers, Westchester County Records and Archives Center.

22. Vale, *Fanaticism*, Part II, pp. 23–24.

23. Oddly enough, given his purported disdain for "Gentile law"—but not so odd, given that he was misrepresenting the truth—Matthias sometimes lapsed into a legalese that sounded a jarring note in the midst of his prophecy at his trial in 1834: "Mr. Folger, Mr. Pierson, and Mr. M[ills] frequently declared to me that they believed I was the Father, and that I was qualified to establish God's kingdom upon earth, and that *Zion Hill was transferred to me; with all the appurtenances thereunto belonging." New York Commercial Advertiser*, 2 October 1834. (Emphasis added.)

24. Pierson had earlier embraced the notion of match spirits. In 1832, after his wife had been dead two years, he had a vision that he was the "spiritual husband" of a woman in his Bowery Hill prayer group, because the spirit of his wife now inhabited the body of this "spiritual wife." Nothing seems to have come of this union, but Pierson continued to miss his wife, whose spirit evidently later came to rest in the body of Ann Folger at the same time that she was Matthias's match spirit. Stone, *Matthias and His Impostures*, p. 114.

25. Vale, *Fanaticism*, Part I, p. 72.

26. Ibid., Part II, pp. 17–20.

27. Ibid., Part I, p. 82; Part II, p. 23.

28. Ibid., Part II, pp. 76–77.

29. Stone, *Matthias and His Impostures*, pp. 162–164, 208, 262. Matthias also believed that ministers and lawyers, along with physicians, were the greatest evils in the world (p. 262). At this very same time in Kirtland, Ohio, Joseph Smith of the Church of Jesus Christ of Latter-day Saints received a revelation that proscribed the use of wine, strong drinks, tobacco, and hot drinks, and recommended herbs, fruits, flesh, and grain, a revelation that became part of the Mormon *Doctrine and Covenants* 88:137–89:5, pp. 175–176. The Mormons, like Matthias, had been influenced by Samuel Thomson's system of natural medicine. See Nathan O. Hatch, *The Democratization of American Christianity* (New Haven: Yale University Press, 1989), pp. 29–30.

30. The certificates appear in the 1850 edition of the *Narrative of Sojourner Truth*. Latourette told Gilbert Vale later that Isabella was "exemplary" as a worker, "a child of God, and eminently gifted and favoured by God, (she used to preach at camp meetings;) and indeed gave her the very best character for morals, truth, industry, and intelligence." Vale, *Fanaticism*, Part II, p. 112.

31. Vale, *Fanaticism*, Part II, p. 3; *New York Courier and Enquirer*, 3 October 1835.

32. Vale, *Fanaticism*, Part I, pp. 5, 61–62; Part II, pp. 25, 126.

33. Ibid., Part I, p. 63.

34. [Anonymous], *An Authentic History of Remarkable Persons, Who Have Attracted Public Attention in Various Parts of the World: Including a Full Expo-*

sure of the Iniquities of the Pretended Prophet Joe Smith, and of the Seven Degrees of the Mormon Temple; also an Account of the Frauds Practised by Matthias the Prophet, and Other Religious Impostors (New York: Wilson & Company, Brother Jonathan Press, 1849), p. 43.

35. Vale, *Fanaticism*, Part I, p. 54; Part II, p. 108.

36. *New York Courier and Enquirer*, 20 April 1835; *New York Sun*, 8 June 1835; Johnson and Wilentz, *The Kingdom of Matthias*, pp. 176–177.

37. The date of Matthias's death is not entirely certain. See Johnson and Wilentz, *The Kingdom of Matthias*, p. 177.

CHAPTER 8   Isabella's New York City

1. Rhoda Golden Freeman, "The Free Negro in New York City in the Era Before the Civil War," unpublished Ph.D. dissertation, Columbia University, 1966, pp. 98–112. Discrimination only began to let up when blacks started fighting back through the courts. They formed a Legal Rights Association in 1855, after the Reverend James W. C. Pennington was thrown out of a Sixth Avenue streetcar.

2. Lewis Tappan, *The Life of Arthur Tappan* (New York: Hurd & Houghton, 1871), pp. 62–69, 97–103, 112, 138–143, 153–162.

3. Tappan quoted in Edmund Fuller, *Prudence Crandall: An Incident of Racism in Nineteenth-Century Connecticut* (Middletown, CT: Wesleyan University Press, 1971), p. 55.

4. Sean Wilentz, *Chants Democratic: New York City and the Rise of the American Working Class, 1788–1850* (New York: Oxford University Press, 1984), pp. 264–265; Tappan, *Arthur Tappan*, p. 203; Leonard L. Richards, *"Gentlemen of Property and Standing": Anti-Abolition Mobs in Jacksonian America* (New York: Oxford University Press, 1970), pp. 28–30, 62, 113–129.

5. *New York Sun*, 19 December 1835; Tappan, *Arthur Tappan*, pp. 272–284.

6. H. Hendricks, "Sojourner Truth," *National Magazine* XVI (1892): 669.

7. [Olive Gilbert and Frances Titus], *Narrative of Sojourner Truth; A Bondswoman of Olden Time, Emancipated by the New York Legislature in the Early Part of the Present Century; with a History of her Labors and Correspondence Drawn from her "Book of Life"* (1878; reprint Salem, NH: Ayer Company, 1990), pp. 74–75.

8. Birth and death dates for Peter Williams, Sr., are not known; Peter Williams, Jr., was born in New Brunswick, New Jersey, in about 1787 and died in New York in 1840. Rhoda Freeman, "The Free Negro in New York City in the Era Before the Civil War," unpublished Ph.D. dissertation, Columbia University, 1966, pp. 28, 31–34, 195, 280, 325, 331, 391–396; George Walker, "The Afro-American in New York City, 1827–1860," unpublished Ph.D. dissertation, Co-

lumbia University, 1975, pp. 25, 132, 212; and J. Carleton Hayden, "Peter Williams, Jr.," in *Dictionary of American Negro Biography*, Rayford W. Logan and Michael R. Winston, eds. (New York: W. W. Norton, 1982), pp. 660–661.

9. *Narrative of Sojourner Truth*, pp. 76, 78. The captain's name is transcribed as Miller. William Jeffrey Bolster, "African-American Seamen: Race, Seafaring Work, and Atlantic Maritime Culture, 1750–1860," unpublished Ph.D. dissertation, Johns Hopkins University, 1992, pp. 6, 262, 299, 307–310, 357, 403; Sidney Kaplan, "Sojourner Truth's Son Peter," in *Negro History Bulletin* XIX, no. 2 (1955): 34.

10. *Narrative of Sojourner Truth*, pp. 77–78, 276.

11. Ibid., p. 76.

12. Vivienne L. Kruger, "Born to Run: The Slave Family in Early New York, 1626 to 1827," unpublished Ph.D. dissertation, Columbia University, 1985, p. 131.

13. The state census of 1855 counted New Yorkers house by house and shows that even where blacks were most numerous, whites often shared the same houses and apartments. Freeman, "The Free Negro in New York City," pp. 219–220.

14. Freeman, "The Free Negro in New York City," p. 430.

15. Ibid., p. 428.

16. Ibid., pp. 299, 428–429.

17. Ibid., p. 428; William S. McFeely, *Frederick Douglass* (New York: W. W. Norton, 1991), pp. 72–74.

18. Freeman, "The Free Negro in New York City," p. 182.

19. New York *Colored American*, 7 January 1837; 2, 26 August 1837; 23, 30 September 1837; 30 June 1838; 17 November 1838; 18 May 1839.

20. *New York Tribune*, 20 July 1854; Freeman, "The Free Negro in New York City," p. 420.

21. Nell Irvin Painter, "Martin R. Delany: Elitism and Black Nationalism," in Leon Litwack and August Meier, eds., *Black Leaders of the Nineteenth Century* (Urbana, IL: University of Illinois Press, 1988), pp. 151–153.

22. Catherine A. Brekus, " 'Let Your Women Keep Silence in the Churches': Female Preaching and Evangelical Religion in America, 1740–1845," unpublished Ph.D. dissertation, Yale University, 1993, pp. 1, 95.

23. *Narrative of Sojourner Truth*, pp. 98–100.

24. Ibid., p. 101.

25. G.[ilbert] Vale, *Fanaticism; Its Source and Influence, Illustrated by the Simple Narrative of Isabella in the Case of Matthias, Mr. and Mrs. B. Folger, Mr. Pierson, Mr. Mills, Catherine, Isabella, &c. &c. A Reply to W. L. Stone, with Descriptive Portraits of All the Parties, While at Sing-Sing and at Third Street.–*

Containing the Whole Truth—and Nothing But the Truth. Part I (New York: G. Vale, 1835), pp. 3–6, 63.

26. *Narrative of Sojourner Truth*, pp. 98, 120–121.

27. Ibid., p. 100.

28. Ibid.

PART II:

CHAPTER 9 Among the Millerites

1. Catherine A. Brekus, " 'Let Your Women Keep Silence in the Churches': Female Preaching and Evangelical Religion in America, 1740–1845," unpublished Ph.D. dissertation, Yale University, 1993, p. 361.

2. Miller worked his biblical numbers in secrecy for many years, until the preaching of the great evangelist Charles Finney inspired him in 1830 to go public with his prediction that the second coming of the saviour would occur in about 1843. Miller, not a charismatic public speaker himself, did his best to alert his fellow Americans of the danger, but his message reached very few until 1839, when a dynamic preacher, organizer, and salesman from Boston, the Reverend Joshua V. Himes, a minister of the Christian Connection who had previously put his energy into Garrisonian abolitionism, took up the cause. In a flurry of modern communication, Himes published the New York *Midnight Cry*, set up a series of widely distributed periodicals, and coordinated the preaching of scores of itinerant preachers.

At least eighteen (or about 5 percent) of the Millerite itinerant preachers were women, and they spoke frequently at camp meetings and appeared regularly in the movement's newspapers. A popular woman preacher edited a Millerite newspaper aimed particularly at women: the *Advent Message to the Daughters of Zion.* This ambitious public relations undertaking elaborated Miller's message and reached hundreds of thousands from Machias in Maine, to the Brooklyns in Connecticut and New York, to Long Island in New York, to Battle Creek in Michigan. Brekus, " 'Let Your Women Keep Silence,' " pp. 138, 354, 373–374. (The *Advent Message to the Daughters of Zion* did not begin to appear until 1844.)

3. New York *Midnight Cry*, 1 December 1842; 30 December 1842.

4. New York *Midnight Cry*, 27 January 1843; 10 February 1843.

5. New York *Midnight Cry*, 20 April 1843.

6. New York *Midnight Cry*, 11 May 1843.

7. New York *Midnight Cry*, 18 May 1843; 25 May 1843; 1 June 1843.

8. New York *Midnight Cry*, 8 June 1843; 22 June 1843.

9. Everett N. Dick, "The Millerite Movement, 1830–1845," in Gary Land, ed., *Adventism in America: A History* (Grand Rapids, MI: Eerdmans, 1986), pp. 18–19, 24.

10. Hymn quoted in Malcolm Bull and Keith Lockhart, *Seeking a Sanctuary: Seventh-Day Adventism and the American Dream* (New York: Harper & Row, 1989), p. 156.

11. David L. Rowe, "Millerites: A Shadow Portrait," in Ronald L. Numbers and Jonathan M. Butler, eds., *The Disappointed: Millerism and Millenarianism in the Nineteenth Century* (2nd ed. Knoxville, TN: University of Tennessee Press, 1993), p. 7; Bull and Lockhart, *Seeking a Sanctuary*, p. 193; Dick, "The Millerite Movement," p. 20.

12. Turner and Walker both quoted in Randall Balmer, "Apocalypticism in America: The Argot of Premillennialism in Popular Culture," *Prospects: An Annual of American Cultural Studies* 13 (1988): 421.

13. Theodore Olson, *Millennialism, Utopianism, and Progress* (Toronto: University of Toronto Press, 1982), p. 15. See also Nell Irvin Painter, *Exodusters: Black Migration to Kansas After Reconstruction* (New York: Alfred A. Knopf, 1977), pp. 184–201.

14. Dick, "The Millerite Movement," p. 16.

15. New York *Midnight Cry*, 20 July 1843; [Olive Gilbert and Frances Titus], *Narrative of Sojourner Truth; A Bondswoman of Olden Time, Emancipated by the New York Legislature in the Early Part of the Present Century; with a History of her Labors and Correspondence Drawn from her "Book of Life"* (1878; reprint Salem, NH: Ayer Company, 1990), pp. 101, 109–110.

16. Willard B. Gatewood, Jr., ed., *Free Man of Color: The Autobiography of Willis Augustus Hodges* (Knoxville, TN: University of Tennessee Press, 1982), p. 59.

17. New York *Midnight Cry*, 22 June 1843.

18. David T. Arthur, "Joshua V. Himes and the Cause of Adventism," in Numbers and Butler, eds., *The Disappointed*, p. 46; New York *Midnight Cry*, 11 November 1842; 10 February 1843. The building had belonged to the Fourth Free Church.

19. Dick, "The Millerite Movement," p. 20; David T. Arthur, "Millerism," in Edwin S. Gaustad, ed., *The Rise of Adventism: Religion and Society in Mid-Nineteenth-Century America* (New York: Harper & Row, 1974), p. 161; New York *Midnight Cry* 18 May 1843. On the difficulty of defining Millerism, see David L. Rowe, "Millerites: A Shadow Portrait," in Numbers and Butler, eds., *The Disappointed*, pp. 4–5.

20. Quoted in Brekus, " 'Let Your Women Keep Silence,' " p. 362.

21. Quoted in ibid., p. 364.

22. Ronald D. Graybill, "The Abolitionist-Millerite Connection," in Numbers and Butler, eds., *The Disappointed*, pp. 143–149; Smith in New York *Midnight Cry*, 7 December 1843.

23. Frank K. Flinn, "Millennial Hermeneutics: 2000 Minus 20," in M. Darrol Bryant and Donald W. Dayton, eds., *The Coming Kingdom: Essays in American*

Millennialism and Eschatology (Barrytown, NY: New Era Books, 1983), p. 1. Millerites, on the other hand, emphasized the authors of the millennialist books of the Bible, Daniel and John.

24. *Narrative of Sojourner Truth*, p. 110.

25. Ibid., pp. 110–111.

26. Ibid., pp. 111–112.

27. Dick, "The Millerite Movement," pp. 23–24; New York *Midnight Cry*, 14 September 1843; 28 September 1843.

28. Dick, "The Millerite Movement," pp. 23–24; Jonathan M. Butler, "The Making of a New Order: Millerism and the Origins of Seventh-Day Adventism," in Numbers and Butler, eds., *The Disappointed*, p. 192.

29. Sarah H. Bradford, *Scenes in the Life of Harriet Tubman* (Auburn, NY: W. J. Moses, 1869), p. 49.

30. *Narrative of Sojourner Truth*, p. 108.

31. Ibid., pp. 106–107. Olive Gilbert presents the conclusion about Truth's "energy and independence of character" as her own.

32. Ibid., p. 106.

33. Ibid., pp. 113–114.

34. Like Sojourner Truth and the New York perfectionists, the Shakers were pentecostals who heard the voice of the Holy Spirit, practiced faith healing, spoke in tongues, and received prophetic revelations. They welcomed men and women, Indians, blacks, and whites, wealthy and poor to join their charismatic and celibate villages, in which property was held in common.

35. *Narrative of Sojourner Truth*, pp. 112–115.

CHAPTER 10   Northampton

1. Millennialism (including second adventism) and utopianism shared a fundamental common assumption: that this world needed to be and would be changed radically. Many Millerites in the leadership and the rank and file had been active in moral reform, tightening the connection between Millerite millennialism and utopianism.

2. David Mack to A. J. Taylor, 23 April 1843, Letters of the Northampton Association of Education and Industry, Vol. 4, Northampton Association of Education and Industry Papers, American Antiquarian Society, Worcester, MA; Alice Eaton McBee, *From Utopia to Florence: The Story of a Transcendentalist Community in Northampton, Mass., 1830–1852* (Northampton, MA: Smith College Studies in History, vol. 32, 1947), p. 49. See also Christopher Clark, *The Communitarian Moment: The Radical Challenge of the Northampton Association* (Ithaca, NY: Cornell University Press, 1995).

3. [Olive Gilbert and Frances Titus], *Narrative of Sojourner Truth; A*

Bondswoman of Olden Time, Emancipated by the New York Legislature in the Early Part of the Present Century; with a History of her Labors and Correspondence Drawn from her "Book of Life" (1878; reprint Salem, NH: Ayer Company, 1990), p. 120.

4. Michael Barkun, *Crucible of the Millennium: The Burned-Over District of New York in the 1840s* (Syracuse, NY: Syracuse University Press, 1986), p. 82.

5. Emerson quoted in Hope Hale Davis, "The Northampton Association of Education and Industry," in *The Northampton Book: Chapters from 300 Years in the Life of A New England Town, 1654–1954* (Northampton, MA: Tercentenary Committee, 1954), p. 114.

6. Susan Strane, *A Whole-Souled Woman: Prudence Crandall and the Education of Black Women* (New York: W. W. Norton, 1990), pp. x, 19, 24, 189, 191, 200, 220, 227; Donald Yacovone, *Samuel Joseph May and the Dilemmas of the Liberal Persuasion, 1797–1871* (Philadelphia: Temple University Press, 1991), pp. 43–55. Crandall became what she called a "Unitarian spiritualist" in the 1850s and settled in Kansas in 1876. In 1886, the state of Connecticut apologized to Crandall and awarded her a $400 per annum pension for the rest of her life. She died in 1890.

7. McBee, *From Utopia to Florence*, pp. 8–13; Davis, "The Northampton Association," p. 110.

8. Frank E. Manuel and Fritzie P. Manuel, *Utopian Thought in the Western World* (Cambridge, MA: Harvard University Press, 1979), p. 653.

9. Record of Proceedings of the Northampton Association of Education and Industry, 8 April 1842, Vol. 2, Northampton Association of Education and Industry Records, 1836–1853.

10. [John Metcalf], *Social Reform: or An Appeal in Behalf of Association, Based Upon the Principles of a Pure Christianity* (Northampton, MA: John Metcalf, 1844), pp. 18–19.

11. Garrison quoted in Arthur E. Beston, Jr., "Fourierism in Northampton: A Critical Note," *New England Quarterly* XIII, no. 1 (March 1940): 110; Barbara Goodwin, *Social Science and Utopia: Nineteenth-Century Models of Social Harmony* (Hassocks, ENG: Harvester Press, 1978), pp. 38–39.

12. Alice Manning, "When Freedom Flourished in Cosmian Hall," Northampton, MA, *Daily Hampshire Gazette*, 7 August 1976; Esther Terry, "Sojourner Truth: The Person Behind the Libyan Sibyl, with a memoir by Frederick Douglass, What I Found at the Northampton Association," *Massachusetts Review* XXVI, nos. 2 and 3 (1985) (no page numbers).

13. Frances P. Judd, "Reminiscences," in Charles A. Sheffeld, ed., *History of Florence, Massachusetts. Including a Complete Account of the Northampton Association of Education and Industry* (Florence, MA: Charles A. Sheffield, 1895), p. 116.

14. Sheffeld, ed., *History of Florence*, p. 105.

15. Davis, "The Northampton Association," p. 111. Prevailing adult wages in Northampton were 10¢ an hour for adults, and a week's room and board cost 75¢.

16. David Mack to John Bailey, 8 June 1844, Letters of the Northampton Association of Education and Industry, Vol. 4, Northampton Association of Education and Industry Papers.

17. Douglass, "What I Found at the Northampton Association," in Sheffeld, *History of Florence*, p. 130; Record of Proceedings of the Northampton Association of Education and Industry, 16 May 1842, Vol. 2, Northampton Association of Education and Industry Records, 1836–1853.

18. Samuel L. Hill to David Mack, 30 June 1846. Northampton Association of Education and Industry Letter Book, Northampton Association of Education and Industry Papers.

19. Sheffeld, ed., *History of Florence*, pp. 101–102.

20. George R. Stetson, "When I Was a Boy," in ibid., p. 121. Stetson's family was also from Brooklyn, Connecticut.

21. Whitney R. Cross, *The Burned-Over District: The Social and Intellectual History of Enthusiastic Religion in Western New York, 1800–1850* (1950; New York: Harper & Row, 1965), pp. 189–190, 240; George Wallingford Noyes, ed., *Religious Experience of John Humphrey Noyes, Founder of the Oneida Community* (New York: Macmillan, 1923), pp. 59, 209–210, 253; Robert Allerton Parker, *A Yankee Saint: John Humphrey Noyes and the Oneida Community* (New York: G. P. Putnam's Sons, 1935), pp. 22, 35–39; and Northampton Association of Education and Industry Records, 1836–1853, Vol. 2, pp. 95, 96.

22. Frederick Douglass, "What I Found at the Northampton Association," in Sheffeld, ed., *History of Florence*, p. 130; Giles B. Stebbins, *Upward Steps of Seventy Years. Autobiographic, Biographic, Historic* (New York: United States Book Company, 1890), pp. 55–57.

23. On the black people at the Northampton Association see Clark, *The Communitarian Moment*, pp. 71–75.

CHAPTER 11 Douglas, Ruggles, and Family

1. Frederick Douglass, "What I Found at the Northampton Association," in Charles A. Sheffeld, ed., *History of Florence, Massachusetts. Including a Complete Account of the Northampton Association of Education and Industry* (Florence, MA: Charles A. Sheffeld, 1895), pp. 131–132. Douglass did not mention the third black adult in the Northampton Association, Basil Dorsey, a fugitive slave who arrived in 1844, after Douglass's visit. Dorsey was a good worker with a pleasing but evidently not very memorable personality, who stayed on as a cotton mill worker in Florence after the dissolution of the Northampton Asso-

ciation. In 1850, the people of Northampton took up a collection that Dorsey added to his own personal savings and used to purchase his freedom. Alice Eaton McBee, *From Utopia to Florence: The Story of a Transcendentalist Community in Northampton, Mass., 1830–1852* (Northampton, MA: Smith College Studies in History, vol. 32, 1947), p. 69.

2. Susan E. Cayleff, *Wash and Be Healed: The Water-Cure Movement and Women's Health* (Philadelphia: Temple University Press, 1987), pp. 2–15, 20–29; Dorothy B. Porter with Edwin C. Rozwenc, "The Water Cures," in *The Northampton Book: Chapters from 300 Years in the Life of A New England Town, 1654–1954* (Northampton, MA: Tercentenary History Committee, 1954), p. 123.

3. Porter with Rozwenc, "The Water Cures," p. 123; Cayleff, *Wash and Be Healed*, pp. 80, 86; McBee, *From Utopia to Florence*, p. 71.

4. Porter with Rozwenc, "The Water Cures," p. 123. Store Department of the Northampton Association of Education and Industry, Day Book No. 4, 1 April 1846, Vol. 1, pp. 194–197, 205, 217, 226–228, 237, 250, 258, 270, 343–350, 355–357, and 365. Northampton Association of Education and Industry Papers, American Antiquarian Society, Worcester, MA.

5. Store Department of the Northampton Association, Day Book No. 4, 1 April 1846, Vol. 1, p. 352. Northampton Association of Education and Industry Papers.

6. Elizabeth married a man named Banks and gave birth to Samuel Banks in Connecticut in 1850. In about 1860, she married again in Battle Creek, Michigan. Berenice Lowe, "The Family of Sojourner Truth," *Michigan Heritage* (Summer 1962): 182, 184.

7. Accounts, Vol. 5, April 1844, Northampton Association of Education and Industry Papers, p. 235.

8. [Olive Gilbert and Frances Titus], *Narrative of Sojourner Truth; A Bondswoman of Olden Time, Emancipated by the New York Legislature in the Early Part of the Present Century; with a History of her Labors and Correspondence Drawn from her "Book of Life"* (1878; reprint Salem, NH: Ayer Company, 1990), pp. 71–73.

9. Darlene Clark Hine, "Rape and the Inner Lives of Black Women in the Middle West: Preliminary Thoughts on the Culture of Dissemblance," *SIGNS* 14, no. 4 (1989): 912–920.

CHAPTER 12 The Narrative of Sojourner Truth

1. William L. Andrews, *To Tell a Free Story: The First Century of Afro-American Autobiography, 1760–1865* (Urbana, IL: University of Illinois Press, 1986), pp. 97, 138. Douglass's narrative was reprinted six times in four years.

2. *International Genealogical Index, 1988 Edition;* Family History Library, Church of Jesus Christ of Latter Day Saints, Salt Lake City, Utah; [Olive Gilbert

and Frances Titus], *Narrative of Sojourner Truth; A Bondswoman of Olden Time, Emancipated by the New York Legislature in the Early Part of the Present Century; with a History of her Labors and Correspondence Drawn from her "Book of Life"* (1878; reprint Salem, NH: Ayer Company, 1990), pp. 276–278; Walter M. Merrill, ed., *The Letters of William Lloyd Garrison.* Vol. III. *No Union with Slaveholders, 1841–1849* (Cambridge, MA: Harvard University Press, 1973), pp. 165, 203, 499; Louis Ruchames, ed., *The Letters of William Lloyd Garrison.* Vol. IV. *From Disunionism to the Brink of War, 1850–1860* (Cambridge, MA: Harvard University Press, 1975), pp. 40, 60–61; Northampton Association of Education and Industry Records, 1836–1853, Vol. 3, p. 229; Vol. 7, pp. 304–327, American Antiquarian Society, Worcester, MA.

3. *Narrative of Sojourner Truth*, pp. 36, 84–85.

4. Jonathan M. Butler, "The Making of a New Order: Millerism and the Origins of Seventh-Day Adventism," in Ronald L. Numbers and Jonathan M. Butler, eds., *The Disappointed: Millerism and Millenarianism in the Nineteenth Century* (2nd ed. Knoxville, TN: University of Tennessee Press, 1993), p. 197.

5. *Narrative of Sojourner Truth*, pp. 115–116. Truth was paraphrasing several biblical verses: Numbers 32:6; Judges 15:16; Luke 3:14; Revelation 19:11–15.

6. *Narrative of Sojourner Truth*, pp. 115–116. Emphasis in the original.

7. Ibid., pp. 116–118.

8. Ibid., pp. 119–120.

9. See ibid., pp. 82–85.

10. Ibid., pp. 72, 122–123.

11. Ibid., p. 124.

12. *William Lloyd Garrison, 1805–1879: The Story of His Life Told by His Children.* Vol. III (Boston: Houghton Mifflin, 1885), pp. 228–231.

13. Printer's file, American Antiquarian Society.

14. *Narrative of Sojourner Truth*, pp. 263, 264; Sojourner Truth to William Lloyd Garrison, Salem, Ohio, 28 August 1851, *Black Abolitionist Papers* (New York: Microfilming Corporation of America, 1981), reel 7, p. 79; Sojourner Truth to William Lloyd Garrison, Detroit, 11 April 1864, *Black Abolitionist Papers*, reel 15, p. 261; Alice Eaton McBee, *From Utopia to Florence: The Story of a Transcendentalist Community in Northampton, Mass., 1830–1852* (Northampton, MA: Smith College Studies in History, vol. 32, 1947), p. 53; Whitney R. Cross, *The Burned-Over District: The Social and Intellectual History of Enthusiastic Religion in Western New York, 1800–1850* (1950; reprint New York: Harper & Row, 1965), pp. 189–191, 196, 240–246, 276, 343.

15. Boston *Liberator*, 24 May 1850. The book had been published in April.

16. According to Alice McBee, Benson's cotton mill failed, and he and his family moved to Wakarusa (now Lawrence), Kansas, where he continued to be ac-

tive in the peace, temperance, and antislavery movements. However, letters between Truth and Garrison and between the Garrisons show that after leaving Northampton, the Bensons spent the early 1850s living on Long Island, New York, where James Boyle boarded with them while his wife was visiting in Ohio. McBee, *From Utopia to Florence*, p. 70. See also Sojourner Truth to William Lloyd Garrison, Salem, Ohio, 28 August 1851, *Black Abolitionist Papers*, reel 7, p. 79; William Lloyd Garrison to Helen E. Garrison, New York, 12 May 1858, Ruchames, ed., *The Letters of William Lloyd Garrison*, Vol. IV, p. 528.

17. McBee, *From Utopia to Florence*, pp. 67–70. Hampshire County, Massachusetts, Registry of Deeds, Book 133, pp. 106–107, 124–125, Northampton, Massachusetts.

18. *Narrative of Sojourner Truth*, pp. 121–122.

CHAPTER 13   Networks of Antislavery Feminism

1. Christopher Clark, *The Communitarian Moment: The Radical Challenge of the Northampton Association* (Ithaca, NY: Cornell University Press), p. 89; New York *National Anti-Slavery Standard*, 15 May 1845, quoted in Dorothy Sterling, *Ahead of Her Time: Abby Kelley and the Politics of Antislavery* (New York: W. W. Norton, 1991), p. 212.

2. *New York Daily Tribune*, 26 October 1850; New York *National Anti-Slavery Standard*, 28 November 1850.

3. New York *National Anti-Slavery Standard*, 28 November 1850.

4. Sojourner Truth to William Lloyd Garrison, Detroit, 11 April 1864, *Black Abolitionist Papers* (New York: Microfilming Corporation of America, 1981), reel 15, p. 261.

5. Chronology, Family Papers of Isaac and Amy Kirby Post, 1817–1918, University of Rochester Library, Rochester, New York; Nancy A. Hewitt, *Women's Activism and Social Change: Rochester, New York, 1822–1872* (Ithaca, NY: Cornell University Press, 1984), pp. 61, 115–116.

6. Russell B. Nye, "Marius Robinson, A Forgotten Abolitionist Leader," *Ohio State Archaeological and Historical Quarterly* LV, no. 2 (April–June 1946): 138–151; Salem (Ohio) *Anti-Slavery Bugle*, 11 January 1851. See also Lawrence Thomas Lesick, *The Lane Rebels: Evangelicalism and Antislavery in Antebellum America* (Metuchen, NJ: Scarecrow Press, 1980), pp. 72, 132, 143, 197.

7. Salem (Ohio) *Anti-Slavery Bugle*, 26 April 1851; Nye, "Marius Robinson," pp. 151–153. Nye is mistaken about Robinson's date of death. He died in 1878 in Salem, where he had become president of the Ohio Mutual Fire Insurance Company. Louis Ruchames, ed., *The Letters of William Lloyd Garrison*. Vol. IV. *From Disunionism to the Brink of War, 1850–1860* (Cambridge, MA: Harvard University Press, 1975), p. 264.

8. Salem *Anti-Slavery Bugle*, 29 March 1851.

CHAPTER 14 Akron, 1851

1. Pittsburgh *Saturday Visiter*, 28 June 1851. Swisshelm insisted on using Dr. Samuel Johnson's spelling of "Visiter."

2. Pittsburgh *Saturday Visiter*, 21 July 1851.

3. Pittsburgh *Saturday Visiter*, 7 June 1851.

4. Pittsburgh *Saturday Visiter*, 2 November 1850.

5. Pittsburgh *Saturday Visiter*, 23 November 1850. Emphasis in original.

6. Pittsburgh *Saturday Visiter*, 23 November 1850. Emphasis in original.

7. Salem (Ohio) *Anti-Slavery Bugle*, 14 June 1851.

8. Boston *Liberator*, 13 June 1851.

9. *Proceedings of the Woman's Rights Convention Held at Akron, Ohio, May 28 and 29, 1851* (Cincinnati: Ben Franklin Book and Job Office, 1851); Pittsburgh *Saturday Visiter*, 7 June 1851; Boston *Liberator*, 13 June 1851. Mary Ann Johnson's husband Oliver had just resigned from the editorship of the *Bugle* to become the editor of the New York *National Anti-Slavery Standard*.

10. Salem *Anti-Slavery Bugle*, 7 June 1851. The omission of a title before Sojourner Truth's name was common in antislavery and feminist newspapers as well as in the mainstream press, although blacks usually accorded each other titles of respect. Generally the people whose names appear in American newspapers with a Mr. or Mrs. were white.

11. Salem *Anti-Slavery Bugle*, 7 June 1851; Rochester *Daily American*, 4 June 1851.

12. Boston *Liberator*, 13 June 1851.

13. Salem *Anti-Slavery Bugle*, 21 June 1851. Other newspapers omit mention of Truth's remarks entirely or report them in brief, such as this from the *Liberator* of 13 June 1851: "Sojourner Truth spoke in her own peculiar style, showing that she was a match for most men. She had ploughed, hoed, dug, and could *eat* as much, if she could get it. The power and wit of this remarkable woman convulsed the audience with laughter. I wish I could report every word she said, but I cannot." The official *Proceedings of the Woman's Rights Convention* makes no mention whatever of Sojourner Truth.

14. See Margaret Jarman Hagood, *Mothers of the South: Portraiture of the White Tenant Farm Woman* (1939; reprint New York: W. W. Norton, 1977), pp. 86–89; and Karen Sayer, *Women of the Fields: Representations of Rural Women in the Nineteenth Century* (Manchester, England: Manchester University Press, 1995), p. 92.

15. When Truth mentions Jesus ("[t]he lady has spoken about Jesus ... "), she makes the only acknowledgment of remarks by other people in the convention that Robinson notes. That other speaker is a woman.

16. Truth is citing John 11:1–12 and Luke 16:19–25. "Dives" means rich man in Latin; it is not a proper name.

17. Boston *Liberator*, 13 June 1851.

18. Sojourner Truth to Amy Post, Ravenna, Ohio, n.d., Post Family Papers, University of Rochester Library.

19. Sojourner Truth to William Lloyd Garrison, Salem, Ohio, 28 August 1851, *Black Abolitionist Papers* (New York: Microfilming Corporation of America, 1981), reel 7, p. 79.

20. Joan D. Hedrick, *Harriet Beecher Stowe: A Life* (New York: Oxford University Press, 1994), p. 223.

21. See Mary Kelley, *Private Woman, Public Stage: Literary Domesticity in Nineteenth-Century America* (New York: Oxford University Press, 1984), p. 9, for a discussion of "puffing," which was often a more commercial transaction than today's "blurbing," which is not done for money. Stowe's puff became the introduction to the late 1853 edition of the *Narrative of Sojourner Truth*. The original, in Stowe's hand, is in the possession of Lisa Baskin of Leeds, Massachusetts, and is used here with permission.

CHAPTER 15 *Vengeance and Womanhood*

1. Quotes in Vincent Harding, *There Is a River: The Black Struggle for Freedom in America* (New York: Harcourt Brace Jovanovich, 1981), pp. 157–160.

2. Ibid., pp. 161, 166, 169–170; Earl Conrad, *Harriet Tubman* (Washington, DC: Associated Publishers, 1943), pp. 130–138.

3. Harding, *There Is a River*, pp. 185–193; Nell Irvin Painter, "Martin Delany and Elitist Black Nationalism," in August Meier and Leon Litwack, eds., *Black Leaders of the Nineteenth Century* (Urbana, IL: University of Illinois Press, 1988), pp. 153–172.

4. The report, as reproduced in the *History of Woman Suffrage*, is rendered in a moderate dialect. Elizabeth Cady Stanton, Susan B. Anthony, and Matilda Joslyn Gage, eds., *History of Woman Suffrage*. Vol. I (New York: Fowler & Wells, 1881), pp. 567–568.

5. Truth's peers would also recall that Vashti's refusal figures in an ongoing gender war and prompts one of Ahasuerus' advisers to remark that "Vashti the queen hath not done wrong to the king only, but also to all the princes, and to all the people that are in all the provinces of the king Ahasuerus." This affront to men in general would have to be redressed by an order from the king to be circulated throughout all 127 provinces, from India to Ethiopia, that wives must obey their husbands. Otherwise, the king's adviser argues, "this deed of the queen shall come abroad unto all women, so that they shall despise their husbands in their eyes, when it shall be reported." Esther 1:16–17. See also Carey

A. Moore, "Book of Esther," in David Noel Freedman, ed., *The Anchor Bible Dictionary*. Vol. 2 (New York: Doubleday, 1992), pp. 633–643.

6. See Esther 9:5; 8:7–17; 9:11–25, and 10:2–3. Today Purim no longer retains this celebration of revenge. It is a time of generalized thanksgiving and the exchange of gifts.

7. Stanton, Anthony, and Gage, eds., *History of Woman Suffrage*, Vol. I, p. 568.

8. New York *National Anti-Slavery Standard*, 10 December 1853.

9. Boston *Liberator*, 14 July 1854.

10. Strain was only of local importance, for local and state histories no longer mention his name.

11. Catherine A. Brekus, " 'Let Your Women Keep Silence in the Churches': Female Preaching and Evangelical Religion in America, 1740–1845," unpublished Ph.D. dissertation, Yale University, 1993; Frances Smith Foster, *A Brighter Coming Day: A Frances Ellen Watkins Harper Reader* (New York: Feminist Press, 1990), p. 127; Rachel Brownstein, *The Tragic Muse: Rachel of the Comédie-Française* (New York: Alfred A. Knopf, 1993), pp. xii, 16, 188.

12. Boston *Liberator*, 15 October 1858.

13. On black women's bodies, see Karla F. C. Holloway, *Codes of Conduct: Race, Ethics, and the Color of Our Character* (New Brunswick, NJ: Rutgers University Press, 1995), pp. 21, 33–38, 61–66.

14. "Letter from Josephine Griffing," Boston *Liberator*, 21 June 1861.

15. John White Chadwick, *A Life for Liberty: Anti-Slavery and Other Letters of Sallie Holley* (New York: G. P. Putnam's Sons, 1899), p. 80.

16. On Jezebel and mammy, see Deborah Gray White, *Ar'n't I a Woman?: Female Slaves in the Plantation South* (New York: W. W. Norton, 1985), and Patricia Hill Collins, *Black Feminist Thought: Knowledge, Consciousness, and the Politics of Empowerment* (Cambridge, MA: Unwin Hyman, 1990).

17. Boston *Liberator*, 15 October 1858. Cf. [Olive Gilbert and Frances Titus], *Narrative of Sojourner Truth: A Bondswoman of Olden Time, Emancipated by the New York Legislature in the Early Part of the Present Century; with a History of her Labors and Correspondence Drawn from her "Book of Life"* (1878; reprint Salem, NH: Ayer Company, 1990), p. 139.

CHAPTER 16 Spiritualism

1. Albert John Wahl, "The Congregational or Progressive Friends in the Pre-Civil-War Reform Movement," unpublished Ph.D. dissertation, Temple University, 1951. On Truth, see pp. 60, 62, 63, 113, 165–166; on Gage, pp. 79, 139, 189, 203, 238; and on Dugdale, pp. 45–46, 135, 148, 182, 189, 238.

2. The evolution of the Seneca Falls convention for women's rights in 1848, the first women's rights meeting in the world, illustrates the confluence of be-

liefs. Hicksite Quaker preacher Lucretia Mott, her friends, and Amy Post were among the main planners of the Seneca Falls meeting. Mott and Elizabeth Cady Stanton, both of whom attended the founding meeting of the Waterloo, New York, Congregational Friends in 1848, had met in London at the World's Anti-Slavery Convention in 1840. As women, they were prohibited from taking part in the deliberations—a prohibition that contributed directly to the subsequent split in the American abolitionist movement. Mott and Stanton determined to assemble a women's rights meeting when they returned to the United States, but this did not occur until eight years later, when both were pulling away from their Hicksite Quaker meeting to form the Congregational Friends Meeting of Waterloo.

Right after that meeting, Mott visited her sister in Auburn, New York, where she spoke again with Stanton. Stanton and Mott, with other Congregational Friends, drew up the call for the conference in Seneca Falls that launched the nineteenth-century women's rights movement. Two weeks after the Seneca Falls meeting, other Congregational Friends, including Amy Post, organized another women's rights meeting in Rochester. These meetings coincided with other sensational occurrences that would soon become allied to the feminist cause. See Wahl, "The Congregational or Progressive Friends," pp. 22, 40, 176–179; Allen C. Thomas, "Congregational or Progressive Friends. A Forgotten Episode in Quaker History," *Bulletin of Friends' Historical Society of Philadelphia* 10, no. 1 (November 1920): 23–24, 28; and Ann Braude, *Radical Spirits: Spiritualism and Women's Rights in Nineteenth Century America* (Boston: Beacon Press, 1989), pp. 13, 57–59.

3. Giles B. Stebbins, *Upward Steps of Seventy Years. Autobiographic, Biographic, Historic* (New York: United States Book Company, 1890), pp. 43–44, 259.

4. Davis quoted in Alice Felt Tyler, *Freedom's Ferment: Phases of American Social History from the Colonial Period to the Outbreak of the Civil War* (1944; reprint New York: Harper Torchbook, 1962), p. 79.

5. George F. Dole and Robert H. Kirven, *A Scientist Explores Spirit* (New York: Swedenborg Foundation, 1992), pp. 67–75; Whitney R. Cross, *The Burned-Over District: The Social and Intellectual History of Enthusiastic Religion in Western New York, 1800–1850* (1950; reprint New York: Harper Torchbook, 1965), pp. 342–343; Braude, *Radical Spirits*, pp. 2–6.

6. E. A. Lukins, "Rochester Knockings," Rochester, April 18, 1851, Salem (Ohio) *Anti-Slavery Bugle*, 3 May 1851.

7. Salem *Anti-Slavery Bugle*, 17 May 1851. Emphasis in original.

8. Ibid.

9. Lucy Colman, *Reminiscences* (Buffalo: H. L. Green, 1892), p. 24.

10. Berenice Bryant Lowe, *Tales of Battle Creek* (Battle Creek, MI: Miller Foundation and Historical Society of Battle Creek, 1976), pp. 54–56, 239.

PART III
CHAPTER 17 The "Libyan Sibyl"

1. Charles H. Foster, *The Rungless Ladder: Harriet Beecher Stowe and New England Puritanism* (Durham, NC: Duke University Press, 1954), p. 72.

2. Susan Coultrap-McQuin, *Doing Literary Business: American Women Writers in the Nineteenth Century* (Chapel Hill, NC: University of North Carolina Press, 1990), p. 98.

3. Van Wyck Brooks, *The Dream of Arcadia: American Writers and Artists in Italy, 1760–1915* (New York: E. P. Dutton, 1958), p. 198. The other well-known American writers in Europe were James Fenimore Cooper, William Wordsworth Longfellow, and Washington Irving.

4. Coultrap-McQuin, *Doing Literary Business*, p. 97; Joan D. Hedrick, *Harriet Beecher Stowe: A Life* (New York: Oxford University Press, 1994), p. 296.

5. See Patricia R. Hill, "Writing Out the War: Harriet Beecher Stowe's Averted Gaze," in *Divided Houses: Gender and the Civil War*, Catherine Clinton and Nina Silber, eds. (New York: Oxford University Press, 1992), pp. 263–264, 267–268.

6. Hedrick, *Harriet Beecher Stowe*, p. 270; Edward Wagenknecht, *Harriet Beecher Stowe: The Known and the Unknown* (New York: Oxford University Press, 1965), p. 131.

7. Harriet Beecher Stowe, "Sojourner Truth, the Libyan Sibyl," *Atlantic Monthly* XI (April 1863): 473.

8. Ibid., p. 479.

9. Ibid., pp. 473, 477, 480. My analysis also draws on the work of two critics: Patricia Hill's "Writing Out the War: Harriet Beecher Stowe's Averted Gaze," pp. 260–278, and Jane Crosthwaite, "Women and Wild Beasts: Versions of the Exotic in Nineteenth Century American Art," *Southern Humanities Review* XIX, no. 2 (Spring 1985): 97–116. On Rachel, see Rachel Brownstein, *The Tragic Muse: Rachel of the Comédie-Française* (New York: Alfred A. Knopf, 1993), p. 206.

10. See Nell Irvin Painter, "Sojourner Truth in Life and Memory: Writing the Biography of an American Exotic," *Gender and History* 2, no. 1 (Spring 1990): 3–16.

11. Stowe, "Sojourner Truth, the Libyan Sibyl," pp. 474, 477.

12. Ibid., pp. 479, 474.

13. See John Wideman, "Frame and Dialect: The Evolution of the Black Voice," *American Poetry Review* (September–October 1976): 34–37.

14. In the *Narrative of Sojourner Truth*, Truth says she never saw Eliza Fowler's

mother again after the news came of Eliza's murder by Fowler in Alabama. [Olive Gilbert and Frances Titus], *Narrative of Sojourner Truth; A Bondswoman of Olden Time, Emancipated by the New York Legislature in the Early Part of the Present Century; with a History of her Labors and Correspondence Drawn from her "Book of Life"* (1878; reprint Salem, NH: Ayer Company, 1990), pp. 57–58.

15. Stowe, "Sojourner Truth, the Libyan Sibyl," p. 478.

16. Harriet Beecher Stowe, *The Minister's Wooing* (1859; reprint Boston: Ticknor & Fields, 1867), pp. 138–144, 174–180, 275–281, 329, 347–350, 356, 446–452. In her father's Litchfield, Massachusetts, household, Stowe had known a black woman named Candace, who did the Beechers' laundry. Hedrick, *Harriet Beecher Stowe*, p. 18.

17. Stowe, "Sojourner Truth, the Libyan Sibyl," pp. 480–481. The two statues were displayed at the 1862 London International Exposition.

18. Henry James, *William Wetmore Story and His Friends, From Letters, Diaries, and Recollections.* 2 vols. (Boston: Houghton Mifflin, 1903), Vol. 1, pp. 64, 66.

19. Ibid., Vol. 1, pp. 32–33, 321.

20. Brooks, *The Dream of Arcadia*, p. 122.

21. Charles de Tolnay, *Michelangelo: Sculptor, Painter, Architect*, trans. Gaynor Woodhouse (Princeton, NJ: Princeton University Press, 1975 [n.d. of original publication]), p. 30. The *Libyan Sibyl* is illustrated in plate 72.

22. W. W. Story to Charles Eliot Norton, 15 August 1861, in James, *William Wetmore Story and His Friends*, Vol. 2, pp. 70–71, 75–76. The *Libyan Sibyl* and its companion, *Cleopatra*, were the best of Story's work. He died in Rome in 1895 without ever again reaching this level of artistry, which even at mid-century was recognized as limited. A replica of the *Libyan Sibyl* is in the Metropolitan Museum of Art in New York, the gift of the senior Henry Cabot Lodge.

23. Stowe, "Sojourner Truth, the Libyan Sibyl," pp. 476–477, 480. My analysis differs from that of Margaret Washington, who says that "the immediate impression of Sojourner that [Stowe] advanced was candid and memorable." *The Narrative of Sojourner Truth*, Margaret Washington, ed. (New York: Vintage Books, 1993), p. xi.

For a thoughtful and passionate discussion of the proliferation of misinformation about black women, see Erlene Stetson, "Silence: Access and Aspiration," in *Between Women: Biographers, Novelists, Critics, Teachers and Artists Write About Their Work on Women*, Carol Ascher, Louise DeSalvo, and Sara Ruddick, eds., (Boston: Beacon Press, 1984), pp. 238, 243–248.

24. Stowe, "Sojourner Truth, the Libyan Sibyl," p. 480.

25. Ibid., p. 476. Stowe had used a stripped-down version of the Truth quote

in a column criticizing President James Buchanan for pro-slavery, pro-southern sentiments in the *Independent*, 20 December 1860.

26. Frederick Douglass, *Life and Times of Frederick Douglass* (1881; facsimile ed. New York: Citadel Press, 1983), p. 282. Douglass ultimately gets the better of this exchange with Truth in his autobiography: "My quaint old sister was of the Garrison school of non-resistance, but she too became an advocate of the sword, when the war for the maintenance of the Union was declared."

27. This authentication of "Frederick, *is God dead?*" comes from the original work of Carleton Mabee, who is the first to locate the exchange with certainty. See Mabee, *Sojourner Truth: Slave, Prophet, Legend* (New York: New York University Press, 1993), pp. 83–86.

28. Gilbert Haven, *The Mission of America: A Discourse Delivered Before the New England M.E. Conference at the High Street Church, Charlestown, MS., on the Occasion of the Annual State Fast, April 2d, 1863* (Boston: J. P. Magee, 1863), p. 37.

29. Many others who had encountered Truth in the 1850s only thought to capture her in print after Stowe had published "The Libyan Sibyl." Sallie Holley, for instance, was a Rochester abolitionist who had heard Truth in Ohio in 1851. Holley, a Garrisonian, belonged to Sojourner Truth's circle. After "The Libyan Sibyl," even Holley, who had visited with Truth informally, could see Truth only through Stowe's lenses. Reporting to the *Liberator* on a speech that Truth had delivered in Rochester in August 1864, Holley quoted Stowe liberally and made Truth into "this strange powerful woman—Africa transplanted in America, hardly naturalized." Holley, following Stowe, made Truth strange, but she could now see her as a personality. John White Chadwick, *A Life for Liberty: Anti-Slavery and Other Letters of Sallie Holley* (New York: G. P. Putnam's Sons, 1899), p. 80.

30. "Letter from Sojourner Truth." Boston *Commonwealth*, 3 July 1863.

31. See "Myth Today," in Roland Barthes, *Mythologies*, ed. and trans. Annette Lavers (1957; reprint New York: Farrar, Straus & Giroux, 1972), pp. 109–159; and Leo Braudy, *The Frenzy of Renown: Fame and Its History* (New York: Oxford University Press, 1986), pp. 9, 468, 591–592.

CHAPTER 18 "Ar'n't I a Woman?"

1. Clara Cornelia Holtzman, "Frances Dana Gage," unpublished M.A. thesis, Ohio State University, 1931, pp. 36–39. For a view of Gage through the eyes of her friend and admirer, the pioneer Civil War nurse Clara Barton, see Stephen B. Oates, *A Woman of Valor: Clara Barton and the Civil War* (New York: Free Press, 1994), pp. 145–148, 153, 189–197, 362.

2. Swisshelm describes her own actions in the Pittsburgh *Saturday Visiter*, 28 June 1851.

3. Pittsburgh *Saturday Visiter*, 7 June 1851; 30 August 1851; and 11 October 1851. The quotation is in the 11 October 1851 issue.

4. Pittsburgh *Saturday Visiter*, 18 October 1851.

5. For example, in "The Market-Woman of San Domingo," Gage describes a mixed-race woman, formerly a slave in Baltimore, who was "tall, symmetrical, almost white, with hair glossy, and wavy, and black as (not a raven's wing) but as the diamonds of the coal mine, just brought to light and flashing the hues of the rainbow in the sun. Unlike those about her, her head was unturbaned, and her hair was gorgeous." New York *Independent*, 24 December 1863.

6. For different readings of Gage's version of Sojourner Truth, see Jean Fagan Yellin, *Women and Sisters: The Antislavery Feminists in American Culture* (New Haven: Yale University Press, 1989), pp. 81–87, and Erlene Stetson and Linda David, *Glorying in Tribulation: The Lifework of Sojourner Truth* (East Lansing, MI: Michigan State University Press, 1994), pp. 112–118, 125.

7. For a thoughtful discussion on the writing of history and the use of historical sources, see Michel de Certeau, *The Writing of History*, trans. Tom Conley (New York: Columbia University Press, 1988), pp. 56–113.

8. See "The Rhetoric of the Image," Roland Barthes, *Image–Music–Text*, ed. and trans. Stephen Heath (New York: Farrar, Straus & Giroux, 1977), pp. 32–51.

9. Elizabeth Cady Stanton, Susan B. Anthony, and Matilda Joslyn Gage, eds., *History of Woman Suffrage*. Vol. 3 (New York, Fowler & Wells, 1883), p. 613. Gage gave a series of lectures in the summer of 1854. Philadelphia *Woman's Advocate*, 26 February 1856; undated letter [ca. 1856] from Gage to Susan B. Anthony in the Papers of Frances Dana Barker Gage, 1808–1884, the Schlesinger Library, Radcliffe College, Cambridge, MA.

10. Frances Dana Gage to Elizabeth Cady Stanton, 4 September [1853?], in Patricia G. Holland and Ann D. Gordon, eds., *The Papers of Elizabeth Cady Stanton and Susan B. Anthony* (Wilmington, DE: Scholarly Resources, Inc., 1990), reel 7, p. 817.

11. Frances Dana Gage to Susan B. Anthony, McConnellsville, Ohio, 5 April 1852, in the Seneca Falls, NY, *Lily*, May 1852, quoted in Holland and Gordon, eds., *The Papers of Elizabeth Cady Stanton and Susan B. Anthony*, microfilm, reel 7, pp. 199–200. Anthony read Gage's letter to the founding convention of the Woman's New York State Temperance Society in Rochester, New York.

12. *Proceedings of the Free Convention Held at Rutland, VT., June 25th, 26th, 27th, 1858* (Boston: G. B. Yerrinton & Son, 1858), pp. 74–76; Pittsburgh *Saturday Visiter*, 10 May 1851.

13. Pittsburgh *Saturday Visiter*, 29 June 1850.

14. Pittsburgh *Saturday Visiter*, 16 November 1850, and Philadelphia *Woman's Advocate*, 21 June 1856.

CHAPTER 19 Partisan and Aristocrat

1. [Olive Gilbert and Frances Titus], *Narrative of Sojourner Truth; A Bondswoman of Olden Time, Emancipated by the New York Legislature in the Early Part of the Present Century; with a History of her Labors and Correspondence Drawn from her "Book of Life"* (1878; reprint Salem, NH: Ayer Company, 1990), pp. 140–141.

2. Ibid., p. 141. Truth's version of her appearances in Steuben County, Indiana, which she most likely dictated to Frances Titus in the mid-1870s in Battle Creek, does not mesh seamlessly with Josephine Griffing's contemporaneous account in the Boston *Liberator*. I have fused these two accounts, doubtless oversimplifying the chronology of events.

3. "Letter from Josephine Griffing," Boston *Liberator*, 21 June 1861. Very strictly speaking, Truth was mistaken: The Confederacy never used black men in combat roles and only considered this expedient in 1865. But most likely she was commenting on General Benjamin Butler's not returning fugitive slaves to their Confederate owners on the pretext that they were contraband of war. See Allan Johnson, *Surviving Freedom: The Black Community of Washington, D.C., 1860–1880* (New York: Garland Publishing, 1993), p. 114.

4. Giles B. Stebbins, *Upward Steps of Seventy Years. Autobiographic, Biographic, Historic* (New York: United States Book Company, 1890), p. 115.

5. "Letter from Josephine Griffing," Boston *Liberator*, 21 June 1861. Griffing's second letter on Truth in Steuben County, Indiana, is in *Liberator*, 28 June 1861.

6. "Letter from Josephine Griffing," Boston *Liberator*, 21 June 1861.

7. Caldwell quoted in Carleton Mabee with Susan Mabee Newhouse, *Sojourner Truth: Slave, Prophet, Legend* (New York: New York University Press, 1993), pp. 95, 117.

8. Norman McRae, *Negroes in Michigan During the Civil War* (Lansing, MI: Michigan Civil War Centennial Observance Commission, 1966), pp. 90–122. After the passage of the Enrollment Act of 3 March 1863, three-year volunteers received a military bounty of $300, five-year volunteers $400. The bounties were paid in installments (McRae, pp. 45–46).

9. Bernard C. Nalty, *Strength for the Fight: A History of Black Americans in the Military* (New York: Free Press, 1986), pp. 43, 46. Even the black regiments from Massachusetts had white officers. Black officers above the rank of sergeant did not appear in larger than token numbers until the Vietnam War.

10. *Narrative of Sojourner Truth*, p. 173.

11. Elizabeth Cady Stanton, Susan B. Anthony, and Matilda Joslyn Gage, eds., *History of Woman Suffrage*. Vol. 3 (1883; reprint Salem, NH: Ayer Company, 1985), p. 532.

12. *Narrative of Sojourner Truth*, p. 126.

13. "Letter from Sojourner Truth," New York *National Anti-Slavery Standard,* 13 February 1864; San Francisco *Pacific Appeal,* 27 February 1864; Sojourner Truth to William Lloyd Garrison, Detroit, 11 April 1864, *Black Abolitionist Papers* (New York: Microfilming Corporation of America, 1981), reel 15, p. 261.

CHAPTER 20   Truth in Photographs

1. Photographic portraiture spread to large numbers of people shortly after photography was invented in 1839; daguerreotypes made portraits commonplace in the 1840s, and Frederick Douglass and Frances Dana Gage both sat for daguerreotype likenesses. The Frederick Douglass daguerreotype is dated about 1847 (National Portrait Gallery, Washington, DC, *History of Photography* 4 [July 1980], frontispiece); the Frances Dana Gage daguerreotype, undated, is in the possession of Jerry Barker Devol, Devola, Ohio. On photography in the mid-nineteenth century, see David S. Reynolds, *Walt Whitman's America: A Cultural Biography* (New York: Alfred A. Knopf, 1995), pp. 280–286.

2. André Rouille, "The Rise of Photography (1851–70)," in *A History of Photography: Social and Cultural Perspectives,* trans. Janet Lloyd, Jean-Claude Lemagny and André Rouille, eds. (Cambridge, ENG: Cambridge University Press, 1987), p. 40; William C. Darrah, *Cartes de Visite in Nineteenth Century Photography* (Gettysburg, PA: W. C. Darrah, 1981), pp. 1–2, 10–12, 19, 24; Leo Braudy, *The Frenzy of Renown: Fame and Its History* (New York: Oxford University Press, 1986), pp. 450–453.

Cartes-de-visite were so popular with soldiers that the New York firm of E. and H. T. Anthony & Co. produced them by the thousands—up to 3,600 daily. See Timothy Sweet, *Traces of War: Poetry, Photography, and the Crisis of the Union* (Baltimore: Johns Hopkins University Press, 1990), p. 81.

3. See Kathleen Collins, "The Scourged Back," *History of Photography* 9 (January–March 1985): 43–45, "Portraits of Slave Children," *History of Photography* 9 (July–September 1985): 187–210, and "Photographic Fundraising: Civil War Philanthropy," *History of Photography* 11 (July–September 1987): 173–187.

4. The drawing is by Charles C. Burleigh, Jr., son of his feminist abolitionist namesake. Burleigh, Jr., was a baby during the 1840s, when Sojourner Truth lived at the Northampton Association. He drew from imagination, inspired by Stowe's "Sojourner Truth, the Libyan Sibyl."

5. Although her Rochester friend, Amy Post, eventually paid for the first photographs, it was Truth who placed herself strictly within the conventions of bourgeois portraiture. On Post's paying for Truth's photographs: Frances Titus to Esther Titus, Battle Creek, 10 May and 11 July 1863, Post Family Papers, Box 5, University of Rochester Library. Truth said the 1864 photos were "much bet-

ter" than those taken in Battle Creek. See "Letter from Sojourner Truth," New York *National Anti-Slavery Standard*, 13 February 1864.

6. Harriet Beecher Stowe, "Sojourner Truth, the Libyan Sibyl," *Atlantic Monthly* XI (April 1863): 473.

7. Mary Elizabeth Massey, *Bonnet Brigades* (New York: Alfred A. Knopf, 1966), p. 157.

8. Elizabeth Cady Stanton, Susan B. Anthony, and Matilda Joslyn Gage, eds., *History of Woman Suffrage*. Vol. 2 (1882; reprint Salem, NH: Ayer Company, 1985), p. 898.

9. Susan Sontag speaks of the three-quarters gaze as conveying an "ennobling abstract relation to the future." *On Photography* (New York: Farrar, Straus & Giroux, 1977), p. 38. See also Roland Barthes, *Image–Music–Text*, ed. and trans. Stephen Heath (New York: Farrar, Straus & Giroux, 1977), pp. 23, 32–51, and *Mythologies*, ed. and trans. Annette Lavers (1957; reprint New York: Farrar, Straus & Giroux, 1972), pp. 91–93.

10. See Deborah Willis, ed., *Picturing Us: African-American Identity in Photography* (New York: New Press, 1994), and Henry Louis Gates, Jr., "The Trope of a New Negro and the Reconstruction of the Image of the Black," *representations* 25, (Fall 1988): 129–155.

11. See Elizabeth Alexander, " 'Can You be BLACK and Look at This?': Reading the Rodney King Video(s)," and Ed Guerrero, "The Black Man on Our Screens and the Empty Space in Representation," both in *Black Male: Representations of Masculinity in Contemporary American Art* (New York: Whitney Museum of American Art, 1994), pp. 90–110, 181–189. Allan Sekula, "The Body and the Archive," in *The Contest of Meaning: Critical Histories of Photography*, ed. Richard Bolton (Cambridge, MA: MIT Press, 1989), pp. 343–346.

12. Alan Trachtenberg, *Reading American Photographs. Images as History: Mathew Brady to Walker Evans* (New York: Hill & Wang, 1989), pp. 53–54.

13. "Letter from Sojourner Truth," Boston *Commonwealth*, 3 July 1863.

14. [Frances Titus], "Memorial Chapter, Giving the Particulars of Her Last Sickness and Death," *Narrative of Sojourner Truth* (Battle Creek, MI: Review and Herald Office, 1884), p. 27.

15. Kathleen Collins, "Shadow and Substance: Sojourner Truth," *History of Photography* 7 (July–September 1983): 183–205; Darrah, *Cartes de Visite in Nineteenth Century Photography*, p. 19.

16. My interpretation of the meaning of Truth's photographs runs counter to influential analyses by Gisèle Freund, Walter Benjamin, and Eduardo Cadava, who see studio photographic portraiture as a kind of alienation or death. In these analyses, the sitter, surrounded by a replica of a bourgeois interior, becomes herself a prop—an object akin to a corpse. See Eduardo Cadava, *Words of Light: Theses on the Photography of History* (forthcoming), pp. 123–125, 173 (note 76).

CHAPTER 21 Presidents

1. "Letter from Sojourner Truth," New York *National Anti-Slavery Standard*, 13 February 1864; Lucy Colman, *Reminiscences* (Buffalo: H. L. Green, 1892), p. 66.

2. This meeting does not appear in either woman's narrative. However, a friend of Tubman's reported the meeting in 1864, and a journalist corroborated it in 1896. See Frank B. Sanborn, Boston *Commonwealth*, 17 August 1864, and Rosa Belle Holt, "A Heroine in Ebony," *The Chautauquan* XXIII (July 1896): 459–462, both quoted in Earl Conrad, *Harriet Tubman* (Washington, D.C.: Associated Publishers, 1943), pp. 183–184.

3. Truth had left her husband at John Dumont's when she walked away from slavery and later went to New York City. After Tubman escaped from slavery, her husband, who was free, remained in Maryland and took another wife. Conrad, *Harriet Tubman*, p. 32.

4. Sarah H. Bradford, *Scenes in the Life of Harriet Tubman* (Auburn, NY: W. J. Moses, 1869), p. 20.

5. Ibid., p. 55; Conrad, *Harriet Tubman*, pp. 71, 142.

6. Tubman quoted in Conrad, *Harriet Tubman*, p. 183.

7. Mary Elizabeth Massey, *Bonnet Brigades* (New York: Alfred A. Knopf, 1966), pp. 194–195.

8. Colman, *Reminiscences*, p. 63. On Keckley's memoir, see James Olney's introduction to Elizabeth Keckley, *Behind the Scenes. Or, Thirty Years a Slave, and Four Years in the White House* (1868; reprint New York: Oxford University Press, 1988), pp. xxxiii–xxxiv.

9. In the Charles S. Johnson manuscript entitled "Arthur A. Schomburg," Schomburg reports that the Lincoln Bible belonged to Fisk University, a gift of Robert Lincoln. According to the report, the Bible was "of the usual pulpit size, bound in violet-colored velvet. On the corners were bands of solid gold, and carved upon a plate, also of gold, not less than one-fourth of an inch thick, on the lefthand corner, was a design representing the President in a cotton-field knocking the shackles off the wrist of a slave, who held one hand aloft as if invoking blessings upon the head of his benefactors. At the feet of Lincoln was a scroll upon which was written 'Emancipation'; on the other cover was a similar plate bearing the inscription: 'To Abraham Lincoln, President of the United States, the friend of Universal Freedom. From the loyal colored people of Baltimore, as a token of respect and gratitude. Baltimore, July 4th, 1864.'" Berenice Bryant Lowe Collection, Sojourner Truth Papers, Section VIII, Michigan Historical Collections, Bentley Historical Library, University of Michigan, Ann Arbor.

10. Boston *Liberator*, 23 December 1864.

11. [Olive Gilbert and Frances Titus], *Narrative of Sojourner Truth; A Bondswoman of Olden Time, Emancipated by the New York Legislature in the*

Early Part of the Present Century; with a History of her Labors and Correspondence Drawn from her "Book of Life" (1878; reprint Salem, NH: Ayer Company, 1990), p. 178.

12. For a careful and complete analysis of Truth's meeting with Lincoln and the myths that have grown up around it, see Carleton Mabee, "Sojourner Truth and President Lincoln," *New England Quarterly* LXI, no. 4 (December 1988): 519–529. Without plumbing the depths of mythmaking (including Truth's own) about her visit with Lincoln, a 1995 article for general readers takes a more critical approach than earlier non-scholarly discussions of Truth at the White House. See Henry Chase, "Memorable Meetings: Classic White House Encounters," *American Visions: The Magazine of Afro-American Culture* (February–March 1995): 30–31.

13. Colman, *Reminiscences*, p. 66.

14. Compare Lincoln's disinterest in Truth with his flattering reception of Harriet Beecher Stowe, also widely mythologized: "So this is the little lady who made this big war!"

15. Colman, *Reminiscences*, p. 67.

16. Keckley, *Behind the Scenes*, p. 158; Colman, *Reminiscences*, p. 52.

17. Giles Stebbins memorial of Sojourner Truth, Detroit, 3 November 1885, in Detroit *Tribune*, 4 November 1885. Burton Historical Collection, Detroit Public Library.

18. As anti-black prejudice hardened in the 1880s, Douglass presented a more appreciative appraisal of Lincoln, saying that he was impressed by the President's "entire freedom from popular prejudice against the colored race." Both quotes are in George M. Fredrickson, "A Man But Not a Brother: Abraham Lincoln and Racial Equality," *Journal of Southern History* XLI, no. 1 (February 1975): 39.

19. Colman, *Reminiscences*, p. 68; Carleton Mabee with Susan Mabee Newhouse, *Sojourner Truth: Slave, Prophet, Legend* (New York: New York University Press, 1993), pp. 126–127, 157.

20. Constance McLaughlin Green, *The Secret City: A History of Race Relations in the Nation's Capital* (Princeton, NJ: Princeton University Press, 1967), p. 79.

21. Stebbins memorial to Truth, 1885.

22. *Narrative of Sojourner Truth*, p. 223.

CHAPTER 22 Washington's Freedpeople

1. Gladys Maria Fry, "The Activities of the Freedmen's Aid Societies in the District of Columbia," M.A. thesis, Howard University, 1954, pp. 50–51.

2. Constance McLaughlin Green, *Washington: Village and Capital, 1800–1878* (Princeton, NJ: Princeton University Press, 1962), pp. 247, 258, 299.

3. Greeley quoted in ibid., p. 312.

4. The quote is from Elden E. Billings, "Social and Economic Conditions in Washington During the Civil War," in Francis Coleman Rosenberger, ed., *Records of the Columbia Historical Society of Washington, D.C., 1963–1965* (Washington, DC: Columbia Historical Society, 1966), pp. 191–192.

5. [Olive Gilbert and Frances Titus], *Narrative of Sojourner Truth; A Bondswoman of Olden Time, Emancipated by the New York Legislature in the Early Part of the Present Century; with a History of her Labors and Correspondence Drawn from her "Book of Life"* (1878; reprint Salem, NH: Ayer Company, 1990), pp. 184–185.

6. Sojourner Truth to Amy Post, Washington, 1 October 1865, Post Family Papers, Box 6, University of Rochester.

7. Sarah H. Bradford, *Scenes in the Life of Harriet Tubman* (Auburn, NY: W. J. Moses, 1869), pp. 46–47; Earl Conrad, *Harriet Tubman* (Washington, DC: Associated Publishers, 1943), pp. 188–189.

8. Laura Haviland to Amy Post, Washington, 22 February 1866, Post Family Papers, Box 6, University of Rochester; New York *National Anti-Slavery Standard*, 13 November 1869; Alfreda Duster, ed., *Crusade for Justice: The Autobiography of Ida B. Wells* (Chicago: University of Chicago Press, 1970), pp. 18–20; Frances Smith Foster, ed., *A Brighter Coming Day: A Frances Ellen Watkins Harper Reader* (New York: Feminist Press, 1990), p. 46.

9. Swisshelm lost her clerkship in 1866 after a bitter attack on President Johnson in her newspaper. She returned to her Swissvale estate near Pittsburgh in 1866, wrote her autobiography *Half a Century* (1880), and died in 1884. See *Crusader and Feminist: Letters of Jane Grey Swisshelm, 1858–1865*, Arthur J. Larsen, ed. (Saint Paul: Minnesota Historical Society, 1934), pp. 25–30.

10. "Letter from Sojourner Truth," Boston *Liberator*, 23 December 1864.

11. Nichols had closed down the second contraband camp in the District, known as Duff's Green, which was located where the Folger Library now stands. The first camp had been in the old Capitol building. Nichols moved the Duff's Green contrabands to Camp Barker, at the corner of 12th Street and Vermont Avenue, N.W. By the spring of 1863 Camp Barker no longer sufficed to house the rapidly growing refugee population, which was resettled in a series of new camps, including the Freedmen's Village in Arlington Heights, Virginia, where Sojourner Truth would live for more than a year. Allan Johnson, *Surviving Freedom: The Black Community of Washington, D.C., 1860–1880* (New York: Garland Publishing, 1993), pp. 107, 121–123.

12. Between 1860 and 1870, the black population of Washington increased 223 percent, with the increase made up almost entirely of very poor people, only some of whom were accommodated in freedmen's camps. Johnson, *Surviving Freedom*, pp. 107, 121–123; Constance McLaughlin Green, *The Secret City: A*

History of Race Relations in the Nation's Capital (Princeton, NJ: Princeton University Press, 1967), p. 62.

13. Freedmen's Hospital, attached to Howard University Medical School, was one of the few medical schools to which blacks had access in the late nineteenth and early twentieth centuries. See Thomas Holt, Cassandra Smith-Parker, and Rosalyn Terborg-Penn, *A Special Mission: The Story of the Freedmen's Hospital, 1862–1962* (Washington, DC: Howard University, 1975), p. 13.

14. Green, *Washington*, p. 273.

15. Keith E. Melder, "Angel of Mercy in Washington: Josephine Griffing and the Freedmen, 1864–1872," in Rosenberger, *Records of the Columbia Historical Society*, p. 250.

16. After the Freedmen's Bureau took over freedpeople's relief in 1865, the effort became an inextricable mix of public and private funding and staffing. William Merritt, a wealthy Battle Creek resident and close friend of Truth's informal manager in the late 1860s, 1870s, and 1880s, Frances Titus, held the mortgage on her house. *Narrative of Sojourner Truth*, pp. 289–290; Carleton Mabee, "Sojourner Truth Fights Dependence on Government: Moves Freed Slaves Off Welfare in Washington to Jobs in Upstate New York," *Afro-Americans in New York Life and History* 14, no. 1 (January 1990): 10.

17. Lois Elaine Horton, "The Development of Federal Social Policy for Blacks in Washington, D.C., After Emancipation," unpublished Ph.D. dissertation, the Florence Heller Graduate School for Advanced Studies in Social Welfare, Brandeis University, 1977, p. 87.

18. U.S. Congress, 39th Congress, 2nd Session (1866–67), Senate Executive Documents, No. 6, "Reports of Assistant Commissions of Freedmen" (vol. 1, serial 1276), District of Columbia, pp. 36–37.

19. "Letter from Sojourner Truth," Boston *Liberator*, 23 December 1864.

20. Quoted in Carleton Mabee with Susan Mabee Newhouse, *Sojourner Truth: Slave, Prophet, Legend* (New York: New York University Press, 1993), p. 139.

21. Sojourner Truth to Amy Post, Washington, 1 October 1865, Post Family Papers, Box 6, University of Rochester.

22. Felix James, "Freedmen's Village, Arlington, VA: A History," M.A. thesis, Howard University, 1967, p. 32.

23. Melder, "Angel of Mercy in Washington," pp. 255–257; Nancy A. Hewitt, *Women's Activism and Social Change: Rochester, New York, 1822–1872* (Ithaca, NY: Cornell University Press, 1984), p. 198.

24. Johnson, *Surviving Freedom*, pp. 162–163.

25. U.S. Congress, 39th Congress, 2nd Session, "Reports of Assistant Commissions of Freedmen," p. 39.

26. Horton, "The Development of Federal Social Policy," p. 93.

27. Eighty percent of those placed were transported before mid-1867. The black proportion of the population of Washington had increased from 19 percent in 1860 to 30 percent in 1867. Ibid., pp. 15, 96.

28. Griffing quoted in Johnson, *Surviving Freedom*, pp. 160, 166.

29. Mabee, "Sojourner Truth Fights Dependence on Government," p. 19; Melder, "Angel of Mercy in Washington," p. 259; Johnson, *Surviving Freedom*, p. 187.

30. Sojourner Truth to Josephine Griffing, Rochester, 30 March 1867, Post Family Papers, Box 6, University of Rochester.

31. Mabee, "Sojourner Truth Fights Dependence on Government," p. 18; "Letter from Sojourner Truth," New York *National Anti-Slavery Standard*, 19 October 1867.

CHAPTER 23   Woman Suffrage

1. The Declaration of Sentiments of the first women's rights convention at Seneca Falls, New York, in 1848 had included a demand for suffrage only as its ninth resolution, which was the only one not to pass unanimously. With Frederick Douglass's support, Stanton was able to muster a bare majority. Elizabeth Cady Stanton, Susan B. Anthony, and Matilda Joslyn Gage, eds., *History of Woman Suffrage*. Vol. 1 (New York: Fowler & Wells, 1881), pp. 72–73; Ellen Carol DuBois, *Feminism and Suffrage: The Emergence of an Independent Women's Movement in America, 1848–1869* (Ithaca, NY: Cornell University Press, 1978), pp. 39, 41.

2. Rosalyn Terborg-Penn finds ten black men and six black women identifiable as suffragists before the Civil War. Rosalyn M. Terborg-Penn, "Afro-Americans in the Struggle for Woman Suffrage," unpublished Ph.D. dissertation, Howard University, 1977, p. 33. Although William Lloyd Garrison, the most prominent abolitionist of the antebellum era, did not attend woman suffrage meetings after the Civil War, he was an advocate for votes for women. Like many others, including Truth, he sided with the American Woman Suffrage Association when the woman suffrage movement split over black male suffrage in 1869. Walter M. Merrill and Louis Ruchames, eds., *The Letters of William Lloyd Garrison*. Vol. VI. *To Rouse the Slumbering Land, 1868–1879* (Cambridge, MA: Harvard University Press, 1981), pp. 1–2.

3. Truth's friend Amy Post was prominent in the Rochester branch of the Women's Loyal League. Nancy A. Hewitt, *Women's Activism and Social Change: Rochester, New York, 1822–1872* (Ithaca, NY: Cornell University Press, 1984), p. 196.

4. Ibid., pp. 199, 207. The theme of comparative degradation had figured in women's rights rhetoric since the 1848 Seneca Falls Declaration of Sentiments, which included this indictment of man's power over woman: "He has withheld

from her rights which are given to the most ignorant and degraded men—both natives and foreigners." Stanton, Anthony, and Gage, eds., *History of Woman Suffrage*, Vol. 1, p. 70.

5. DuBois, *Feminism and Suffrage*, p. 54; Hewitt, *Women's Activism and Social Change*, p. 207.

6. Truth was one of several speakers for the Equal Rights Association at its Rochester convention in December 1866. Parker Pillsbury and Charles Remond also spoke. Hewitt, *Women's Activism and Social Change*, p. 208.

7. Terborg-Penn, "Afro-Americans in the Struggle for Woman Suffrage," p. 35.

8. Frances Smith Foster, "Frances Ellen Watkins Harper (1825–1911)," in Darlene Clark Hine, ed., *Black Women in America: An Historical Encyclopedia* (Brooklyn, NY: Carlson Publishing, 1993), pp. 532–537.

9. Frances Smith Foster, ed., *A Brighter Coming Day: A Frances Ellen Watkins Harper Reader* (New York: Feminist Press, 1990), p. 15.

10. In 1868 the white women typesetters associated with Stanton and Anthony in the Working Women's Association practically echoed Harper: One of the typesetters doubted that the vote, of itself, was "the greatest panacea for the correction of all existing evils." DuBois, *Feminism and Suffrage*, pp. 134–135.

11. The last two paragraphs of this speech, which I have quoted, are to be found on the errata sheet of the hardcover edition, not in the softcover reprinting of Foster, ed., *A Brighter Coming Day*, p. 219.

In 1897, Frances Watkins Harper spoke at a reception for Harriet Tubman that one of William Lloyd Garrison's sons planned and the AWSA hosted in the offices of its organ, the Boston *Woman's Journal*. Earl Conrad, *Harriet Tubman* (Washington, DC: Associated Publishers, 1943), p. 215.

12. Elizabeth Cady Stanton, Susan B. Anthony, and Matilda Joslyn Gage, eds., *History of Woman Suffrage*. Vol. 2 (1882; reprint Salem, NH: Ayer Company, 1985), p. 183. Years later Stanton and Anthony would mistake the middle initial of one of their equal rights colleagues who turned into one of their sharpest critics, George T. Downing, who was black. After Downing had parted company with Stanton and Anthony following their opposition to the Fourteenth and Fifteenth Amendments, Downing appears with a middle initial of W. (*History of Woman Suffrage*, Vol. 2, 1869, p. 377), and of F. (1868, 1874, pp. 537, 758).

13. Stanton, Anthony, and Gage, eds., *History of Woman Suffrage*, Vol. 2, p. 193.

14. Ibid., Vol. 2, p. 391.

15. On Truth's biblical imagery in this speech, see Erlene Stetson and Linda David, *Glorying in Tribulation: The Lifework of Sojourner Truth* (East Lansing, MI: Michigan State University Press, 1994), pp. 178–180.

16. Stanton, Anthony, and Gage, eds., *History of Woman Suffrage*, Vol. 2, p. 193.

17. Ibid., Vol. 2, pp. 214–216, 220–221.

18. Ibid., Vol. 2, p. 224.

19. Ibid., Vol. 2, pp. 224–225.

20. Ibid., Vol. 2, pp. 926–927.

21. Ibid., Vol. 2, pp. 353–355.

22. Ibid., Vol. 2, p. 383.

23. Ibid., Vol. 2, p. 391.

24. Ibid., Vol. 2, p. 342.

25. Foster, "Frances Ellen Watkins Harper," p. 533. On Lucy Stone's dislike of Elizabeth Cady Stanton and Susan B. Anthony after 1867, see Andrea Moore Kerr, *Lucy Stone: Speaking Out for Equality* (New Brunswick, NJ: Rutgers University Press, 1992), pp. 142, 196–197.

26. [Olive Gilbert and Frances Titus], *Narrative of Sojourner Truth; A Bondswoman of Olden Time, Emancipated by the New York Legislature in the Early Part of the Present Century; with a History of her Labors and Correspondence Drawn from her "Book of Life"* (1878; reprint Salem, NH: Ayer Company, 1990), pp. 299–302.

27. Ibid., pp. 217–220; *New York Herald,* 12 May 1870, p. 10; Stanton, Anthony, and Gage, eds., *History of Woman Suffrage,* Vol. 2, p. 766. According to the *Herald* report, working women's issues took up a great deal of time at both the AWSA and the NWSA, which were both meeting in New York at the same time.

28. *Narrative of Sojourner Truth,* p. 218.

29. Ibid., pp. 231–232.

CHAPTER 24 Kansas

1. [Olive Gilbert and Frances Titus], *Narrative of Sojourner Truth; A Bondswoman of Olden Time, Emancipated by the New York Legislature in the Early Part of the Present Century; with a History of Her Labors and Correspondence Drawn from Her "Book of Life"* (1878; reprint Salem, NH: Ayer Company, 1990), pp. 198–199, 219; Richard Cordley, Emporia, Kansas, "Sojourner Truth," Boston *Congregationalist,* 3 March 1880.

2. *Narrative of Sojourner Truth,* p. 221. The New York *National Anti-Slavery Standard* for 1869 and 1870 regularly carried news of Indians, and in 1870, when the paper became the *National Standard* after the ratification of the Fifteenth Amendment, American Indians became one of the paper's main subjects of discussion.

3. *Narrative of Sojourner Truth,* p. 193.

4. Ibid., p. 221.

5. Ibid., pp. 236–237.

6. *New York Tribune,* 13 March 1871, quoted in Carleton Mabee with Susan

Mabee Newhouse, *Sojourner Truth: Slave, Prophet, Legend* (New York: New York University Press, 1993), p. 157.

7. *Narrative of Sojourner Truth*, p. 195.

8. Recent scholarship corroborates Truth's sense that the freedpeople of Washington were stagnating economically and occupationally, and their situation did not improve before 1880. See James Oliver Horton and Lois E. Horton, "Race, Occupation, and Literacy in Reconstruction Washington, D.C.," in James Oliver Horton, *Free People of Color: Inside the African American Community* (Washington, DC: Smithsonian Institution Press, 1993), pp. 192–195.

9. *Narrative of Sojourner Truth*, p. 237.

10. Ibid., pp. 197, 221, 239.

11. Ibid., p. 235.

12. Ibid., pp. 215–216.

13. This demand appears under several auspices in the New York *National Anti-Slavery Standard:* Stephen S. Foster, 22 May 1869; the Friends of Human Progress, 12 June 1869; David Plumb, 5 June 1869; Charles Stearns (of Georgia), 31 July 1869; Wendell Phillips, 25 September 1869; Aaron M. Powell to the National Colored Labor Convention, 18 and 25 December 1869; National Labor Convention delegation to Grant to get forfeited southern railroad lands for freedpeople's settlement, 8 January 1870.

14. See Nell Irvin Painter, *Exodusters: Black Migration to Kansas After Reconstruction* (1977; reprint New York: W. W. Norton, 1992), pp. 71–117.

15. New York *National Anti-Slavery Standard*, 4 March 1871. In late 1869, Aaron Powell of the *Standard* published this petition calling for a federal land commission to oversee the allocation of public land to freedpeople: *"To the Forty-first Congress of the United States:* The undersigned respectfully and earnestly ask your honorable body to authorize at once the appointment by the President of a Land Commission, to be composed of well-known, disinterested friends of the freed people, with authority to appoint a limited number of Agents, whose duty it shall be to cooperate with individuals and associations among the hitherto enslaved, for the selection and purchase of eligible lands for homestead, to hold titles thereof for a given period, until by installments they shall have been paid for at actual cost to the Government, when the money so employed, not to exceed two millions of dollars, shall be refunded to the national treasury." New York *National Anti-Slavery Standard*, 25 December 1869.

16. *Narrative of Sojourner Truth*, p. 198.

17. Boston *Zion's Herald*, 23 February 1871.

18. New York *National Anti-Slavery Standard*, 4 March 1871; *Narrative of Sojourner Truth*, pp. 201, 203, 257, 288.

19. *Narrative of Sojourner Truth*, p. 199.

20. Ibid., pp. 280, 297–299.

21. Ibid., pp. 297, 289, 199–206, 263, 257, 267, 270, 294.

22. Ibid., pp. 215–216. This newspaper account is reprinted in Sojourner Truth's *"Book of Life"* in the 1870s and 1884 editions of her *Narrative.*

23. Ibid., p. 240.

24. Sojourner Truth obituary, Philadelphia *Christian Recorder,* 13 December 1883; *Narrative of Sojourner Truth,* pp. 200, 240, 225; Battle Creek *Daily Journal,* 26 November 1883, Sojourner Truth File, Willard Public Library, Battle Creek. Both "African" and "sibyl" are misspelled in the original.

25. Elizabeth Cady Stanton, Susan B. Anthony, and Matilda Joslyn Gage, eds., *History of Woman Suffrage.* Vol. 2 (1882; reprint Salem, NH: Ayer Company, 1985), pp. 926–928; Unidentified newspaper clipping, ca. 1878, Berenice Bryant Lowe, Sojourner Truth Papers, Section IX, Michigan Historical Collections, Bentley Historical Library, University of Michigan, Ann Arbor.

26. See *Narrative of Sojourner Truth,* pp. 199, 200, 202, 204, 216, 218, 220–222, 225, 227–228, 243, and 246.

27. New York *National Anti-Slavery Standard,* 4 March 1871.

28. *Narrative of Sojourner Truth,* p. 273.

29. Battle Creek *Journal,* 14 June 1871. Truth also spoke to spiritualists in the late 1860s. Rochester, *Union and Advertiser,* 26 August 1868.

30. *Narrative of Sojourner Truth,* p. 240.

31. Mabee, *Sojourner Truth,* identifies Byron M. Smith as a land agent, p. 159.

32. *Narrative of Sojourner Truth,* pp. 245, 248.

33. Ibid., p. 247.

34. Ibid., pp. 245, 246–247.

35. Cordley, "Sojourner Truth."

36. *Narrative of Sojourner Truth,* pp. 248, 264, 269.

37. Helen Benson Garrison to William Lloyd Garrison, Roxbury, 6 August 1874, Box 1, Garrison Papers, Wichita State University; Walter M. Merrill and Louis Ruchames, eds., *The Letters of William Lloyd Garrison.* Vol. VI. *To Rouse the Slumbering Land, 1868–1879* (Cambridge, MA: Harvard University Press, 1981), p. 338.

38. Effie J. Squier, "Sojourner Truth, New York," *The Christian at Work,* 28 September 1882, p. 12.

39. Unidentified obituary [Battle Creek *Daily Journal?*], 8 March 1875, Sojourner Truth Red Books by Dorothy Martich, Vol. 1, p. 14, Willard Public Library, Battle Creek; Berenice Lowe, "The Family of Sojourner Truth," *Michigan Heritage* (Summer 1962): 184.

40. Sojourner Truth to William Still, Battle Creek, 4 January 1876, American

Negro Historical Society Papers, Leon Gardiner Collection, Box 9G, Historical Society of Pennsylvania, Philadelphia.

41. Sojourner Truth to William Still, Battle Creek, 4 January 1876; "Sojourner Truth," Philadelphia *Evening Bulletin*, 28 July 1876.

42. [Frances Titus], "Memorial Chapter, Giving the Particulars of Her Last Sickness and Death," *Narrative of Sojourner Truth* (Battle Creek, MI: Review and Herald Office, 1884), p. 29.

43. See Painter, *Exodusters*, pp. 184–211, and Chicago *Daily Inter-Ocean*, 13 August 1879.

44. "Memorial Chapter," *Narrative of Sojourner Truth*, p. 19.

45. See Painter, *Exodusters*, pp. 213, 245–250, and William S. McFeely, *Frederick Douglass* (New York: W. W. Norton, 1991), pp. 299–302.

46. "Memorial Chapter," *Narrative of Sojourner Truth*, p. 20.

47. Battle Creek *Daily Journal*, 24 February 1880, Sojourner Truth File, Willard Public Library, Battle Creek, Michigan.

48. Quoted in Mabee, *Sojourner Truth*, p. 166.

49. On the politics of the late nineteenth century, see Nell Irvin Painter, *Standing at Armageddon: The United States, 1877–1919* (New York: W. W. Norton, 1987).

CHAPTER 25   The End of a Life

1. [Olive Gilbert and Frances Titus], *Narrative of Sojourner Truth; A Bondswoman of Olden Time, Emancipated by the New York Legislature in the Early Part of the Present Century; with a History of her Labors and Correspondence Drawn from her "Book of Life"* (1878; reprint Salem, NH: Ayer Company, 1990), p. 307.

2. Harriet Beecher Stowe, "Sojourner Truth, the Libyan Sibyl," *Atlantic Monthly* XI (April 1863): 480.

3. Frances Dana Gage, "Sojourner Truth," New York *Independent*, 23 April 1863.

4. Sojourner Truth to Amy Kirby Post, Detroit, 18 January 1869, Post Family Papers, Box 6, University of Rochester Library; New York *National Anti-Slavery Standard*, 18 December 1868; 26 December 1868.

5. Sojourner Truth to William Still, Battle Creek, 4 January 1876, American Negro Historical Society Papers, Leon Gardiner Collection, Box 9G, Historical Society of Pennsylvania, Philadelphia; "Memorial Chapter, Giving the Particulars of Her Last Sickness and Death," *Narrative of Sojourner Truth* (Battle Creek, MI: Review and Herald Office, 1884), p. 19; "Sojourner Truth," Philadelphia *Evening Bulletin*, 28 July 1876; "Sojourner Truth," Boston *Woman's Journal*, 8 August 1876. The *Woman's Journal* article by Lucy Stone acknowledged

the error of the rumor of Truth's death but ran an appraisal of her life's work anyway.

6. Chicago *Inter-Ocean*, 1 January 1881; Philadelphia *Christian Recorder*, 27 January 1881, p. 4; Philadelphia *Woman's Journal*, 14 November 1903.

7. Effie J. Squier, "Sojourner Truth, New York," *The Christian at Work*, 28 September 1882, p. 12.

8. Samuel J. Titus reminiscences, in Henry J. A. Wiegmink, *Early Days of Battle Creek*. Vol. 3 (n.p. [Battle Creek]: Mamie Wiegmink, 1954), p. 1127, Burton Historical Collection, Detroit Public Library.

9. Battle Creek *Enquirer and News*, 26 November 1981, Sojourner Truth Brown Files, Willard Public Library, Battle Creek, Michigan.

10. Squier, "Sojourner Truth," p. 12.

11. Battle Creek *Citizen*, 1 December 1883, Sojourner Truth Brown Files, Willard Public Library, Battle Creek.

12. On family strains: Sojourner Truth to Amy Post, Washington, DC, 3 July 1866, Post Family Papers, Rochester University Library. On William Boyd's desertion: notice dated 7 August 1872, Sojourner Truth Red Books, Vol. 1, p. 15, Willard Public Library, Battle Creek.

13. Berenice Lowe, "The Family of Sojourner Truth," *Michigan Heritage* (Summer 1962): 181–184.

14. Squier, "Sojourner Truth," p. 13.

15. Stowe, "Sojourner Truth, the Libyan Sibyl," p. 474.

16. See Kenneth Manning, *Black Apollo of Science: The Life of Ernest Everett Just* (New York: Oxford University Press, 1983), and David Levering Lewis, *W. E. B. Du Bois: Biography of a Race, 1868–1919* (New York: Henry Holt, 1993).

17. Sojourner Truth Red Books, Vol. 1, pp. 15–16, Willard Public Library, Battle Creek.

18. Joy Bennett Josey, "Sojourner Truth's Memory Lives On," Battle Creek *Enquirer and News*, 26 November 1981, Sojourner Truth Brown Files, Willard Public Library, Battle Creek.

19. Battle Creek *Enquirer and News*, 12 June 1932, Sojourner Truth Brown Files, Willard Public Library, Battle Creek.

20. Battle Creek *Nightly Moon*, 24 November 1883, Sojourner Truth Brown Files, Willard Public Library, Battle Creek; "Memorial Chapter," p. 7.

21. Berenice Bryant Lowe, *Tales of Battle Creek* (Battle Creek, MI: Miller Foundation and Historical Society of Battle Creek, 1976), p. 241.

22. "Memorial Chapter," pp. 9–11. See also Giles Stebbins's report on Truth's funeral in the Boston *Woman's Journal*, 8 December 1883.

23. "Memorial Chapter," pp. 14–15.

24. Philadelphia *Christian Recorder,* 13 December 1883.

25. *New York Globe,* 1 December 1883.

26. Nashville *Daily American,* 1 March 1884.

27. Elizabeth Cady Stanton, Susan B. Anthony, and Matilda Joslyn Gage, eds., *History of Woman Suffrage.* Vol. 3 (New York: Fowler & Wells, 1883), pp. 531–532.

28. Boston *Woman's Journal,* 1 December 1883.

29. Battle Creek *Daily Journal,* 26 November 1883, Sojourner Truth Brown Files, Willard Public Library, Battle Creek.

30. Cited in "Memorial Chapter," p. 15.

CHAPTER 26 The Life of a Symbol

1. [Frances Titus], "Memorial Chapter, Giving the Particulars of Her Last Sickness and Death," *Narrative of Sojourner Truth* (Battle Creek, MI: Review and Herald Office, 1884), pp. 10–11.

2. [Olive Gilbert and Frances Titus], *Narrative of Sojourner Truth; A Bondswoman of Olden Time, Emancipated by the New York Legislature in the Early Part of the Present Century; with a History of Her Labors and Correspondence Drawn from Her "Book of Life"* (1878; reprint Salem, NH: Ayer Company, 1990), pp. 263–264.

3. Titus copyrighted the expanded version in 1875, but the most commonly circulated copies bear the publication date 1878.

4. *Narrative of Sojourner Truth,* pp. 234, 253.

5. Ibid., p. 254.

6. Titus's letters to Amy Post are full of spiritualist imagery.

7. Berenice Bryant Lowe Collection, Folder 13, Michigan Historical Collections, Bentley Historical Library, University of Michigan, Ann Arbor; Dorothy Martich, "Sojourner Truth Chronology," Willard Public Library, Battle Creek, Michigan. Two other neighbors helped pay for the gravestone. Titus's marker endured until about 1916, when it was replaced. The Sojourner Truth Memorial Committee, headed by Forest H. Sweet, a Battle Creek antiquities and autographs dealer, erected the current marker in 1946. Sweet to the University of North Carolina Press, Battle Creek, 5 February 1947. University of North Carolina Press Records, Sub-group 4, Fauset, A. H., *Sojourner Truth, God's Faithful Pilgrim,* University Archives, Wilson Library, University of North Carolina at Chapel Hill.

8. Battle Creek *Enquirer,* 30 November 1894, in Dorothy Martich, "Sojourner Truth Chronology," Willard Public Library, Battle Creek.

9. Unidentified newspaper article ca. 1940 in Lowe Collection, Section VIII; Dorothy Martich, "Sojourner Truth Chronology," Willard Public Library, Battle Creek.

10. According to Hertha Pauli, whose book contains no notes, Courter painted the Truth and Lincoln picture for the 1893 World's Fair. Diana Corbin sat for the figure of Truth. Hertha Pauli, *Her Name Was Sojourner Truth* (New York: Appleton-Century-Crofts, 1962), p. 241.

11. *Narrative of Sojourner Truth*, p. 129.

12. Ibid., p. 130. This incident has never been corroborated by evidence that Truth visited the Senate in the early 1860s. She was there in 1870, when she collected the autographs of several senators, but no testimony describes the exchange in the roseate light that Titus presents.

13. Elizabeth Cady Stanton, Susan B. Anthony, and Matilda Joslyn Gage, eds., *History of Woman Suffrage.* Vol. 1 (New York: Fowler & Wells, 1881), pp. 116–117.

14. Lide Parker (Smith) Meriwether Papers, Folder 1, Schlesinger Library, Radcliffe College, Cambridge, MA.

15. Harriet Carter, "Sojourner Truth," *The Chautauquan* VII, no. 8 (May 1887): 477.

16. Ida M. Tarbell, "The American Woman: Part IV, Her First Declaration of Independence," *The American Magazine* LXIX (1909–10): 476, 480.

17. Herbert Aptheker, ed., *The Collected Works of W. E. B. Du Bois: Writings in Periodicals. Selections from the Horizon* (White Plains, NY: Kraus Thompson, 1985), p. 99.

18. John W. Cromwell, *The Negro in American History: Men and Women Eminent in the Evolution of the American of African Descent* (Washington, DC: American Negro Academy, 1914), pp. 105–106.

19. Ibid., pp. 112–114. Cromwell includes a single footnote—to Henry James, *William Wetmore Story and His Friends, From Letters, Diaries, and Recollections.* 2 vols. (Boston: Houghton Mifflin, 1903), Vol. II, p. 70. Emphasis in original.

20. Freeman Henry Morris Murray, *Emancipation and the Freed in American Sculpture: A Study in Interpretation* (1916; reprint Freeport, NY: Books for Libraries Press, 1972), pp. 5–8.

21. Vivian Njeri Fisher, "Hallie Quinn Brown," in *Black Women in America*, Darlene Clark Hine ed. (Brooklyn, NY: Carlson Publishing, 1993), pp. 176–178.

22. Hallie Q. Brown, *Homespun Heroines and Other Women of Distinction* (1926; reprint Freeport, NY: Books for Libraries Press, 1971), pp. 14–15, 17.

23. Ibid., pp. 15, 17. On a similar note, Frances Goodrich and Albert Hackett, scripwriters of the 1955 Broadway play *Anne Frank*, invented the line that ends the play: "In spite of everything, I still believe that people are really good at heart," and substituted it for Frank's multi-page recognition of the "suffering of millions." Scholars in current reference volumes on the American theater have erroneously assumed that this last line in the play is also the last line in Anne Frank's diary. See Frank Rich, "Betrayed by Broadway," *New York Times*

Book Review, 17 September 1995, p. 11.

24. Benjamin Brawley, *Negro Builders and Heroes* (Chapel Hill, NC: University of North Carolina Press, 1937), pp. 76–79.

25. University of North Carolina Press Records, Sub-group 4, Fauset, A. H., *Sojourner Truth: God's Faithful Pilgrim*, University Archives, Wilson Library, University of North Carolina at Chapel Hill. Fauset was the brother of the Harlem Renaissance writer Jessie Fauset.

26. Arthur Huff Fauset, *Sojourner Truth: God's Faithful Pilgrim* (1938; reprint New York: Russell & Russell, 1971), pp. 127–134, 135, 139–140, 146–149. Like Brawley, Fauset dates the Akron speech as 1852, not 1851. Aside from the frontispiece, Truth in old age, from the *Narrative*, this biography lacks illustrations.

27. Victoria Ortiz, *Sojourner Truth: A Self-Made Woman* (Philadelphia: J. B. Lippincott, 1974), p. 149.

28. Walter White, "Sojourner Truth: Friend of Freedom," in "American Movers and Shakers: No. 5," *New Republic* 118 (24 May 1948): 16–18.

29. Jacqueline Goggin, "Politics, Patriotism, and Professionalism: African-American Women and the Preservation of Black History, 1890–1960," unpublished 1993 paper in author's possession; Glenda Gilmore to Nell Irvin Painter, Charlotte, North Carolina, 11 July 1995; Helen E. Tyler, *Where Prayer and Purpose Meet: The WCTU Story: 1874–1949* (Evanston, IL: Signal Press, 1949), p. 275.

30. See Louis Filler, *The Crusade Against Slavery: 1830–1860* (New York: Harper & Row, 1960), p. 38; James M. McPherson, *The Struggle for Equality: Abolitionists and the Negro in the Civil War and Reconstruction* (Princeton, NJ: Princeton University Press, 1964), pp. 230, 172; Carleton Mabee, *Black Freedom: The Nonviolent Abolitionists from 1830 through the Civil War* (London: Macmillan Company, 1970), p. 83; Benjamin Quarles, *Black Abolitionists* (New York: Oxford University Press, 1972), pp. 178–179.

31. Pauli was the sister of the Nobel Prize physicist Wolfgang Pauli, and came to the United States after the fall of France in 1940, having previously sought refuge in France following the Nazi occupation of Austria. Pauli obituary, *New York Times*, 11 February 1973, in Dorothy Martich's Red Sojourner Truth Books, Vol. 3, p. 119, Willard Public Library, Battle Creek.

32. Pauli, *Her Name Was Sojourner Truth*, p. 3.

33. Ibid., pp. 3, 4, 6, 23, 172–174. Pauli hints broadly, for instance, that John Dumont forced Isabella to have sex with him, although the *Narrative of Sojourner Truth* does not contain any such suggestion.

34. Jacqueline Bernard, *Journey Toward Freedom: The Story of Sojourner Truth* (1967; reprint New York: Feminist Press, 1990), p. 183.

35. See note 27 above.

36. "A Candidate on Pilgrimage: Shirley Chisholm Visits Sojourner Truth

Grave, Dedicates Housing," Battle Creek *Enquirer and News*, 29 April 1972, in Dorothy Martich's Red Sojourner Truth Books.

37. Battle Creek *Enquirer and News*, 30 May 1976, in Sojourner Truth Brown Files, Willard Public Library, Battle Creek.

38. Bert James Loewenberg and Ruth Bogin, eds., *Black Women in Nineteenth-Century American Life: Their Words, Their Thoughts, Their Feelings* (University Park, PA: Pennsylvania State University Press, 1976), pp. 234–235.

39. Linda K. Kerber and Jane Sherron DeHart, *Women's America: Refocusing the Past* (1982 edition New York: Oxford University Press, 1987), pp. 213–214.

40. See Phyllis Marynick Palmer, "White Women/Black Women: The Dualism of Female Identity and Experience in the United States," *Feminist Studies* 9, no. 1 (Spring 1983): 151–170.

41. bell hooks, *Ain't I a Woman: Black Women and Feminism* (Boston: South End Press, 1981).

42. Deborah Gray White, *Ar'n't I a Woman? Female Slaves in the Plantation South* (New York: W. W. Norton, 1985); Elizabeth Fox-Genovese, *Within the Plantation Household: Black and White Women of the Old South* (Chapel Hill, NC: University of North Carolina Press, 1988).

43. *Washington Post*, 23 November 1991; Associated Press dispatch in the *Oakland Tribune*, 15 July 1995.

44. See Deborah E. McDowell, "Transferences: Black Feminist Thinking: The 'Practice' of 'Theory,'" in *"The Changing Same" Black Women's Literature, Criticism, and Theory* (Bloomington, IN: Indiana University Press, 1995), pp. 156–175; Donna Haraway, "Ecce Homo, Ain't (Ar'n't) I a Woman, and Inappropriate/d Others: The Human in a Post-Humanist Landscape," in *Feminists Theorize the Political*, Judith Butler and Joan W. Scott, eds. (New York: Routledge, 1992), pp. 86–100; Denise Riley, "Does Sex Have a History?" in *"Am I That Name?" Feminism and the Category of "Women" in History* (Minneapolis: University of Minnesota Press, 1988), pp. 1–17.

45. Carleton Mabee with Susan Mabee Newhouse, *Sojourner Truth: Slave, Prophet, Legend* (New York: New York University Press, 1993); Erlene Stetson and Linda David, *Glorying in Tribulation: The Lifework of Sojourner Truth* (East Lansing, MI: Michigan State University Press, 1994).

CODA

1. This task was aided immeasurably by the publication of *The Black Abolitionists Papers. Vol. IV: The United States, 1847–1858* (Chapel Hill, NC: University of North Carolina Press, 1991), which made Marius Robinson's 1851 report of Truth's comments easily accessible for the first time (pp. 81–83).

2. Nell Irvin Painter, "Representing Truth: Sojourner Truth's Knowing and Be-

coming Known," *Journal of American History* 81, no. 2 (September 1994): 461–492.

3. On the resilience of what he calls "myth" and I am calling "symbol," see Roland Barthes, *Mythologies*, ed. and trans. Annette Lavers (1957; reprint New York: Farrar, Straus & Giroux, 1972), pp. 130, 135.

4. Michael O'Malley, *"AHR Forum:* Response to Nell Irvin Painter," *American Historical Review* 99, no. 2 (April 1994): 408. O'Malley took his quote from Linda K. Kerber and Jane Sherron DeHart, eds., *Women's America: Refocusing the Past* (3rd ed. New York: Oxford University Press, 1991), p. 230.

5. See Barry Schwartz, *George Washington: The Making of an American Symbol* (Ithaca, NY: Cornell University Press, 1987).

6. Valerie Reitman, "Tale of Betsy Ross, It Seems, Was Made Out of Whole Cloth," *Wall Street Journal*, 12 June 1992.

7. Timothy Egan, "Chief's 1854 Lament Linked to Ecological Script of 1971," *New York Times*, 21 April 1992.

Acknowledgments

WRITING this book drew me into a new world too broad and strange for solitary passage. To the extent I have covered it, I owe a thousand thanks for generosities from strangers, acquaintances, colleagues, and friends. I deeply appreciate the knowledge conveyed and the fellowship shared in the exploration of the life and symbol of Sojourner Truth.

I began with a specific inspiration: the first volume of Arnold Rampersad's magnificent *Life of Langston Hughes,* which I read shortly after it appeared. By encouraging my return to biography, a genre I had largely put aside after *The Narrative of Hosea Hudson* in 1979, Rampersad on Hughes brought me Truth. Since 1986 many fine biographies have appeared, but three sensitive classics escorted my Sojourner Truth venture: William S. McFeely's *Frederick Douglass*; David Levering Lewis's *W. E. B. Du Bois*; and Thadious Davis's *Nella Larsen.** Thank you for inspiration.

Nancy Hewitt, and Jean Fagan Yellin and John C. Van Horne

*Arnold Rampersad, *The Life of Langston Hughes.* 2 vols. (New York: Oxford University Press, 1986, 1988); William S. McFeely, *Frederick Douglass* (New York: W. W. Norton, 1991); David Levering Lewis, *W. E. B. Du Bois: Biography of a Race, 1868–1919* (New York: Henry Holt, 1993); Thadious M. Davis, *Nella Larsen, Novelist of the Harlem Renaissance: A Woman's Life Unveiled* (Baton Rouge, LA: Louisiana State University Press, 1994).

accompanied my first ventures into print with Truth, in *Gender and History* and *An Untrodden Path,* respectively.* Then others in many places offered assistance. In Ulster County, New York, Carleton Mabee, Dorothy Dumond, Amy Kesselman, and Carl Van Wagenen introduced me to Truth's home territory. At the University of Rochester, Mary Hugh and Karl Kabelac were warmly helpful. In the summer of 1991 a Peterson Fellowship at the American Antiquarian Society made all the difference in the world. The AAS opened the antebellum North to this post–Civil War historian. Nancy Burkett had encouraged my application, and after my stay in Worcester, Dennis Laurie and Georgiana Barnhill helped tie up loose ends. The AAS staff, renowned for their helpful expertise, fully deserve their glowing reputation. At the Schlesinger Library at Radcliffe College, Eva Hoffman gave her time. Dorothy and Michael Martich of Battle Creek offered comradely guidance into Truth memorializing. The staff at the Bentley Historical Library at the University of Michigan at Ann Arbor have been helpful in person and by mail. Robin and Deirdre Kelley made me part of their family in Ann Arbor. Kenneth E. Rowe and Sarah Blair offered guidance in the Methodist Archives at Drew University. I am also grateful to Edwin Sanford at the Boston Public Library; Virginia Christenson in Florence, Massachusetts; Bruce Brooks at the Lilly Library in Florence; the Sophia Smith Collection at Smith College; and Ray Matthews in the Family History Library of the Church of Jesus Christ of Latter-Day Saints in Salt Lake City.

Information from many thoughtful scholars saved me years of blind wandering. For keeping Sojourner Truth and me in mind, I thank Harriet Hyman Alonso, Lisa Baskin, Jennifer Baszile, Elizabeth Bethel, Jeffrey Bolster, Eileen Boris, Anne Braude, Catherine Brekus, Richard Brown, Hazel Carby, Lee Chambers-Schiller, Yvonne Chireau, Christopher Clark, Nancy Cott, Jane Dailey, Lowell M. Durham, Jr., the Frederick Douglass Papers Project at Yale University, Kevin Gaines, Paula Giddings, Glenda Gilmore, William

*See Nell Irvin Painter, "Sojourner Truth in Life and Memory: Writing the Biography of an American Exotic," *Gender and History* 2, no. 1 (Spring 1990) and "Sojourner Truth in Feminist Abolitionism: Difference, Slavery, and Memory," in Jean Fagan Yellin and John C. Van Horne, eds., *An Untrodden Path: Women's Political Culture in Antebellum America* (Ithaca, NY: Cornell University Press, 1994), pp. 139–158.

Gilmore-Lehne, George Gorse, Ramón Gutiérrez, Joan Hedrick, Richard P. Heitzenrater, Patricia Hill, Darlene Clark Hine, Lynn Hudson, Philip Lapsansky, Thomas C. Leonard, Donald Matthews, William McFeely, Jacqueline McLeod, Michael Merrill, A. G. Miller, Stephen Nissenbaum, Tom O'Brien, Linda Reed, C. Peter Ripley, Patricia Schechter, William Seraile, Lyde Cullen Sizer, Dorothy Sterling, Ian Straker, John Sweet, Rosalyn Terborg-Penn, Jan Todd, Alan Trachtenberg, Bradford Verter, Shane White, and Karolyn Wrightson. Toni Morrison generously shared her knowledge of publishing.

Over the years several research assistants have contributed to this undertaking, beginning with my own beloved Dona and Frank Irvin of Oakland, California, and continuing with Martha Wharton in Northampton, Crystal Feimster in Chapel Hill, and Becky Jones, Eduardo Pagán, Walter Johnson, Nataki Finch, and Charles Reeves in Princeton. BB Walker, Judith Jackson-Fossett, and Christine Unger supported this work in myriad, necessary ways. I am profoundly grateful to all of them.

Many colleagues have read my drafts and given valuable criticism: Carole Beal, Jon Butler, James Cone, Giles Constable, Ellen DuBois, David Hackett, Jane and Leo Marx, Elaine Pagels, Peter Paris, Jane and William Pease, Daniel Rodgers, Christine Stansell, Kathryn Watterson, Deborah Gray White, Sean Wilentz, Gayraud S. Wilmore, Patricia Woolf, and Jean Fagan Yellin.

This journey cost the earth, and I am grateful to Robert Gunning and Ruth Simmons for their role in Princeton University's generous monetary and spacial support. Grant FA-30715-92 from the National Endowment for the Humanities contributed to my support in 1992–93. I took my baby steps in this project at the Center for Advanced Study in the Behavioral Sciences, where their legendary support system, plus grants from the Andrew W. Mellon Foundation and the National Endowment for the Humanities (grant FC-20060-85), created a perfect place for discovery.

A few steadfast giants made the completion of this book possible. To each of you I want to say: I could not have written without you. Charlotte Sheedy believed in the project for years before the book came into sight and then let the world know about it. Edwin Barber really edits, the kind of hard-headed gentleman editor they say doesn't exist any more. Ed made a work of scholarship readable. Elaine Wise has accomplished more different kinds of chores than I could ever enumerate. Without her versatility, patience, intelligence, and good humor, I would have crumpled years ago. Richard Newman, the angel of this project, has read, rallied, informed, and supported since my first naive presentation to the Association for the Study of the History of Black Religion in 1990. His shower of citations broadened the book enormously.

The Big Three—Nellie McKay, Mary Kelley, and Thadious Davis—friends of a lifetime, took every step and misstep beside me, reading, rereading, talking, bracing. Surviving my life of scholarship, not just this book, depends upon their steadfast sustenance.

My husband, Glenn Shafer, read each of innumerable drafts, the last patiently, painstakingly aloud. Glenn kept our lives going in the summer of 1995, permitting my single-minded concentration on finishing. He holds the key to my scholarship, happiness, and the whole of my life.

Index

Page numbers in *italics* refer to illustrations.